BODIES IN SOCIETY

BODIES IN SOCIETY

Essays on Christianity
in Contemporary Culture

MARGARET R. MILES

CASCADE *Books* • Eugene, Oregon

BODIES IN SOCIETY
Essays on Christianity in Contemporary Culture

Copyright © 2008 Margaret R. Miles. All rights reserved. Except for brief quotations in critical articles or reviews, no part of this book may be reproduced in any
manner without prior written permission from the publisher. Write: Permissions,
Wipf and Stock Publishers, 199 W. 8th Ave., Suite 3, Eugene, OR 97401.

Cascade Books
A Division of Wipf and Stock Publishers
199 W. 8th Ave., Suite 3
Eugene, OR 97401

www.wipfandstock.com

ISBN: 978-1-55635-421-2

Cataloging-in-Publication data:

Miles, Margaret Ruth.

    Bodies in society : essays on Christianity in contemporary culture / Margaret R.
Miles.

    xiv + 228 p. ; 23 cm. Includes bibliographical references.

    ISBN: 978-1-55635-421-2

    1. Body, Human—Religious aspects—Christianity. 2. Christianity and culture. I.
Title.

BT 741.3 .M56 2008

Manufactured in the U.S.A.

Contents

Part III Christianity in North American Society

Acknowledgments

Chapters of this book appeared in an earlier form in various journals and books. The author and publisher gratefully acknowledge permission to reprint from these publications:

1   "The Pursuit of Lifefulness: In Search of a Method" was originally published in *Studia Mystica* 7:4 (1984) 63–69.

2   "Revisioning an Embodied Christianity" was originally published in *Unitarian Universalist Christian* 42 (1987) 5–13.

3   "Violence against Women in the Historical Christian West and in North American Secular Culture: The Visual and Textual Evidence," was originally published in *Shaping New Vision: Gender and Values in American Culture*, edited by Clarissa W. Atkinson, Constance H. Buchanan, and Margaret R. Miles, 11–29. Ann Arbor: UMI Research Press, 1987.

4   "Textual Harassment: Desire and the Female Body" was originally published in *The Good Body: Asceticism in Contemporary Culture*, edited by Mary G. Winkler and Letha B. Cole, 49–63. New Haven: Yale University Press, 1994.

5   "Celibacy as Sexual Orientation" was originally published as the Foreword in *Sex, Priests, and Power: Anatomy of a Crisis*, A. W. Richard Sipe, ix–xiv. New York: Brunner/Mazel, 1995.

6   "Religion and Food: The Case of Eating Disorders" was originally published in *JAAR* 63 (1995) 549–64.

7   "Voyeurism and Visual Images of Violence" was originally published in *Christian Century* 101:10 (1984) 305–6. Copyright © *Christian Century*. Reprinted by permission from the March, 1984, issue of the *Christian Century*.

8   "Religion and Values in Contemporary North American Popular Film" was originally published in *Christian Spirituality Bulletin* 3:1 (1995).

10 "Larry Flynt in Real Life" was originally published in *Christian Century* 114:14 (1997) 419–20. Copyright © 1997 *Christian Century*. Reprinted by permission from the April, 1997, issue of the *Christian Century*.

11 "What You See is What You Get" was originally published in *Religion and Prime Time Television*, edited by Michael Suman. Copyright © 1997 by Westport, CT: Praeger, 1997. Reproduced with permission of Greenwood Publishing Group, Inc., Westport, CT.

12 "Fashioning the Self" was originally published in *Christian Century* 112:8 (1995) 273–76. Copyright © 1995 *Christian Century*. Reprinted by permission from the March, 1995, issue of the *Christian Century*.

15 "The Passion for Social Justice and *The Passion of the Christ*" was originally published in *Mel Gibson's Bible: Religion, Popular Culture, and "The Passion of the Christ,"* edited by Timothy K. Beal and Tod Linafelt, 121–28. Chicago: University of Chicago Press, 2006.

17 "Pilgrimage as Metaphor in a Nuclear Age" was originally published in *Theology Today* 45:2 (1988) 166–79.

18 "Imitation of Christ: Is it Possible in the Twentieth Century?" was originally published in *Princeton Seminary Bulletin* 10:1 (1989) 7–22.

19 "Hermeneutics of Generosity and Suspicion: Pluralism and Theological Education" was originally published in *Theological Education* 23, Supplement (1987) 34–52.

20 "Theory, Theology, and Episcopal Church Women" was originally published in *Episcopal Women: Gender, Spirituality, and Commitment in an American Masculine Denomination*, edited by Catherine M. Prelinger, 330–44. New York: Oxford University Press, 1992. Reprinted by permission of Oxford University Press, Inc. www.oup.com.

21 "From the Garden to the Academy: Blame, Battle, or a Better Way" was originally published in *Journal of Feminist Studies in Religion* 17:1 (2001) 101–11.

Introduction

"The object was to learn to what extent the effort to think one's own history can free thought from what it silently thinks, and so enable it to think differently."

—Michel Foucault, *The Use of Pleasure*

THINKING LIFE

So little of what most of us call thinking actually *is* thinking. It is, rather, an internal soundtrack composed of a hodge-podge of repetitious self-talk, opinion, and cut-and-pasted second-hand ideas. "We are not used to looking at [and thinking about] the real world at all."[1] Iris Murdoch urges attentiveness to the world, uncolored by the demands of self: "Should we not . . . endeavor to see and attend to what surrounds and concerns us, because it is there and is interesting, beautiful, strange, worth experiencing, and because it demands (and needs) our attention, rather than living in a vague haze of private anxiety and fantasy?"[2]

In contemporary North American public culture, thinking has a bad name. And indeed, scholars, the designated thinkers in a society, are often tempted to think abstractly; the present and the concrete are often alien. Indeed, not only the content of scholarship, but also its traditional practices isolated the "great man" from everyday concerns and tasks. Until quite recently most professional thinkers were supported by people who washed their socks, put food on their table, and protected them from distractions.[3] Traditional scholars required a great deal of maintenance.

1. Foucault, *The Use of Pleasure*, 9.

2. Murdoch, *Metaphysics as a Guide to Morals*, 64, 218.

3. Inclusive language is neither required nor accurate here, since the model of the scholar was a male model to which, at best, a few women could aspire.

Scholars' roles in societies are irreducibly privileged, but many scholars now recognize that it is not sufficient simply to acquaint students with bodies of knowledge; it is necessary also to endeavor continuously to demonstrate connections between the topics we study and the pressing problems of the world outside the academy. Presently many women and men in the academic world think concretely within the context of their own lives and with recognized and acknowledged accountability to broader communities with whom they think, and to whom they make themselves answerable. They think concretely about such issues as reproductive technologies, world hunger, and the effects of media entertainment.

Although we often consider such engaged critical scholarship new, the third-century philosopher Plotinus pointed out that thinking and living depend intimately on each other and cannot be separated.

> If the truest life is life by thought,
> and is the same thing as the truest thought,
> then the truest thought lives,
> and contemplation, and the object of contemplation
> at this level is living and life,
> and the two together are one.[4]

The earliest Christian prayers, sermons, and hymns also acknowledged the interdependence of life end thought. They indentified Christ's gifts as knowledge and life.

The essays in this volume represent my efforts to think concretely about three interconnected features of contemporary North American society: media, gender assumptions and arrangements, and theological institutions. Republished essentially as they were originally published, the essays reveal my lifelong interest in identifying personal and communal deadness in order to seek the goal of the liturgical prayer, "We beg you, make us truly alive." This is not a new project, as this fourth-century prayer by Serapion of Thmuis indicates. The identification of spots of deadness and practical methods for overcoming them has often concerned historical Christians. For example, ascetic practices were advocated as a method for addressing the habits that dull the sharp quick sense of life. Augustine and his Christian contemporaries thought of *concupiscentia* as the enemy of life. They defined *concupiscentia* not solely as sexual lust, but also as lust for power—orientations of attention and affection strong enough to deflect individuals from the source of being. Medieval monks added lust

---

4. Plotinus *Ennead* 3.8.8.

for possessions to Augustine's list, countering sexual lust with celibacy, lust for power with obedience, and lust for possessions with poverty.[5] The "seven deadly sins" were so named because they were found to deaden lives.

It has been said that all theology is occasional theology, that is, it both responds to particular circumstances and employs the tools at hand for approaching inherited questions. That is certainly true of these essays. Those that were written in the 1980s assume a nuclear threat that is presently not on the front burner. Essays written during the 1990s cite figures for religious populations in America that were inaccurate as soon as they were published. Similarly, figures for poverty, violence, and other social factors are, even in the best of studies, approximate and, at best, accurate only for the historical moment studied. As is true of all written works, the more timely a work is, the less it can claim to be timeless. But the opposite is also true: the more a work claims to be timeless, the more a reader should seek to understand the particular social circumstances in which it was written. For indeed, all theology is occasional theology.

THINKING BODIES

A foundational theme traversing these essays is how "selves" are formed, both by social forces and by intentional choices. Augustine said that if one seeks to know who a person most essentially is, one must ask what s/he loves. Clearly, desire and delight compose the self. And have intimately to do with body.[6]

Thinking bodies fruitfully is an important and difficult human task. Christianity, the religion of the Incarnation, places a particular urgency on rethinking bodies, whether in the context of Roman colosseum entertainment or in contemporary North American media culture; in both, bodies are spectacle. Christianity supplies the example of a founder who lived lovingly in a body, in the world. But the doctrine of the Incarnation has been slenderly developed. Theologians' attention has been devoted to souls and something called "spirituality," a neologism approximating the traditional word "piety," but neglecting to take into account the practice of Christianity. Moreover, it is not just human bodies that need concrete and committed thought, but the bodies of all living creatures and the world's body. The ecological crisis of our time desperately calls for rethinking our values and practices. Augustine's teaching that the commu-

---

5. Bonner, "Libido and Concupiscentia in St. Augustine."

6. The phrase "the body" will be found in my essays that were written before the mid-1990s, but I do not use the phrase anymore because it connotes either the male body of traditional scholarship, or a generic entity that no one has ever seen or touched. Bodies are particular, marked by age, sex, race, illness or health, and myriad other qualities.

nity of human responsibility is limited to that of "rational minds" may have been adequate to a time in which the natural world seemed invulnerable. We cannot blame historical people for not predicting and preventing a world in which natural resources are irrecoverably damaged by human greed and waste. But we can, and must, recognize that their decisions and practices are not helpful—indeed, are destructive—in our time. We must explore the implications of "the grace of the Creator in giving us a body."[7]

Section two, "Society," includes essays that represent an interest that originated in my use of artworks as historical evidence.[8] Seeking more democratic evidence for the common life of historical communities in the Christian West, I found that religious artworks, analyzed in relation to the liturgies, social arrangements, and institutions in which they were created, provide a perspective on religious life that sometimes augmented, sometimes nuanced, and sometimes contradicted, the evidence supplied by historical texts. Artworks, until the Renaissance seen almost exclusively by Christian communities in churches, were an essential communication medium of historical societies. Recognizing this, it seemed to me less than responsible to ignore the media communications of twentieth-century North American culture. I focused on popular movies, examining a movie as one voice in a complex social and cultural conversation occurring at the time of its production and circulation in first-run theaters. Several essays included in this volume exemplify my method for examining "religion and values in the movies."[9]

The great social and intellectual movements of the last half of the twentieth century have shaped and informed my thinking and writing: critical and cultural studies, feminism, queer theory, race studies, and Marxist critique of capitalist economy. Among these, the study of gender constructions and their effects in Western European and North American societies has been my particular focus. My approach has been to "mainstream" gender studies, insisting that social inequality is not a "women's issue," nor one of "political correctness," but a matter that affects all members of a society. Although women may suffer

---

7. Ponticus, *The Praktikos and Chapters on Prayer*, 31.

8. With the exception of chapters 3 and 7, my work on art historical topics is not represented in this volume. It is to be found in my books, *Image as Insight: Visual Understanding is Western Christianity and Secular Culture*; *Carnal Knowing: Female Nakedness and Religious Meaning in the Christian West*; *The Word Made Flesh: A History of Christian Thought*, and *A Complex Delight: The Secularization of the Breast*, 1350–1750.

9. My book, *Seeing and Believing: Religion and Values in the Movies* offers a method for analyzing popular films in the context of public conversations and concerns contemporary with their production and release.

more from constraining gender assumptions and arrangements, men also suffer within the roles they are expected to play. The quality of relationships suffers for everyone when women do not have access to equal respect, opportunity, and pay. The same can be said for other issues of the present time and society. The trivializing term "political correctness" mocks those who seek, in small and large ways, to alleviate human impoverishment, both physical and spiritual in this, the wealthiest country in the world.

THINKING INSTITUTIONS

Most teachers enter the profession because we enjoy learning. Once we are safely installed in a tenured position, however, we often isolate ourselves within a field in which we keep up with reading, but do not expose ourselves to the discomfort of fundamental new learning. After teaching for many years, I accepted an administrative position as Dean of the Graduate Theological Union, Berkeley. I made that move, puzzling as it was to several of my friends, because I wanted to learn to think an institution. This was fundamental new learning for me and quite daunting. How was I supposed to have learned how to organize a large budget? No one mentioned it when I was interviewed and I somehow had not expected it—perhaps a more-or-less deliberate blind eye on my part. There was, in my experience, little overlap between the "skill sets" of a teacher and author and those of an administrator.

However, the experience of attempting to match budget line items to needs and demands was quite eye-opening. It revealed why a fundamental dissonance between faculty perspectives and those of an administrator exists. In order to reduce this dissonance, institutions often seek administrators among faculty members: a term in the dean's office brings understanding of administrators' problems, reducing traditional hostilities.

I also wanted to see the profession of teaching from a larger perspective than that of a faculty member immersed in a subfield but not necessarily acquainted with the larger field of religion and theology. I thought it would be a fascinating challenge to see if and how an institution could be made better, because all academic institutions must constantly adjust and improve, or slide downhill. My reflections on my endeavor to think an institution appear in chapter 21. In the end, however, I realized that I am not a born administrator. Born administrators, at least as I imagine them, do not lie awake at night vexed with the problems that flourish in institutions. I also missed the classroom conversations that inspire and refine scholarly projects. My term in the dean's office was, in brief, a rich and sometimes painful "learning experience."

A PERSONAL NOTE

The text that has directed my life and work appears in a plaque over my desk: "Delight is, as it were, the weight of the soul. Where the soul's delight is, there is its treasure."[10] That insight has proved invaluable to me. At a time when people with doctorates in History were not getting jobs, and every realistic counselor advised me to pick a "sexier" field, I loved historical study, and stayed with it. My delight both energized my study and carried me forward to rich opportunities throughout my life. Staying close to one's delight is not a guarantee, certainly, but it worked for me. In the end, of course, we all live by faith, whether we acknowledge it or manage to conceal it from ourselves.

Augustine's amazing statement at the end of his *Confessions*: "My weight is my love; by it I am carried wherever I am carried,"[11] is, for me, the articulation of a *project*, a goal, not a simple statement of fact. At the end of his long narration of the conversion that altered his life and thought, Augustine could claim that the glacial psychic *weight* of anxiety, fear, ambition, and sexual lust he described in detail throughout the *Confessions* had shifted to love. The subject of the *Confessions* is the pain, the hard work, and the grace that created that shift. In the end, that is what I would most like to be able to say with honesty, "my weight is my love."

---

10. Augustine *De musica* 6.11.29.

11. Augustine *Confessions* 13.9.

PART I

Bodies

1

The Pursuit of Lifefulness

In Search of a Method

The film, *My Dinner with André*, is the record of a conversation, over dinner in an elegant restaurant, of two men. Wally, a struggling playwright and part-time actor, is content with his life, happy, as he tells us, if he can just find in the morning his cold leftover coffee without a dead cockroach floating on top. Life is good, Wally repeats, why want more than the comforts and pleasures of an ordinary modern life? André, a financially secure playwright, describes to Wally the series of experiences he has had that have simultaneously revealed to him the deadness of ordinary life and convinced him that there is more. He has traveled, impulsively and widely—to Findhorn, India, and Poland—experimenting with improvisational theater, the mildly occult, and the just plain wacky. The conversation of these two comprises the entire film; no flashbacks to the strange events described by André interrupt continuous images of Wally's curious, puzzled face, and André's thin, intent face.

Yet the film is spellbinding; it focuses and formulates the ancient human longing to be fully alive and the equally ancient quandary over the best method of achieving a rich, intense, and fulfilling life. Neither André's nor Wally's view is caricatured or dismissed: Wally's suggestion that it is the life of comfort and contentment that achieves the greatest human happiness is not made to appear dull or unimaginative in comparison with André's frankly exotic experiences. Nor does André's uncritical enthusiasm for occult games and encounter groups appear irresponsible in contrast with Wally's uncomplaining commitment to work and small pleasures. The film focuses the question of how to avoid the "living death," sketches two contemporary answers, and leaves the audience to resolve the question—in lifestyle, if not in concept.

André characterizes the strongest longing of human beings in various ways as he describes his experiences: "But you see, what I think I experienced was for the first time in my life to know what it means to be truly alive. . . . It was a feeling of recognizing everything, of being able to be aware of the reality and the specialness of even the most ordinary things."[1] But André found it impossibly difficult to maintain the feeling of sensitive empathic aliveness. He found, on the contrary, that it is "quite possible to do all sorts of things and at the same time be completely dead" (105).

Together André and Wally identify the major causes of the ordinary deadness of human life as comfort and the habits that insulate against real feeling, real seeing, and real awareness. André says, discussing the effect of the electric blanket that Wally has been given for Christmas: "that kind of comfort just separates you from reality in a very direct way . . . comfort can be dangerous" (76–77). The habits of everyday life are also deadening. André tells of a man who, to combat the effect of habits, practiced

> certain exercises, like for instance, if he were right-handed, all day he would do everything with his left hand. All day—writing, eating, everything—opening doors—in order to break the habits of living, because the great danger for him, he felt, was to fall into a trance, out of habit. And he had a whole series of exercises, very simple ones, that he invented to just keep seeing, feeling, remembering. (75)

André's solution to the effect of comfort and daily habits is an extreme one, "a training program to learn how to be a human being" (108), in which one acts "completely on impulse"; "I think you really do have to become a king of hobo or something, you know . . . go out on the road" (106). His method is extreme because his condition was extreme: "I had gone for a good eighteen months unable to feel except in the most extreme situations" (107). André's experiences included being "buried" alive for a half hour in the dead of night in the middle of a bush forest on Long Island; eating sand with a young Japanese Buddhist priest on the Sahara desert ("that was how desperate we were. We were searching for something, but we couldn't tell if we were finding anything," 42); and a solemn christening ceremony, arranged by his friends, in which he was renamed in a flower-filled Polish castle.

But deadness is not, according to André, primarily an individual condition; rather it is a highly contagious social disease: "we're all in a trance. We're

---

1. Quotations from *My Dinner with André* are from the screenplay by Wallace Shawn and André Gregory, 38.

walking around like zombies" (63); "We don't see the world. We don't see ourselves" (78). And this situation is "much more dangerous, really, than one thinks. . . . And . . . it's not just a question of individual survival, but that someone who's bored is asleep. And someone who's asleep will not say no" (92).

Consciousness raising is not the solution: drama, art, literature, and the media present "a terrifying chaotic universe full of rapes and murders" (88), but serve only to reinforce in people a sense of the intractable pervasiveness of the problems of the world. They receive the impression that "there's absolutely no way out and there's nothing they can do. They end up feeling passive and impotent. And so the experience has helped to deaden them" (88). "Even those works which were once outcries against the darkness can now only contribute to the deadening process" (87).

Wally provides examples of his own to reinforce André's analysis of the problem and its dimensions, but he objects to André's prescription: "I mean, isn't it a little upsetting to come to the conclusion that there's no way to wake up people anymore except to involve them in some kind of christening in Poland or some kind of strange experience on top of Mount Everest?" (89). Wally's solution to the problem of feeling "truly alive" is to accept one's life and to enjoy its small pleasures:

> I'm trying to earn a living, I'm trying to pay my rent and my bills. I mean, I live my life, I enjoy staying home with Debbie, I'm reading Charlton Heston's autobiography, and that's that. . . . And, I mean, I have a list of errands and responsibilities that I keep in a notebook, and I enjoy going through my list and carrying out the responsibilities and doing the errands and then crossing them off my list. . . . I don't think I feel the need for anything more than all this. (97)

Both André and Wally propose, in contemporary language, ancient solutions to the age-old question of how to feel—to be fully alive. Wally's solution is presented, for example, in the *Epic of Gilgamesh* (third milennium BC), by Siduri, winemaker for the gods. Siduri advises Gilgamesh to give up his frenzied quest for immortality and accept—and enjoy—the "lot of humanity":

> Gilgamesh, where are you hurrying to? You will never find that life for which you are looking. When the gods created humans they allotted to them death, but life they retained in their own keeping. As for you, Gilgamesh, fill your belly with good things; day and night, night and day, dance and be merry, feast and rejoice. Let your clothes be fresh, bathe yourself in water, cherish the little child that holds

your hand, and make your wife happy in your embrace; for this too
is the lot of humans.[2]

André's uncompromising quest for lifefulness, on the other hand, has been
the theme of countless heroic sages of ancient myth, drama, and ritual.

The recognition of human longing for a "sharp quick sense of life" has
also been a constant theme of historic Christianity. Before Christian faith was
articulated by doctrines, before it was embodied in participation in a community, before it was understood as involving rectified moral commitments,
it was described simply as a change from deadness to life. The fourth-century
Eucharistic prayer attributed to Serapion of Thmuis formulates what early
Christians found in Christian faith: "We beg you, make us truly alive." If
we take seriously and literally the insistence of early Christian authors that
Christian faith is primarily an orientation to the source of life, to "Life itself"
(Augustine), we see that both recognition of the longing of human beings
for lifefulness and the provision of practical methods of disentangling the
deadening effects of comfort and daily habit have been a central feature of the
teaching of the Christian churches.

The practical method to which I refer is asceticism, one of the least understood and most rejected features of historic Christianity. Because we have
confused an enormous range of practices, goals, and rationales under the
rubric "asceticism," we do not distinguish between the gentle, dehabituating
practices advised by many spiritual leaders and the far more attention-getting harsh and dualistic practices involving self-induced pain. Many historic
authors caution against such bodily abuse while at the same time urging the
frequent practice of dehabituating exercises, carefully and individually tailored to address a particular person's compulsive behavior or addictive habits.
The undeniable existence of body-damaging and life-shortening practices in
some historic reports should not cause us to reject gentler methods, some of
which are amazingly similar to those proposed in our contemporary setting
by André Gregory. The temporary sacrifice of comforts and suspension of
habits—even "taking to the road" in pilgrimage—were the standard tools of
medieval Christians who wanted to feel "truly alive?"

The confident hedonism of contemporary North American culture has
concealed the truth—amply revealed in the writings of modern novelists—
that the uninhibited pursuit of sex, power, and possessions is a prescription

---

2. Sanders, *Epic of Gilgarnesh*, 99.

for cumulative deadness—"not the death of dying, but the living death."[3] As André put it, "we're going around all day like unconscious machines . . . we're walking around like zombies" (63).

Gentle ascetic practices can dissolve the daily comforts and habits that keep human beings insulated, unfeeling, and unaware of political and social injustice. If, as various historic authors claim, such practices are effective in identifying and addressing cultural as well as individual blindness and deadness, we may need to acknowledge the need for a recovery of at least a part of traditional asceticism.

What might an asceticism for our time look like? First, the only rationale for asceticism consonant with the decisive Christian affirmation of the human body articulated in the doctrines of creation, the Incarnation of Jesus Christ, and the resurrection of the body, is that which assumes the unity of human being. Whatever affects the body, affects the soul, so that change in habitual patterns of activity renders the soul vulnerable to new sensitivity and awareness.

Secondly, gentle ascetic practices that aim at lifefulness through dehabituation are as good—as clarifying and healing—for body as for soul. Short fasts, fasts from the media, physical exercise, disciplined prayer and meditation, periods of celibacy, of solitude, or of silence: any of these practices can overcome the habits and minor addictions of everyday life and result in increased clarity of insight and what St. Thomas Aquinas called, "the renewal of the senses."

Finally, ascetic practices such as I have suggested are often recommended by historic authors and by contemporary gurus solely for purposes of individual spiritual growth. As Wally objected, however, the "salvation" of the few is an unaffordably luxurious cultural product in a nuclear age in which the fate of each of us is so inseparable from the fate of all of us. The possibility of the nuclear destruction of human life must call into question esoteric quests for personal happiness. Even though real changes in sensitivity, awareness, and the development of a global perspective must *begin* with individuals, it cannot end with individuals.

Moreover, André's quest was privileged and expensive; as Wally said, "everybody knows that he's got some money hidden away somewhere—I mean, how the hell else could he have been flying off to Asia or wherever he went and still have been supporting his family?" (19). Few people can "take to the road," as André advised. The social, educational, and financial privilege

3. Percy, *The Second Coming*, 311.

assumed by André's method implies, as Wally recognized, that people without these resources must expect that deadness will inevitably infiltrate and erode their lives:

> Because I mean—the awful thing is let's face it, André—I mean if you say that it really is necessary to take everybody to Everest, then it's really tough, because everybody can't be taken to Everest. (89)

Ascetic practices, on the other hand, work more realistically with less dramatic but nevertheless effective methods: self-observation, and simple "exercises" that correct habitual or compulsive behavior. Such tools were, and are, democratic, flexible, and capable of being precisely and individually designed.

Similarly, ascetic practices can be useful in combatting the temptation of Wally's method to insular quietism. As Wally admitted, "I'm ignoring a whole section of the real world. . . . I mean, if I were actually to confront the fact that I'm sort of sharing this stage with the starving person in Africa somewhere, well then I wouldn't feel so great about myself" (83). A short fast, for example, would help Wally concretely to experience his connectedness to the world's hungry people through his own body's hunger. It could challenge his commitment to achieving a comfortable life, in its own way as isolated from the reality of human suffering as André's life ("I'm not trying to get rid of the few things that provide relief and comfort. On the contrary, I'm looking for more comfort" 77.) Also, in addition to requiring that one ignore the "whole enormous world out there" (83), in Wally's method, as André pointed out, "there's always the danger that things can go dead" (106).

A Christian asceticism for our time must begin with the acknowledgment that although "a sharp quick sense of life" is ultimately the gift of participating in "Life itself," there are some simple and humble ways by which we can take responsibility for eliminating pockets of deadness in our lives. Historically, ascetic practices were not the elitist exercises of a leisured class. And they were repeatedly urged, not only for private spirituality but for political awareness. André and Wally demonstrate, in their discussion of the longing to be "truly alive" and the methods by which they hoped to achieve this, that the recovery of asceticism has, in our time, become a social responsibility.

2

Revisioning an Embodied Christianity[1]

I would like to explore with you today an aspect of historical Christianity that hasn't received the attention that other features of Christianity have, i.e., the centrality of human bodies in Christianity. But I want first to describe to you something of how I got to puzzling over historical ideas about human bodies. I am a historian and a theologian; this means, on the one hand, that I'm interested in the religious ideas of the past for their own sake, for their beauty and profundity and their usefulness in the lives of particular human beings who, like us, had to manage slippery worlds in fragile human bodies. But I also have some non-traditional interests in reconstructing pieces of the past.

First, I want to ask whether the past—the study of history—can offer us any suggestions about the present, about ourselves and our world. The present usefulness of historical ideas is not an easy quest if we are to maintain simultaneously the full complexity and particularity of the historical situation in which the ideas were formulated as well as the complexity and particularity of our own situation.

The second interest that determines my historical method is resistance to the unexamined assumption that the ideas of a few historical people who enjoyed the privileged education and leisure for reading and writing theological texts were normative for and characteristic of whole communities. I want to know what religious messages were available to a fourteenth-century woman, for example, who could reasonably expect to die in childbirth at sixteen or twenty-three or thirty, and this information is not available to me in theological texts. So I find I must explore the visual images, seen daily and throughout her life, on the walls of her parish church if I want to know the religious information from which she could construct her self-images and her ideas of relationship,

1. This essay was first delivered as the keynote address at the Unitarian Universalist Christian Fellowship annual meeting on May 18, 1986, in Cambridge, Massachusetts.

community, world, and God. And then, in order to check the temptation to project my own sensitivities in interpretations of the past, I must seek out the visual associations and interpretive tools available to this woman—popular devotional texts, read aloud in town squares, liturgies, sermons, religious drama. I must first imagine and then find the sort of historical evidence that enables me to reconstruct the social situation, gender arrangements, cultural interests and conditioning, and methods of social control of Christian communities. I am after a more integrated historical subject than the ideas of the most atypical members of historical communities can give me., i.e., the ideas of literate, often monastic men. I want to know what most people were doing, not just what a few of them were thinking.

Finally in this catalog of interests that directs my historical work, though I am an Episcopalian, I feel in solidarity with what I take to be one of the strong interests of Unitarian Universalists, namely a critique of historical and contemporary Christian ideas and practices that marginalize or exclude or oppress human beings. I am committed to identification of both the history of oppression and the history of creative and fruitful use of Christian ideas for the shaping of human lives. Today we'll focus on an idea that is, I think, usable and productive in our present situation; last week I was in Ohio, lecturing on the ideas and images of the Christian past that have permitted—if not promoted—violence against women, in order to make some suggestions about our own society in which violence against women, far from being a crime of the past in our enlightened age, is on the increase and reaching epidemic proportions.

What I find when I look at the Christian past is just this bewildering mixture of empowering, challenging, and comforting ideas and practices, and the willful and theologically rationalized marginalization and exclusion of some—even most—human beings from active roles in the formation, organization, and administration of Christian churches. And so I—and you—must do a painstaking job of identifying the useful and usable aspects of Christian faith and those aspects that have fostered marginalization and oppression. To those who are concerned with "orthodoxy," the acknowledgment that one can—and must—evaluate/judge/reject some aspects of Christian tradition looks dangerous. And yet, all that is really non-traditional about this task of "sorting" is the explicit acknowledgment of it. As I read theologians of the past, they all implicitly did just this: they found, focused on, and emphasized some aspects of Christian faith as useful and usable and then, instead of explicitly critiquing and rejecting other aspects/ideas/practices they usually simple ignored them. But in so doing, they adjusted the weight, the central-ity, the emotional intensity of Christian faith in dramatically new directions. What else is Luther's discovery of his foundational principle, "the just shall live by faith?" What else was Michael Servetus' observation that the doctrine of the Trinity is not to be found in Scripture? Examples could be multiplied. (The strategy used by most theologians of the past in order to mask their innovations was their claim to be identifying the "true" Christianity, the Christianity of the "early church.")

Moreover (and back to the mixture of oppression and empowerment), not only have certain ideas and persons been privileged over others in the long and stormy history of Christianity, but also certain parts or functions of human beings have been honored and valued more than others. For example, theologians have often seemed exclusively interested in something called the human "soul." We have designated this "soul" as the proper subject of human religiousness and the object of redemption. We have designed spiritualities addressed to the soul, and have often seemed to be concerned about souls as the only aspect of human beings requiring and deserving religious attention.

There is, I think, a certain irony and contradiction in this preoccupa-tion with souls in Christianity, the religion of the Incarnation, the Word made flesh. So let's examine another possibility, an embodied spirituality. Let's think for a few minutes together about how our understanding—and perhaps our practice—of Christianity might change if we understood our bodies, as well as our souls, as fully engaged in the Christian life. I would like to challenge the assumption that the task of religion is accomplished when it has informed people only of how to cultivate and develop their souls. I'll describe some ways that historical Christians imaged and communicated the role of human bodies in Christian faith and then I will sketch a picture of what an embodied spirituality for our own time might look like.

But let me first describe to you something of the process by which I realized that the Incarnation means something quite concrete about our common life and work.

I shed the fundamentalist religion of my childhood home as blithely as I dropped violin lessons as soon as I reached adulthood and left home. After rejoicing in untarnished secularity for a decade, I came upon Augustine in graduate study and became fascinated, in a scholarly way, of course, with his ability to express the landscape and the seasons of the psyche in theological language. I heard—this veteran of Sunday school and sermons heard—for the first time in the safely neutral environment of a graduate seminar, that theological language is a comprehensive, nuanced, and accurate articulation of the psyche, its journeys, its roadblocks, and its discoveries.

As a child, I had been punished by having to memorize whole chapters of the Bible, always threatened with "Next time, Psalm 119." Predictably, scriptural language had not impressed me as saying anything important about myself. A mechanical, recitation sing-song, whether in my head or aloud, had precluded the communication of meaning. Augustine's language, however, was close to the words on which my psyche had been formed, yet without allowing that automatic reversion to recitation. Theological words came to have meaning: "sin, temptation, salvation," even "God": these words made sense in terms of the beginning self-understanding I had built in seven years of psychotherapy. Until I read Augustine, I had used a combination of poetic and psychological language to formulate what I was discovering about myself and the world. Theological language, however, had an advantage in that it had originally formed my psyche. It also struck me as at once more profound and more comprehensive than either psychological language or poetry.

For the next five years I continued to read Augustine and to ponder his language and ideas. I thought about my life in theological language. But I did not attend church, ever. Instead, I went on long hikes, or I painted, or lay in the California sun. Then one Saturday, the oddest irrational urge struck me; I wanted to go to church the next day. This was in every way an unwelcome urge, but, like a good Californian, I decided not to talk myself out of it, but to explore it. The next day I went to the nearest church, an old, red, spired Episcopal church in Sonora, California, in the heart of the Gold Rush country.

What I realized almost immediately by doing this was that no one is a Christian by self-identifying with a set of concepts, beliefs, or attitudes. The decisive motion is not intellectual, but physical. One puts one's body among other bodies in a building dedicated to communal worship; one takes into one's body the Body of Christ. For the religion of the Incarnation, there's no other way to be a Christian. Ideas, concepts, even doctrine must, in R. G. Collingwood's phrase, "collapse into immediacy," be acted out. Words—scriptural, creedal, doctrinal—receive their setting and their meaning only in physical participation in the worship of a Christian community. Christian faith is decidedly not simply a matter of "getting your mind right."

Nor, of course, is Christian faith a matter of performing ritual gestures at the right place at the right time. "The Word became flesh," the statement that sets forth the astonishing historical fact of the Incarnation of Jesus Christ, describes a balance of concepts and human life that affirms and integrates both. The Word is not an abstract word, to be comprehended by thought alone, no matter how profound. "The Word became flesh," and the human body is no longer merely flesh, but can breathe spirit, life, and truth.

And so for centuries Christians have tried to understand and incorporate what the Incarnation means. We have tried to describe, in philosophical and theological formulae, how it "worked." Having once learned, however, that understanding can be the result of going and of doing rather than of thinking, I began to ask whether, in fact, there were other people who understood by doing rather than by analysis and explanation. I changed my major from philosophy to history. And this is what I found.

The historical fact that Christ as God entered the visible world of nature, bodies, and objects meant to the Christians of the first three centuries that a cosmic seismic shift had occurred in the condition of being human. But long before the implications of this shift were articulated and explored, either in doctrines or creeds or philosophies, Christians were observed by their secular neighbors to have some strange preoccupations and activities. They rose before dawn to assemble together and to sing hymns; they ate a common meal, and they described this meal in such strong terms that when pagans overheard Christians they accused them of cannibalism. In addition, and even more oddly, Christians volunteered to take care of bodies, both living and dead bodies, not just of their own families but also of the poor surrounding them.

Secular Romans found this a bizarre preoccupation. This immediate, almost instinctive urge of Christians to care for the sick, the hungry, the old, and the poor aroused comment from their neighbors. Furthermore, Christians seemed to feel it was their religious duty to do so, a duty as pressing as their ritual assemblies. The really odd feature of Christian activity was their voluntary burying of the dead, again, not just of their own families or congregations, but of the poor who would otherwise have been unceremoniously dumped in a huge common grave. Contemporary Romans, horrified by the possibility of burial in one of these pits, joined burial societies in which the mutual responsibility of burying was pledged and guaranteed. Nobody wanted the job—except the Christians. Corpses were considered "ill-omened" and in most religions of the late Roman world, a period of ritual purification was required before a person who had attended a deathbed or marched in a funeral procession could again participate in a ritual.

Equally bewildering to their secular neighbors, Christians insisted on gathering the bones of those who had been executed for refusal to renounce the Christian sect. They put these bones in a place of honor and described them as capable of possessing the sanctity of the living holy person. Surely this was, as one secular Roman put it, a "fleeing from the light" of classical antiquity, a failure to understand that it is the mind that is to be honored and cultivated, while the human body must be ignored, disparaged, and "scorned." I emphasize the oddness of Christians' behavior in the context of Roman culture in order to indicate that behavior that we may be tempted to categorize under "general goodness," was in fact not something they could have learned from secular life. Rather, they cared for living bodies and dead bodies because they understood that the Incarnation of Christ had once and for all settled the issue of the value of human bodies.

It was several centuries before Christian theologians recognized that the Christian affirmation of the human body implied in the doctrines of creation, the Incarnation of Jesus Christ, and the resurrection of the body, was incompatible with the model of human being of the classical philosophical schools. In these schools, human being was understood as stacked components, with body on the bottom, and rational mind on the top. From the earliest days, however, ordinary Christians acted in humble, practical ways on a new understanding of the value and permanent integrity of the human body. Without a rationalizing rhetoric, they understood it to be part of the Christian life to respect and to care for both living and dead bodies. These people had, I think, understood and incorporated the Incarnation into the fabric of their daily lives and activities. They were not immediately articulate about that understanding, especially in writing, and so we must "read" their unusual behavior rather than theological texts in order to surmise their motivation. These people—ordinary, for lack of a better word—were not the culturally and educationally privileged of their time that could wield and shape language. Rather, theirs was a language of action. It may be a difficult language for us to translate; we have been told so many times that we now believe it, that if we cannot explain something we do not understand it. Generations of church historians have attended to the literary evidence of historic Christianity on the assumption that the people who articulated concepts best, understand them best.

Understanding the Incarnation may be much more a matter of feeling the presence of Christ in one's body than of being able to explain the Incarnation philosophically or theologically. Christianity, understood not primarily as a nexus of ideas but as concrete participation in a body—the Body of Christ—provides a very strong formulation of the centrality of physical existence, as do the doctrines of creation and the resurrection of the body. The basis of community for people who do not define themselves by their ideas is also given in physical existence, the great lonely—and yet universal—experiences of birth, growth, maturation, physical vulnerability, pain, illness, ecstasy, age, sex, death.

Something like the perspective I have sketched is much closer to that of most historical people, and probably of most contemporary people, than is identification with a self-constituting subjective activity of thought. Most historical people were necessarily engrossed and preoccupied with the necessities of physical life—food, childbearing, and fear of imminent swift death. They were not shielded from recognizing the brevity of human life by modern technology and the modern practice of keeping the old, the sick, and the dead out of sight. To most historical people, the meaning of the Incarnation was very intimate and direct: the salvation of the body, now in hope, and ultimately in resurrection to a body gloriously minused of pain, hunger, disease, and ever-threatening death. Christ didn't come to save only the soul, Tertullian wrote, why would he have bothered to come to earth in a human body he did not intend to save? The import of the Incarnation was, in a phrase repeated many times by early Christian authors, that what Christ assumed, Christ saved. Since Christ bears our flesh, Christ redeemed our flesh.

I suspect that the trinitarian and christological controversies carried on with passion and often with venom by educated men had little to do with helping most Christian people to understand the Incarnation. If, instead of rehearsing again the theological and philosophical difficulties debated, we were to keep our attention on the practical ways that most Christians acted out their understanding of the reality of the Incarnation, we would need to take note of Christian practices contemporary with the great theological controversies that were specifically related to and validated by the Incarnation of Christ.

First, liturgy. Christ's visibility in the visible world, the world of the senses meant that the senses needed to be engaged and affirmed in the worship of Christ. To be present is to have the senses engaged, to be there. In the earliest sites of Christian worship of which we have evidence, there were religious symbols and pictures. Candles burned. There was song and readings and admonition. We read of a fourth-century church in which herbs were spread on the floors—marjoram, basil, myrtle, and bay—so that when the congregation walked on them, the building was filled with their aroma. People moved about; the earliest offertories were explicitly and insistently inclusive in that every member of the congregation was expected to come to the altar, bearing a gift at once symbolic of the offering of the whole person and useful in the charitable work of the church. We read of olives, wax, oil, chickens, bread, and wine as characteristic gifts. Those aspects of human being engaged in worship, the central act of Christian community, were honored and affirmed; the worship of early Christians was emphatically, and for theological reasons, a sensory experience.

Furthermore, the sacraments irreducibly involved a material and a spiritual aspect; they thus reflected and addressed the human condition—both spirit and matter. Tertullian wrote:

> To such a degree is the flesh the pivot of salvation, that since by it the soul becomes linked with God, it is the flesh that makes possible the soul's election by God. For example, the flesh is washed (in baptism) that the soul may be made spotless; the flesh is anointed (with chrism) that the soul may be consecrated: the flesh is signed (with the sign of the cross), that the soul too may be protected; the flesh is overshadowed by the imposition of the hand that the soul may be illuminated by the Spirit; the flesh feeds on the body and blood of Christ so that the soul may become fat with God. (*De came Christi*, X.)

Secondly, they understood the usefulness of ascetic practices, of altering the habitual condition and activities of daily life for purposes of alerting themselves to usually well-defended patterns of thought and behavior. They understood that upsetting one's habits made the soul vulnerable, sensitive to its own inertia, its life-denying sin. The body as method, as access to the soul, was an indispensable feature of the spiritual lives of those who struggled as "athletes" toward the goal of self-knowledge, the intermediate goal toward the ultimate goal of the kingdom of heaven. The ascetic life, however, was not understood as confined to those who sought the barren wastes of the Egyptian desert, but was broadly defined as including those who, whatever the external condition of their life, understood their life as spiritual discipline. Even—or especially, as Clement of Alexandra claimed—marriage provided the conditions of intimacy and vulnerability optimally conducive to recognition of ones own weakness, anxiety, and dishonesty. And common life in monastic community is described by Pachomius as eminently suited to learning all about one's temptations to impatience, anger, and self-righteousness.

In all these practical ways, historical Christians revealed their understanding that the Incarnation affected daily life, devotion, and worship. We often fail to recognize that what even Athanasius called "disputes over words" are not the only historical testimony for serious, committed realization of the Incarnation of Jesus Christ. The Incarnation must correct our propensity for converting everything into an intellectual problem. "Do not try to describe ineffable matters by words alone," wrote Simeon, the New Theologian of the Eastern Church, "for this is an impossibility. . . . But let us contemplate such matters by activity, labor, and fatigue. . . . In this way we shall be taught the meaning of such things as the sacred mysteries."

What might an embodied spirituality for our time look like? First, it might involve a difference in the way we think about our participation in worship and sacraments, a re-weighting of our sense of how we participate, a conscious recognition that our bodies are not incidental to worship but an integral part of the spiritual development of whole human beings.

If Christianity were simply a system of ideas, a conceptual scheme, or if it were a subjective state of a certain sort, physical presence at the corporate worship of a community would be unnecessary. It would even distract us from concentration on certain ideas or the cultivation of certain emotion or attitude. But worship is not primarily a gathering of the likeminded. It is a gathering of fragile, vulnerable, transitory human bodies to be present with one another in the mystery of our being and in the faith that human existence originates in, and is drawn toward, love. Christianity is, historically and presently, primarily about human communities based on the shared experiences of physicality, life cycle, physical pain, and physical ecstasy, experiences that are powerful and that we don't know how to integrate, that Christian faith and the Christian community helps us to integrate. And what about historical Christians' interest in asceticism? Will that have any place in an embodied spirituality?

Asceticism hasn't a good press nowadays. It is one of the least understood and most rejected features of historic Christianity. Because we have confused an enormous range of practices, goals, and rationales under the pejorative rubric "asceticism," we do not distinguish between the gentle dehabituating practices advised by many spiritual leaders and the far more attention-getting harsh and dualistic practices involving self-induced pain. Many historic authors caution against such bodily abuse, surely inappropriate in the religion of the Incarnation, while at the same time urging the frequent practice of dehabituating exercises, carefully chosen and individually tailored to address a particular person's compulsive behavior or addictive habits. The undeniable existence of body-damaging and life-shortening practices in some historic reports should not cause us to reject gentler methods. Ascetic practices work realistically with undramatic but nevertheless effective methods: self-observation, temporary abstinence from a good thing to which we've become addicted, and simple exercises that identify and correct habitual or compulsive behavior.

Gentle ascetic practices can temporarily dissolve the daily comforts and habit that keep human beings insulated, unfeeling, and unaware of political threat and social injustice. If, as various historic authors claim, such practices are effective in identifying and addressing cultural as well as individual blindness and deadness, we who live in a nuclear world need to acknowledge the need for a recovery of at least a part of traditional asceticism.

Short fasts, fasts from the media, physical exercise, disciplined prayer and meditation, periods of celibacy, of solitude, or of silence: any of these practices—all as good for body as for soul—can overcome the habits and minor addictions of everyday life and result in increased clarity of insight and what St. Thomas Aquinas called "the renewal of the senses."

Finally, an embodied spirituality involves committed service to the bodies of others. To me, in my historical situation, for example, taking the body as seriously as God did in coming to us in a human body, means that I must protest the threat to human bodies and the body of the earth by the build-up of nuclear weapons. It means that I must work for just social arrangements and against the forms of oppression of human beings in our day.

I have emphasized the importance of the practical and the physical in worship and spirituality, not in order to disparage the language that articulated and preserved the central affirmation of Christian faith—the Incarnation. Nevertheless, I have wanted to explore the aspect of the Incarnation that seems to me to have been—ironically—frequently slighted in preoccupation with the correct verbal formula—human bodies and physical life with its beauty, trials, and redemption.

The Incarnation has been, and is being, understood and appropriated in the simple, humble, practical ways I have suggested as well as in many other practical ways. A multitude of saints through the ages has lived, as we must, our understanding that "the Word became flesh."

③

Violence against Women in the Historical Christian West and in North American Secular Culture

The Visual and Textual Evidence

Let's start with a story, an old, old story, not really one woman's story, but a story repeated in some or all of its details numberless times in the lives of countless women. The story from the Hebrew Bible book of Judges relates the story of a nameless woman who was betrayed, raped, tortured, murdered, and dismembered. The concubine of a powerful ruling-class man, this nameless woman was offered by her master, as the text calls him, to some men who threatened violence against him as they travelled through a foreign territory.

> So the man seized his concubine and put her out to them; and they raped and abused her all night until the morning. And as the dawn began to break, they let her go. As the morning appeared, the woman came and fell down at the door of the man's house where her master was, till it was light.
>
> And her master rose up in the morning, and when he had opened the doors of the house and went out to go on his way, behold, there was his concubine, lying at the door of the house with her hands on the threshold. He said to her, "Get up, let us be going." But there was no answer. Then he put her upon the ass; and the man rose up and went away to his home. And when he entered his house he took a knife, and laying hold of his concubine he divided her, limb by limb into twelve pieces and sent her throughout all the territory of Israel.[1]

He did this, according to the text, to protest this cavalier treatment of his property. Commenting on the story in her book, *Texts of Terror*, Hebrew Bible scholar Phyllis Trible writes: "Of all the characters in scripture, she is the least. Appearing at the beginning and close of a story that rapes her, she

1. Judges 19:25b–29 adapted from RSV.

19

is alone in a world of men. Neither the other characters nor the narrator recognizes her humanity. She is property, object, tool, and literary device. Without name, speech, or power, she has no friends to aid her in life or mourn her in death."[2]

This is an old story, but is it not also a current story? Parts of it sound strangely contemporary for a story about two thousand years old. In the United States today, a woman is raped once every six minutes; one in ten women will be a rape victim sometime in her life; 20 to 30 percent of girls now twelve years of age will suffer violent sexual assault in their lifetimes. In the first three years of the 1980s, there were approximately three-quarters of a million attempted or completed rapes, according to FBI statistics.[3] In addition, a woman is beaten every eighteen minutes in the United States; each year three to six million women are beaten by their sexual partner or ex-partner. In one state alone—Massachusetts—a woman is murdered by her husband or partner every twenty-two days.[4]

Sexual violence against women is also a racist crime: black women are nearly six times as likely to be rape victims as white women.[5] And it is a class crime: the incidence of violence against women is significantly higher in poor families, in racial minority families, and in urban families.[6] Violence, far from being a thing of the past in our enlightened age, is on the increase, and women are its primary victims. But violence against elderly people, children, and vulnerable men is also growing in American culture. Rape is only one form—though a particularly heinous one—of the pervasive violence that is a major threat to Americans, draining human resources and requiring massive strategies for containment and the rehabilitation of its victims and perpetrators. Analysis of the ideological rationalization of and support for violence toward those most affected—women—will help us to begin to unravel the complex cultural strands that keep violence at record highs in American culture.

Women who are fortunate enough never to have been sexually molested often do not realize how much we adjust our lifestyle to avoid victimization. These "precautions" constitute an implicit recognition of the danger; the threat of assault and rape is enough to make us rearrange our lives, reflect-

2. Trible, *Texts of Terror*, 80–81.

3. Pellauer, "Moral Callousness," 42.

4. September 18, 1986, statistics, Memo to staff, Harbor Me Battered Women's Shelter, Boston, Massachusetts.

5. Pellauer, "Moral Callousness," 43.

6. Fortune, *Sexual Violence*, 90.

ing our constant state of terror. Yet our precautions are often futile efforts to lessen the possibility of attack. A high percentage of rapes take place in somebody's home, many of these by assailants known to the victim. There is no possible way for any woman to be thoroughly enough protected that we can feel safe; there is no "safe" way to dress, no "safe" way to behave that will guarantee that we will never be victims of a sexual assault.

Is rape a universal crime, simply a biological fact of life? Because of its distance from us in time and space, the story with which we began seems to imply that rape has been prevalent in every society in every time. If rape is universal, surely there is nothing we can do about it except hope that some *other* woman will be in the wrong place at the wrong time and become a victim. Rape is not, however, a universal crime. The misconception that rape is universal is one of the factors that keeps women feeling passive and helpless in the face of the statistics. Peggy Reeves Sanday's cross-cultural studies of rape revealed that in 40 percent of the societies she studied rape was absent or rare. Rape is not universal but is, Sanday writes, "a learned response which comes from the way societies are organized."[7]

Similarly, Beryl Lieff Benderly, in her article "Rape Free or Rape Prone," writes:

> Certain behavioral patterns and attitudes are common to rape-prone societies. These societies tolerate violence and encourage men and boys to be tough, aggressive, and competitive. Men in such cultures generally have special, politically important gathering spots off-limits to women. . . . Women take little or no part in public decision making or religious rituals: men mock or scorn women's work and remain aloof from childbearing and rearing. These groups usually trace their beginnings to a male supreme being.[8]

North American Christian and post-Christian culture is certainly not unique in its record of violence against women; it is, however, the serious common moral duty of women and men in all rape-prone societies to identify the ideas and images, the attitudes and practices that support, promote, and rationalize violence. If rape is not universal—something we must resign ourselves to and learn to live with—then we must be prepared to detect the images and ideas in American culture that formulate and support the misogyny that results in violence against women.

7. Sanday, *Female Power and Male Dominance*, 42.
8. Benderly, "Rape Free or Rape Prone," 42.

The second misconception that keeps us feeling helpless in the face of the startling figures on violence against women in our own culture is that rape has a biological cause in the powerful sexual urges of males, that it is, in some sense, "natural." This idea is without basis in fact, according to Sanday's cross-cultural studies that identified societies in which rape occurs rarely or not at all. Nevertheless it is pervasive enough in western culture to come from places as various as the Marquis de Sade—and my mother. Men can't "help themselves," my mother told me when I was a teenager, and thus it was "up to me" to see to it that I didn't arouse them. The Marquis de Sade wrote:

> It appears beyond contradiction that Nature has given us the right to carry out our wishes upon all women indifferently; it appears equally that we have the right to force her to submit to our wishes. . . . It is beyond question that we have the right to establish laws which will force women to yield to the ardors of him who desires her; violence itself being one of the results of this right, we can legally employ it. Has not Nature proved to us that we have this right, by allotting us the strength necessary to force them to our desires?[9]

Sexual violence against women is not universal and it is not hormonal, whether the biological basis is construed as an irresistibly powerful sexual urge or as superior physical strength. Moreover, sexual violence is not sexual. Marie Marshall Fortune, in her book *Sexual Violence: The Unmentionable Sin*, calls rape a "pseudosexual act motivated by aggression and hostility."[10] Clinician Nicholas Groth in his study of rapists quotes what he describes a typical description of a rape by the offender:

> I was enraged when I started out. I lost control and struck out with violence. After the assault I felt relieved. I felt I had gotten even. There was no sexual satisfaction; in fact, I felt a little disgusted. I felt relieved of the tension and anger for awhile, but then it would start to build up again. The crime just frustrated me more. I wasn't sexually aroused. I had to force myself.[11]

Marie Marshall Fortune writes: "The belief that male sexual aggression is natural, biologically driven behavior and is 'so overwhelming that the male is the one to be acted upon by it' is a myth that we can no longer afford to perpetuate." Implicit in this myth of male helplessness in the face of a mas-

---

9. Dinnage, *Marquis de Sade*, quoted in Fortune, *Sexual Violence*, 132–33.

10. Fortune, *Sexual Violence*, 116.

11. Groth, *Men Who Rape*, 27.

sive biological drive is a pessimistic view of men. Ironically, it is feminists who question this helplessness hypothesis most strongly. Believing that rape is neither inevitable nor natural to males, feminists insist that men "take responsibility for their sexual and aggressive behavior."[12] If particular social practices—such as male gender conditioning that trains boys to be tough, aggressive, and competitive—are connected to the rape-prone societies studied by Benderly, it is clear that these practices must be identified and changed if misogyny is to be healed. But the dominant ideas, values, and visual images of the American public must also be scrutinized by feminists since these inform social practices.

PATRIARCHAL ORDER: EVE AS DERIVATIVE

What are the ideas and images of historical Western Christianity and contemporary secular culture that constitute the particular conceptual foundation of violence in American culture? My analysis will not exhaust the subject but will aim, rather, at stimulating further work to identify, protest, and change the concepts, images, and conditions that promote violence against women in our society. Moreover, instead of exploring some of the dramatic cultural support for violence against women—such as pornography—I will focus on ideas and images that support violence simultaneously in more readily accessible and more foundational ways. The most pervasive foundations of violence against women are so ordinary, so unexceptional, and therefore so unnoticed that they are seldom challenged. Pornography, an industry larger than the record and film industries *put together*, may be enormously important as the major eroticization of violence of our culture,[13] but there are other rationalizations of, and support for, violence against women. These are more superficial in that they lie more on the surface of American culture; at the same time they are more foundational in that they are built into the assumptions and institutional structures of American culture in the family and child rearing, in educational institutions, and in churches, synagogues, and government.

It is important also to recognize that misogynist ideas and images are not the only messages given in Judaism and Christianity to and about women; there are other ideas and images that were often used by women for their empowerment, as validations of their activity, and as warrants for a degree of independence. Historical Christianity, on which I will focus in discussing medieval

12. Fortune, *Sexual Violence*, 116–18.
13. Dworkin, *Pornography: Men Possessing Women*, 201.

and Renaissance visual images, is a frustrating mixture. If it were unambiguously misogynist, feminists could feel free to reject it; if it presented a comprehensive affirmation of women, feminists could find in it tools for present empowerment. Since Christianity carries both possibilities simultaneously, it is necessary to do a painstaking job of identifying the misogynist *and* the useful and usable strands, the history of oppression *and* of women's creative use of ideas and images that gave them credibility and leverage in relation to their societies. It is well to keep in mind that a kind of anachronistic violence against historical women can be done by historians who assume that they tolerated and masochistically enjoyed a religion and culture that oppressed and persecuted them. A respectful attitude toward the struggles of historical women requires that we remain open to seeing the possibility that they were often able to create for themselves lives of amazing beauty and richness by the creative use of their religious and cultural resources.[14]

It is not, however, the project of this chapter to explore the resourceful selective interpretations by which women constructed their self-images and ideas of relationship, world, and God with the help of Christian ideas and images. Our project is the identification of the most common biblical concepts contributing to misogyny and the continued use of these concepts in the present. It is astonishing to detect the continuity of rationales for the subordination of women across what we usually take to be the gulf between the historic religious cultures of the West and contemporary American culture. Although patriarchal religious ideas and visual images are still strong in their religious setting in large sectors of the American public, their translation in the secular media has insured both their continuing influence and their constant availability to Americans. Secularization has not apparently rejected, but rather taken over many ancient religious judgments about the role and value of women. We will shortly take a closer look at this continuity.

First, let us consider three pervasive and powerful ideas of Jewish and Christian cultures that continue to contribute heavily to the misogyny in American culture that scapegoats women. The first of these ideas is that patriarchal order is the right ordering of society, reflecting cosmic order. Patriarchal hierarchy has been amazingly constant from the Ten Commandments of the Hebrew Bible, which list a man's wife along with his cattle and house as one of his possessions, to the laws of modern American culture, which in most states, despite efforts to change them, still stipulate that rape within marriage

14. See, for example, Miles, "Images of Women in Fourteenth-Century Tuscan Painting," *Image as Insight*, chapter 4, 63–93.

is impossible since a husband always has the right of sexual access to his wife. Tertullian, an influential North African Christian author of the third century, explained the Genesis account of the creation of men and women like this: "This second human being was made by God for man's assistance, and that female was forthwith named woman."[15] In the texts of historic Christianity, the creation of Eve after Adam is repeatedly cited as "proof" of women's inherent need to he controlled by men. As several contemporary authors are showing, other interpretations of the creation myth are certainly possible; the consistent interpretation of Eve as a "second human being" created to help man, is puzzling unless we find political reasons why it was thus interpreted through centuries of patriarchal order in the Christian West. For example, John Boswell, the Yale historian, has argued that the creation myth of Genesis 1 clearly states an ascending progression of creation: first inanimate matter, then animals, then intelligent being—man, and, as the apex and crown of creation, intelligent and life-bearing woman. What seemed to Boswell an "obvious" reading is one that is seldom found in the history of interpretation of Genesis.[16]

Most people in historic Western communities did not, however, write or read scriptural or theological texts. And, although they heard expressions of ideas of patriarchal order in sermons, in religious drama, in public readings of devotional texts, in hymns, scripture, and liturgy, the written and spoken word was perhaps not the most powerful communication of misogynist attitudes to illiterate people. Visual images, seen by everyone in the community every day on the walls of their local church, were a constant and fundamental source of instruction and conditioning for whole communities. Historical people did not have television, newspapers, magazines, or billboards. Thus the images they saw daily were few and usually remained the same throughout their lives. It is perhaps impossible for us to reconstruct from our own experience of a glut of media images the powerful influence of medieval "media," that is, religious paintings and sculpture. We cannot do more here than to suggest some characteristic visual themes and pictorial treatments that, seen repeatedly in the central community gathering-place, the church, contributed to and validated violence against women.

15. Tertullian, *De velandis virginibus* 5, 30.

16. Lecture, Harvard Divinity School, April 1985. Another exception to standard interpretations of the Genesis 1 account of the creation of women as secondary human beings is Agrippa von Nettesheim's 1509 "Declamation on the Nobility and Excellence of the Feminine Sex." In Opera, vol. 2, 504–7. Lyon, n.d.; photo. repr. Hildesheirm 1970.

The texts written and read by a small minority of culturally and educationally privileged people in historic communities might have been less influential had the idea of Eve's creation as a "second human being" not been visually reinforced and extended in many paintings and sculptures, which show Eve emerging bodily from a gaping hole in the side of the sleeping Adam. Repeated depiction of this scene on the facades of cathedrals and in paintings in local parish churches enabled people not only to hear or read, but also to *picture* the secondary creation of the first and prototypical woman.

The establishment of patriarchal order in early Christianity, the exclusion of women from leadership roles in the church, and the theological rationalization of patriarchal order in family and society have been described by several feminist historians.[17] The preoccupation of church leaders with the danger of insubordination led them to urge the gender-specific "virtues" of docility, submissiveness, and obedience for women. Tyrannical domination, the complementary male role, was apparently less to be feared than female insubordination. In the early fifth century, Augustine, discussing the question of why the patriarchs of the Hebrew bible were permitted to have more than one wife, wrote:

> It was permitted for one husband to have several wives, [but] it was not permitted for one woman to have several husbands. . . . For, by a hidden law of nature *things that rule love singularity*; things that are ruled, indeed are subjected not only each one to an individual master, but also . . . many of them are not unfittingly subjected to one master . . . just as many souls are properly subjected to the one God.[18]

"Things that rule love singularity" is followed by the justification and rationale, "just as many souls are properly subjected to the one God." The twin assumptions of male supremacy—through self-identification with God—and women as male property constitute patriarchal order. Rationalized as loving protection of the ruled, the bottom line of patriarchal order is the use of violence toward and even murder of the ruled for their protection. Augustine's epic *City of God* provides the explicit connection between rule and protection that allowed patriarchal rulers families and states to justify their rule to those subjected as "for your own good."[19]

---

17. See especially Schüssler Fiorenza, *In Memory of Her* (1983); see also Miles, "Patriarchy as Political Theology"; and Brooten, "Paul's Views on the Nature of Women and Female Homoeroticism."

18. Italics mine; Augustine *De bono conjungali* 17.20.

19. Augustine *De Civitate Dei* 19.14.

A contemporary example of the murder of a woman for her protection shows the continuity of patriarchal assumptions. James Michener's 1963 novel, *Poland*—thirty-eight weeks on the *New York Times'* best seller list—provides a contemporary example of the continuity of male justification of violence against women as clearly and vividly as if it were contemporaneous with the book of Genesis or with Augustine. After a battle, the protagonist finds in the luxurious headquarters of the defeated enemy the partially decapitated body of a beautiful young slave woman. Reflecting on this grisly scene, he muses that "the man who bought her had obviously loved her deeply, for he had killed her—rather than have her fall into the hands of others."[20] The author apparently expects readers of this novel to assume, along with him, that murderous violence is the ultimate proof of deep love. The short steps from patriarchal order, to ownership, to violence are all in place.

WOMAN, BODY, NATURE, AND SIN

The second influential idea we need to examine is the identification, in Western Christian cultures, of woman with body and nature, and body with sin. From Eve, the instigator of sin and cause of the fall of the human race, to the actual women whose beauty tempted celibate males, women have been reduced in male eyes to body, visibility, and temptation. Just as images of women as sinful functioned as cultural sanctions for male domination, male supremacy ratified the domination, denudation, and use of nature.

Again, historical sculpture and paintings, the media of Western Christianity, encouraged medieval and Renaissance viewers to picture the sinful woman as naked and old, with swollen belly and pendulous breasts. Excessive female flesh was a consistent visual signal of "fleshliness"—a literalistic interpretation of St. Paul's use of "the flesh" as a theological term to designate the predilection to sin of the whole person, especially the soul. A facade bas-relief on the Modena cathedral, Notre Dame du Part, shows Eve, with swollen belly and exaggerated breasts, standing by Adam. His foot is placed on top of hers, a pictorial device for signifying superiority. Female nudity was symbolic of woman's "natural" proclivity to lust. If, in addition, the female body suggested pregnancy, it represented the biological result of female lust.

Since woman was seen as body, biology, and nature, she represented for men everything in themselves that they must discipline and reject if they

---

20. Michener, *Poland*, 200.

are to achieve their potential to be pure intellect, mind, and spirit. Tertullian described male lust as the responsibility of women:

> *You* are the Devil's gateway. *You* are the unsealer of that forbidden tree. *You* are the first deserter of the divine law. You are she who persuaded him whom the Devil was not valiant enough to attack. *You* destroyed so easily God's image, man. On account of *your* deserved punishment, that is, death, even the Son of God had to die.[21]

These quotations from the Church Fathers are not significant because they originated the ideas they express, but because they are tediously characteristic of the male ecclesiastical leadership whose perspective they represent. If these were novel ideas of Tertullian or Augustine, they would probably not have been influential, since in their own time theological texts were read only by a few culturally and educationally privileged males. They are important precisely because they were not novel but were, instead, extraordinarily clear statements of consensus male opinions.

Tertullian says, further, that he can be confident that he recognizes a woman's desire to attract him by the way *he* is affected by the woman's appearance. If a man is aroused by a particular woman, that woman means to arouse him: "Seeing and being seen belong to the selfsame lust."[22]

One result of the identification of woman with body, nature, and sin, is the exaggerated esteem of female virginity that Andrea Dworkin, in her book, *Woman Hating*, calls "a real sexual perversion."[23] If woman is body, sex, and sin, rejection of her "nature" as body/sex/sin is inordinately valued. Thus, although men rape and impregnate women, the woman they value is the untouched, untouchable woman. The virgin/mother of Christ is the prototype. The popular fourteenth-century devotional text, Jacobus de Voragine's *The Golden Legend*, follows the opinions of more esoteric theologians like Augustine and Thomas Aquinas that although the virgin was consummately beautiful, yet there was something about her that absolutely prevented any man from looking at her with desire.[24]

Paintings and sculptures of the Virgin strongly reinforce textual insistence on her obedience, submissiveness, and innocence. Her head is frequently shown with a side cant, a posture of humble acquiescence, as in

21. Tertullian *De cultu feminarum* 1.
22. Tertullian *De velandus virginibus* 2.
23. Dworkin, *Woman Hating*, 73.
24. Vorgaine, *The Golden Legend*, 150.

Botticelli's *Madonna of the Magnificat*. An exaggeratedly high brow, large eyes, and a small mouth are iconographical features repeatedly employed by painters to represent her spirituality and lack of sensuality. Even in paintings of the nursing Virgin, like Rogier van der Weyden's *St. Luke Painting The Virgin*, the potential sensuality of an exposed breast is controlled by her non-sensual facial features.[25]

FEMALE SUFFERING AS SALVIFIC

The final rationalization of misogyny and violence against women that we will discuss is the idea that suffering is the path to transcendence and salvation. This notion has a complicated historical development that, to be fully understood, would require an equally complex examination of the concrete historical situations in which it came to be a prominent Christian idea. The glorification of suffering in Western Christianity has suggested that if suffering is potentially beneficial, even salvific, to impose physical suffering on another human being, far from being reprehensible, may sometimes even be helpful to the victim. From the fifth century BCE forward, the spoken or unspoken law of Western societies has been that the strong take what they will and the weak suffer what they must. The Greeks, who articulated this description of aggression, did not attempt to sweeten it with the rationalization that it was good for the weak to suffer. No heavenly reward that would eventually compensate the sufferer was posited. The Greeks simply acknowledged a brutal law of the jungle.

In Christianity, however, imitation of, and participation in, the suffering of Christ, although variously interpreted, was seen as normative for Christians. Even the most tyrannical oppressor could claim enough suffering to warrant support for the principle that suffering is good for the soul. Suffering in life was seen especially in the medieval period as a way to preclude suffering after death. Present suffering ensured future bliss. Some notorious oppressors took this maxim quite literally, In fifteenth-century England, John, Lord of Arundel, before going off to war, paid a call on the local convent, carrying off sixty nuns to entertain his soldiers on the long sea voyage. Midway through the voyage, however, storms arose, which necessitated lightening the ship's load. The nuns were thrown overboard and perished, to a woman. When John of Arundel died, his will left instructions for posthumous penance for

25. Hollander, in *Seeing Through Clothes*, claims that naked breasts are, in any culture, "the sure conveyors of a complex delight," though cultural definitions of the norm for erotic breasts vary widely (186).

this and other deeds of his adventuresome life. His body, the will stipulated, was to be beaten, wrapped in chains, and buried naked in the earth. The advantage of posthumous penance is obvious,[26] but even in its own cultural setting the notion that such undemanding "suffering" could atone for responsibility for the suffering of the raped and drowned women trivializes the real suffering of the murdered women.

Medieval religious painting, publicly accessible on the walls and altars of churches, repeatedly depicts the suffering of women as salvific—and not only for their own souls; it is their suffering that qualifies them to be effective intercessors for others. The martyrdom of women saints was a favorite theme, a theme that often borders on pornographic eroticization of violence. Paintings of the martyrdom of St. Barbara by Master Franke (*The St. Barbara Altarpiece*, first half of the fifteenth century) and of St. Agatha by Sebastiono del Piombo (first half of the sixteenth century) show these saints having their naked breasts pulled off by giant pincers and sliced off by one burly executioner, while being whipped by another. Martyrdoms of the legendary St. Catherine of Alexandria, like the painting of this subject on the wall of the St. Catherine Chapel in San Clemente, Rome, show St. Catherine being beheaded. From these depictions of violent suffering to depictions of the fainting but dignified Virgin at the foot of the cross, the physical and spiritual suffering of women is shown as one of the primary ways for women to follow Christ. Excluded from emulating other roles of the human Christ, such as teaching or preaching, women often gained social and spiritual power by exaggerated and self-imposed suffering.

Male saints and scriptural figures—especially Christ—are, of course, also shown in texts and images as suffering, but their roles are not focused on salvific suffering. A much broader repertoire of activities is assigned to men than to women in religious images, while the primary religious participation and power of men was priesthood, religious images suggested to women that various forms of suffering were the surest route to participation in religious power. The reward for suffering was also a constant theme of religious paintings and sculpture. In this life, the reward was ecstatic mystical union, such as that shown in the later Bernini sculpture of St. Teresa in the Cornaro Chapel of Santa Maria della Vittoria in Rome. In the next life, present suffering was rewarded more dramatically; bodily assumptions of the Virgin and Mary Magdalen, as well as Coronation of the Virgin scenes, depicted the fulfillment of patient suffering in this life.

26. Cohen, *Metamorphosis of a Death Symbol,* 5.

WOMEN AS SUBORDINATE, EVIL, AND SUFFERING

The most dramatic historical example of the confluence of the three ideas and images we have explored occurred in the fifteenth through the seventeenth centuries in an oppression and persecution of women unparalleled in the history of Christianity. The phenomenon of witch-hunting in the late fifteenth through the early seventeenth centuries is too diverse and complex on the one hand, and too local, petty, and sordid on the other hand to be illuminated by any single explanatory thesis. It is, however, a striking example of the co-operation of misogynist texts and images to produce massive violence against women. Figures for victims of witch persecutions can only be guesswork due to partial and lost records; the most conservative estimate is that of the 100,000 to 200,000 victims approximately 80 percent were women. Henri Bouget, writing in 1590, said that "Switzerland has been compelled to wipe out many of her villages on [the witches'] account," and that Germany was "almost entirely occupied with building fires for them."[27] The human suffering involved cannot be adequately suggested by statistics.

Manuals on witchcraft and its detection and prosecution, like Kramer and Sprenger's *Malleus Meleficarum*, codified and expanded older beliefs about women's moral weakness, gullibility, and wantonness, and concluded that the persecution and execution of witches was God-ordained and God-pleasing. Quoting patristic authors, the *Malleus* says that the root problem of witches and the reason they are mostly women is that such a woman "will not be governed, but will follow her own impulse."[28] Secondly, "All witchcraft comes from carnal lust, which is in women insatiable." The *Malleus Maleficarum* is a catalog of male projection: "The word 'woman' is used to mean the lust of the flesh." Yet, oddly enough, although women cause men to sin through inciting them to lust, one of the chief accusations brought against witches was that they cause impotence. The witches' arrest, judicial torture, and execution by burning was prescribed as the only way to relieve the innocent who suffered from their powers. In fact, it was apparently genuinely believed that the only possible way to impress on a witch the evil of her ways and the urge to true repentance was the extreme suffering of burning; *in extremis*, it was believed, the witch might repent and thus, in spite of all, attain salvation. Therefore, the greatest possible favor one could do for a witch—as for any heretic—was to burn her.

27. Bouget, *An Examen of Witches Drawn from Various Trials*, xxxiii.
28. Kramer and Sprenger, *The Malleus Maleficarum*, xxx.

The Inquisitor's witchcraft handbooks, horrifying in their logical impeccability and cool self-righteousness, however, were texts written in Latin and inaccessible to everyone but the educated. The *Malleus* was published in 1484, but it was not until the sixteenth and seventeenth centuries that the witch persecutions reached their most intense level. The manuals did not inspire the popular frenzy against presumed witches of the sixteenth and seventeenth centuries. Rather, the witch persecutions were a media phenomenon. They could not have happened before the invention of the printing press at the end of the fifteenth century. The first widely circulated printed "newspapers" were not pamphlets containing Protestant reformation theology but broadsheets distributing accounts of the trials, tortures, and executions of presumed witches. The dissemination of this "information" to towns and villages prompted the popular mania for identifying and persecuting witches.[29] When people were told that hailstorms, miscarriages, crop failures, accident, and disease were caused by witches, *and* when they were shown what witches looked like, they learned to look for the cause of their high and constant levels of misery in women familiar to them. As in paintings and sculptures of Eve with an abundance of flesh, printed drawings of witches on sixteenth-century broadsheets, etchings, and engravings featured corpulent women epitomizing the lust that motivated witchcraft. Hans Baldung Grien and Albrecht Dürer are the most famous of the artists who obsessively pictured witches and their alleged activities. Not until ideas and images were brought together did witch-hunting become mass hysteria and popular sport.

CONTEMPORARY WOMEN AND PATRIARCHAL ORDER

We have seen that the first newspapers were illustrated tirades against women; let us turn now to our present situation, to media images of our own time, and ask if traditional misogynist ideas and images are not still selling newspapers. Since media images of our own time are not usually religious images, the continuity of ancient biblical misogyny is masked in North American media. But is it not still there?

How do advertising images function to inform members of the present society of their relative value and position in the society? Verbal captions of advertisements proclaim, by seeming to address everyone, a rhetoric of social equality. Images, however, consistently present young, wealthy, slim, sexually attractive Anglo-Saxon women and men as the satisfied users of their

29. Eisenstein, "Advent of Printing and the Protestant Revolution," 260ff.

products. The verbal text contradicts the powerful subliminal message of the image, which promotes sexism, racism, and ageism. By the endless repetition of visual clichés, it creates marginal people, both women and men, who can never realistically aspire to youth, wealth, the right skin color or sexual preference in order to qualify for the satisfaction promised by the image.

In advertising images, the valued and valuable members of the society are clearly identified; consistent and cumulative messages are given by which we measure ourselves and formulate self-images based on the degree to which we match the images. Both men and women appear in our daily newspapers, but, as one student recently discovered when she analyzed an issue of the Sunday *New York Times*, about 90 percent of the pictures of men appeared in news stories, while about 90 percent of the images of women appeared in advertising. On October 27, 1983—the day Grenada was invaded— the front and back pages of the first section of the *New York Times* illustrated vividly the complementarity of gender images. The front page shows photographs of men, brows furrowed, conferring with one another, and photographs of military men landing in Grenada, greeted with gratitude and enthusiasm. The back page shows a full-page sized "Cosmo girl," partially but inadequately draped, in a seductive pose. Our conditioned expectations that men think and act, while women fulfill themselves and gain whatever power they may have by being beautiful objects, are consistently nourished by media gender imagery.

The three ancient ideas about women examined above are alive and well in today's media. Male supremacy is daily reinforced in implicit if not explicit norms of patriarchal order; identification of women with body and temptation is a staple of media images, and the notion that suffering is salvific is also to be found in press photographs of suffering women and in advertising images: "Life looks better when you do," urges an advertisement for cosmetic surgery. The secularization of these messages makes them seem contemporary, but, as the French proverb has it, "the more things change, the more they remain the same." We have seen that it is precisely these traditional ideas, now artfully clothed in fashionable modern dress, that provide cultural support for misogyny and ultimately for violence against women.

In *The Body and Society*, Bryan Turner has argued that changes in the character of the family unit, industrialization, women's participation in the marketplace, and laws that have to a great extent dismantled the exclusionary practices that established and maintained patriarchy, have given rise to a contemporary American culture that cannot be realistically characterized as patriarchal. If patriarchy is defined as institutional and political subordination of women, we do not presently live in such a society. Yet institutional changes have not created an inclusive society; women still experience sexism, misogyny, and violence in everyday life. In fact, Turner argues, the demise of patriarchy has created the condition of "patrism," or ideological patriarchy. Although "patrism" is unsupported by laws and institutions, it is still a powerful force, a reaction by men who "find their traditional sources of power increasingly open to doubt":

> The collapse of patriarchy has left behind it widespread patrism which is a culture of discriminatory, prejudicial, and paternalistic beliefs about the inferiority of women. . . . Patrism is expanding precisely because of the institutional shrinkage of patriarchy, which has left men in a contracting power position. . . . Institutionalized patriarchy has crumbled along with the traditional family unit and the patristic attitude of men towards women becomes more prejudicial and defensive precisely because women are now often equipped with a powerful ideological critique of traditional patriarchy.[30]

If Turner is correct in identifying a trend in the direction of increasingly inclusive laws and institutions in American culture, then it is important to extend feminist analysis beyond the structures of society to the more subtle oppression of women by patrism—male reaction to the loss of patriarchal laws and institutions. Traditional ideas and images, often in contemporary dress but essentially unaltered and undiminished in virulence, continue to be reiterated, reinforced, and extended in the public practices of everyday life as well as in the media. The ideas and visual images discussed above inform and rationalize numerous everyday occurrences that are too taken-for-granted to be easily changed—jokes, street taunts, sexist language, dress, and sexually-differentiated labor. Social change must still proceed, no doubt, by continuing to insist on laws that protect and institutions that include women. But public life is not the only arena in which change is necessary. Personal attitudes and behavior are also political activities. In making some suggestions about how a public ideology of misogyny can be addressed, then, let us speak personally.

What can we do about it? It is, of course, worse than useless to stand around deploring the communication media of modern society, perhaps the most common and constant carrier of misogyny in North America. The media are here to stay. Yet it is important to raise questions about the values implicit in the daily media dosage of a whole society. Until we are conscious of these implicit values, we are helpless victims. Until we are conscious of the

---

30. Turner, *Body and Society*, 156.

messages we receive daily, we can neither choose those we find life-enhancing nor reject and protest those that promote injustice and violence.

There are two possible kinds of response to misogyny and violence against women. One response is that of providing help for victims of violence. As a result of the present women's movement, Mary Pellauer writes, "intellectual and institutional resources have been generated at an incredible speed. There are now more than 500 battered women's shelters and 1500 rape crisis centers around the country."[31] The difference between the passive voyeurism of the viewer of media violence and active engagement to eliminate violence and to heal its victims is crucial. Most shelters are staffed by volunteers, women who find the opportunity of "doing something about it" personally healing. We can address the moral deadening caused by seeing daily doses of misogynist and/or violent media images about which we can do nothing by offering our presence and help to women who are the victims of violence.

The second response aims at prevention, at the massive social transformation that will be necessary to change our situation as women. Identifying the underlying and constant ideas and images that make violence against women possible and even, in the eyes of some, legitimate, enables us to speak against these ideas wherever we find them—in the home, in institutions, in the media, in churches, and in synagogues.

If our speech is to be effective, however, we must overcome the individualism that enables many of us to think that violence against women is not our problem. "I've never been raped, never been discriminated against, never been hurt," we hear. The crucial step for the creation of the solidarity necessary to protest and change the conditions in which we live as women is to stop thinking only in terms of "my own experience" and to self-identify with women as a "caste," in Mary Daly's term, with women who are always subordinated in patriarchal cultures and in cultures characterized by patrism. Once one has achieved identification with women as a caste, all one needs to do is to read the newspapers in order to feel as one's own the dramatic abuse of women, especially women of color, poor women, and third world women. Once one has made this self-identification, it will no longer do to blame the victim, to think, however unconsciously, that victims of so-called sexual violence have been assaulted because they dressed provocatively, because they "invited" it by going out alone at night, or even by living alone. Blaming the victim functions to keep women feeling safe, feeling that we will not become victims; it keeps us isolated.

31. Pellauer, "Moral Callousness," 49.

How do we claim as our own the experience of another human being? How do we feel experiences we have not had? Feminist author Emily Culpepper once responded to these questions with a simple but profound reply: "We tell each other our stories," she said. In the commitment to listening with empathy and speaking with honesty, the experience of another woman can become one's own experience. The ability to feel the pain of others can then become an ethical resource, empowering women to overcome isolation, individualism, and fear. The first step toward protesting the misogyny and violence of present society and beginning to create a society in which we can love and play and work without fear, is to begin to think communally, collectively.

The second step has already been named. Women must replace paralyzed passivity with activity. The two steps are intimately connected. Women can act effectively only to the extent that we act collectively. Probably every woman has had the experience of speaking about an issue of personal importance in a public gathering. A great effort was required to do so, and after saying her piece she felt guiltily that she had been daring, subverted the discussion, and made an impact. Then the next person spoke, not in response or even rebuttal to her comment, but on an entirely new topic. The discussion went on as if the woman had never spoken. Perhaps a few minutes later someone else mentioned her comment, reinforced it by noting it, or restated it. Then and only then she feels and is heard. A single woman's voice in patriarchal and patristic cultures is inaudible, no matter how strong and loud it may be. But once two or several women have acknowledged or restated the comment, it begins to be heard. Only our collective voices are heard.

Finally, in a culture characterized by patrism, it is not usually by dramatic public statements against women that violence against women is justified and perpetuated, but by the small increments of sexism occurring constantly on a daily intimate level. Even the apparently humorous misogyny of everyday life desensitizes both women and men to misogyny. If misogyny is pervasive, however, it is also accessible; it can be named as it appears, and if it is constantly named and rejected by women it can be changed.

Only by exploration of the deep roots of misogyny in Western scriptures and religious images can the rationalizations for violence against women be recognized in their contemporary forms. For a historian trained to expect that ideas appearing to remain the same across time and space in fact do not act similarly in different cultural settings, it is startling to see the continuity of misogynist ideas and images and the similarity with which they operate to subordinate women in diverse cultures. The next surprise is that, in spite of the pervasiveness and rootedness of misogyny, the subordination of women, and violence against women in Western societies, women have still been able to change the institutionalized, legalized oppression of women in American culture still prevalent a few decades ago. Those real gains, however, cannot be consolidated and advanced unless feminists continue to unmask the patriarchal God as He appears in American culture. Where should women place our attention—on the progress, the fragile beginning of the creation of an inclusive society, or on the mighty forces within and outside individuals that persist in misogyny? We need to have our eye on both—on the progress, so we do not become discouraged, and on the magnitude of the task, so that we do not become prematurely comfortable in feminist enclaves.

4

Textual Harassment

Desire and the Female Body

In his *Lives of the Most Eminent Philosophers*, the Roman author Diogenes Laertius made the puzzling observation that "even the despising of pleasure is pleasurable."[1] The fourth-century Christian Gregory of Nazianzus referred to "the pleasure of no pleasure."[2] More recently, in *Middlemarch*, George Eliot had Celia say that Dorothea "likes giving up."[3] In what sense is "giving up"—asceticism—pleasurable? In this chapter I will suggest that it is necessary to entertain the odd notion that what might be interpreted as "negative" or destructive behavior could have not merely productive but even pleasurable effects.

How would contemporary understandings of eating disorders change if this complex phenomenon were described as a kind of perverse pleasure, the amazing, poignant, sturdy pleasure of a plant seeking light in a crowded forest? If theorists and clinicians attend only to potential or actual destructive effects, I am persuaded, we will fail to identify useful strategies for addressing those less-than-desirable effects. When eating disorders are understood as a dangerous, "kinky" pleasure, the clinical task will be to identify and cultivate more direct and unambiguous satisfactions. In short, effective treatment of the 90 percent of anorexics and bulimics who are women will involve exercising and strengthening female desire, providing it with the support of multiple and diverse models, symbolic authorization, and a repertoire of textual warrants. Examining the social construction of desire and its goal, pleasure, will therefore be central to my argument.

1. Laertius, *Lives of the Most Eminent Philosophers*, 6.2.70.
2. Gregory Nazianzus, *De ordine* 6, quoted by Musurillo, "The Problem," 6.
3. Eliot, *Middlemarch*, 42.

I believe there is an important connection between the social construction of female desire in middle-class North American society and asceticism, "the pleasure of no pleasure." I understand desire not only as sexual desire but also as including a broader repertoire of desire for particular social roles and achievements. Desire is preliminary to pleasure and integrally entailed in its production. Recently, Teresa de Lauretis remarked on the "weakness" of female desire, "its lack of authorization, symbolic representation, support and encouragement."[4] This observation is an important one: if female desire—*eros*—is not cultivated, or if it is construed merely as the complement to male desire, this could help to explain why so many young women practice and enjoy the asceticism of fasting.

There are two fundamentally different approaches to thinking about desire. Forty years ago Herbert Marcuse pictured sexual desire as radically at odds with the constraints of societies, a wild card, undomesticated, on which the individual could base rebellion against society; one's sexuality organized the "true," uncolonized "self."[5] More recently, Michel Foucault argued against Marcuse's model in which an untouched, pristine, free, stock of desire—an individual property—is appropriated by society, trained to serve its economic, emotional, and social ends. Rather, he pictured individual desire as socially produced and conditioned, as called into existence as well as shaped by society.

Using Foucault's model, Frigga Haug, a German feminist, has analyzed female sexualization. She discusses the complex and intricate process by which women learn to please others, to attract the male glance and gaze. Female sexualization, a crucial aspect of socialization she says, is intimately concerned with achieving the right body parts—the right hair, breasts, legs—and behavior—the right walk, the right eye movements. Female desire, then, is socially constructed as the passive complement of male desire rather than as a distinctive female "I want."[6] If a strong and centered desire is not primarily a personal attribute or capacity but is produced by one's socialization, it is evident that the lack of an active, effective, distinctive female desire is the result of a "lack of symbolic authorization" combined with a lack of institutional recognition and confirmation. So women's longings never take form—

4. de Laurentis, "The Essence of Triangle or, Taking the Risk of Essentialism Seriously."

5. Herbert Marcuse, in *Eros and Civilizatio*, extended Freud's analysis of civilization as based on instinctual renunciation and the sublimation of sexuality, in *Civilization and Its Discontents*, and *The Future of an Illusion*.

6. Haug, *Female Sexualization*.

individually or collectively—as a powerful force. Moreover, if Western societies fail to provide authorization and symbolic representations of positive pleasure, the practice of refusing the problematic pleasures "provided" is likely to become pleasurable. "No pleasure," not only as a refusal of the pleasures to which one is socialized but also as a set of performative practices, can develop a "personalized" desire.

Understanding eating disorders as, in some sense, pleasurable provides a conceptual handle that is useful for clinical as well as for theoretical purposes. I will contest both the understanding of eating disorders as an attempt by the powerless to control *something*, and the suggestion that young women starve themselves in order to look like the models they see in the media. Anorexia nervosa will, I think, prove impervious to understanding or treatment until it can be seen as a female strategy for imagining and achieving pleasure. That the range of behavior labeled eating disorders is also dangerously self-destructive and that it also punishes families, communities, and society is evident. But theoretically positioned as *effects* rather than as causes or motivations, punishment of self and others appears as secondary to its production of pleasure.

Asceticism, then, not only *expresses* desire; it also acts to resist socialization. Resistance, we should note, assumes an unwanted socialization to resist. Asceticism is an alternative to the pleasure of assuming the roles and capabilities established by one's society. Unlike that of the person who accepts socialization, the ascetic's desire refuses socially designated objects and instead seeks its object in an activity of alternative self-construction. In its practical strategies for resistance, asceticism exposes the social construction of the gendered "I," challenging and subverting the illusion of naturalness that characterizes the socialized self. Consciously chosen and practiced, asceticism is pleasurable. It becomes counterproductive—more painful than pleasurable, even potentially physically destructive—when fascination with practices and their effects assumes centrality. Asceticism in itself then, is not inevitably "positive" or "negative." In the abstract it is neutral—simply a methodology or tool; close examination of particular practices in specific contexts is required to determine whether ascetic practices accomplish the purposes for which they are intended and, if they do, whether the cost to the individual or to society seems to outweigh the benefits.

I will first consider some descriptions of the connection between desire and pleasure in the dominantly Christian West, examining one influential textual construction of (male) desire, St. Augustine's *Confessions*, in order to demonstrate the specificity of desire as gendered. Then I will sketch an understanding of eating disorders that provides incentives for women to seek and to create more direct and effective pleasures than the "pleasure of no pleasure."

I

In the Christian West, a myth of individual autonomy, self-directedness, a chosen self that is cultivated, exercised, and trained has articulated and examined values continues to exert attractive force. This myth may have a corrective function in societies that are deeply embedded in traditional ideas, practices, and social arrangements. It may also function to encourage individuation in societies in which mass communication media socialize under the guise of entertaining or informing. However, the accuracy and specific productivity of orienting myths as well as their effects in particular social contexts must be continuously examined. If the myth of autonomous individuality has indeed reflected anyone's experience in North American and Western European cultures, it has seldom been true for women. Linked to other people by kinship, marriage, and reproduction, women have rarely represented themselves as solitary "self-actualizing" entities.

As early as the third century of the Common Era, self-shaping desire was recognized to be a male prerogative. In the late Roman period, women who resisted traditional roles in order to create and cultivate a religious "self" whether in one of the philosophical schools, in Christianity, or in Judaism, were spoken of as "becoming male." Chosen, intentional behavior was clearly understood as a male prerogative. Nevertheless, countercultural religious and philosophical communities recognized—had a context for understanding—these women's behavior.

In societies that lack symbolic representations of female aspiration, women who have dared to formulate distinctive desires and to act these out in a deliberately chosen lifestyle have usually encountered scorn, misunderstanding, and, often, violence.[7] Throughout the West, folktales, novels, and—more recently—films depict the flamboyant life of Joan of Arc, or Anna Karenina, Madame Bovary, Isadora Duncan, or Camille Claudel only to conclude with a narration of their alcoholism, insanity, or painful and ignominious death in youth or early middle age. Indeed, these stories can often claim the status

---

7. Differences according to class and race need, of course, to he taken into account; it has certainly always been more likely that a wealthy noblewoman of a dominant race could act as she chose than that a working-class woman could. Nevertheless, women of all classes who resisted female socialization to conventional marriage and motherhood have frequently met dramatic and untimely ends, both in life and in literature.

of biography—real life—thereby reinforcing their effectiveness as cautionary tales and illustrating again Antigone's observation; "As in the past, this law is immutable: for mortals greatly to live is greatly to suffer."

It may be true that to disregard the conventional wisdom advocating a life of moderation and obedience to one's socialization is dangerous to "mortals." Nevertheless, there has been, and currently is, in late twentieth-century North America and Western Europe, social tolerance for the possibility— even the expectation—that young men will enjoy a more or less extended period of social rebellion and sexual experimentation. In the male-designed and administered societies of the West, however, women who attempt to behave in unconventional ways inevitably meet myriad covertly and overtly powerful strategies of restraint and opposition. Through socialization, female desire is strongly directed to traditional roles, roles that are crucial to the reproduction of society, especially in the bearing and rearing of children. Multiple rewards and punishments reinforce this socialization with precisely the necessary amount of forcefulness. The sensory and emotional pleasures entailed in resisting socialization can be considerable.

II

What are the pleasures of "giving up"? The relief of psychic pain can be one such effect. Because body and psyche are interconnected, the psyche's pain can be reproduced in the body, bringing it to the surface where it can find expression. For example, the starving psyche might be acted out as a starving body, replacing involuntary pain with voluntary—chosen and controlled—pain. Asceticism may be, in fact, the most direct way to vent the psyche—a democratic, accessible method of relieving psychic pain. It was Karl Marx who said: "There is only one antidote to mental suffering, and that is physical pain."[8]

Asceticism also offers some sensory pleasures of which historical authors have been well aware. Thomas Aquinas spoke of a "renewal of the senses" that occurs as a result of sensory deprivation. Augustine also acknowledged that the sense of taste, for example, is dehabituated by a fast. He even warned against fasting for what he considered the questionable purpose of clarifying the palate! From Catherine of Genoa, with her predilection for maggots, to the twentieth-century manic depressive John Custance, with his fascination with dirt and excrement, ascetics have repeatedly insisted that ordinarily common or repugnant objects become almost unbearably sensuous when,

---

8. Marx, *Herr Vogt*, quoted in Hyman, *Tangled Bank*, 118.

through various ascetic practices, the senses are stripped of their conditioning to aversion and attraction.[9] In fact, the perennial claim of ascetics is that
asceticism creates more—not less—pleasure.

The common core of these claims for the "pleasure of no pleasure" is
that asceticism dehabituates and sensitizes the senses, forging a permeable
and vivid connection between the living body and the psyche. Perhaps the
question ultimately is: "What sets the body thinking?"[10] In health and ordinary circumstances, psyche and body seem to maintain a tenuous connection
at best; one's body comes to be noticed only when it "acts up." Ascetic practices, however, alter the body world and make the mind notice that it feels,
not more-of-the-same, but different and *differently*.

Moreover, asceticism and hedonism have much in common. In hedonism, the discipline is excess rather than deprivation, but in either case
the body is *worked*. Just as asceticism can be pleasurable, hedonism can be
the sternest asceticism of all;[11] addiction to pleasures regularly requires the
renunciation of comfort and security. Hedonism's effects on the body can
even parallel those of the harshest asceticism in causing pain and disease; hedonism can be *hard on the body*. Moreover, asceticism can be more erotic than
hedonism: instead of creating fatigue and habituation, asceticism saturates
the denied object with affect so that it becomes magic.

In *The Ascetic Imperative in Culture and Criticism*, Geoffrey Galt
Harpham made a breakthrough identification of the powerful dynamic at
work in asceticism.[12] Working on the literature of the fourth-century ascetic
movement in Christianity, he asked himself why men who had left the sexual
stimulation of cities for the isolation of an eremitic life in the Egyptian desert
should constantly be preoccupied with "demons" in the guise of beautiful
and lascivious women. Nor could he doubt that many of these authors—like
Evagrius Ponticus—were highly sophisticated in psychology. To be sure, they
had not read B. F. Skinner's experiments, but they knew that the best way to
avoid temptation was simply to busy oneself with other matters. Given their

---

9. The inversion of socialization is itself pleasurable. In *The Powers of Horror*, Kristeva
has observed that "one of the insights of Christianity . . . is to have gathered in a single
move perversion and beauty as the lining and the cloth of a single garment" (125).

10. Leder, *Absent Body*, 171.

11. As Epicurus clearly saw when he defined pleasure as the absence of pain, rather
than the more "positive" pleasures of sumptuous and excessive diet and drink, parties and
lovemaking, since these inevitably entail physical and emotional pain.

12. Harpham, *Ascetic Imperadve in Culture and Criticism*.

sophistication *and* their preoccupation with sex, Harpham deduced that the dynamic of temptation and resistance was the method by which these ascetics "took hold on their souls"—as one fourth-century ascetic put it. Strong desire, powerfully evoked but denied its object, brings desire to consciousness, makes it accessible. Desire can then be worked with, pointed toward an object of choice, *designed*. Indeed, the primary pleasure of asceticism may be the dynamic of temptation and resistance that enables the ascetic to create a countercultural "self," a consciously chosen and cultivated interior life.

III

What would "authorization of desire look like?"[13] In order to convincingly support my claim that women lack such authorization, I will discuss the gender specificity evident in one of the "great Western texts" on desire, Augustine's *Confessions*. The *Confessions* centrally and primarily concerns satisfying desire, getting—and keeping—the greatest pleasure. It is explicitly about desire, longing, and passion—both physical and spiritual—and both most evidently when Augustine most intends to distinguish spiritual from physical. It is an erotic text, a book preoccupied with bodies, pleasures, and pains. It is not, however, as is usually claimed or assumed, about "human" desire; it is about its author's desire—Augustine's desire.

It is instructive to analyze why and how Augustine became a model of physical and spiritual desire. Having deconstructed this powerful (male) model, we can begin to construct other models more consonant with women's experiences, more challenging and supportive of women, and—not incidentally—more responsive to the desperate need of our endangered planet for more responsible models of subjectivity and desire.

The *Confessions* narrates Augustine's life story in order to demonstrate the mysterious path by which, by pursuing the objects of his desire most aggressively (and destructively, to himself and other people) he was led unerringly to an expansive, intense, and fruitful desire, which he names as the desire for God. Augustine's autobiography has been powerfully influential in constructing what is recognized and authorized as desire in Western societies. The influence of books and ideas should not be exagerated; "great ideas" do not, of course, explain why the world is as it is and why people act as they do. Nevertheless, the *Confessions* contributed to shaping Western values and

13. This section is adapted from my book *Desire and Delight: A New Reading of Augustine's "Confessions."*

therefore to designing social arrangements and institutions, especially hetero-sexuality, marriage, monasticism, and the church.

It is important to acknowledge at the outset that my "reading" of the *Confessions* is necessarily and inevitably affected by my own social location as a late twentieth-century academic Anglo-Saxon woman. It is, more-over, a disobedient reading because I notice and note features of the text that—although there—would, perhaps, be overlooked by an ancient reader or a twentieth-century male reader. In recognizing and acknowledging my perspectival reading, however, I admit only what any honest reader must acknowledge—that is, the lack of a universal, transcendent, or God's-eye perspective from which to interpret.

The strange discovery I made recently in rereading the *Confessions* is that, in my former readings, I had obediently assumed the position of the sympathetic male colleague for whom Augustine wrote. The *Confessions* was not written to be read by a woman; to read it with "understanding" is to read it as a man—an educated skill. The difficult and interesting task, then, is to produce a gendered reading: not only to notice Augustine's actual and textual treatment of women, but also to recognize that the metaphor that dominates his construction of pleasure is male sexuality. Furthermore, Augustine's sexual experience is not accidental or incidental to the primary concerns of the *Confessions*. In spite of his loud and frequent disclaimers, Augustine learned more than he acknowledged from his own experience of sex; he learned what Audre Lorde has called "the deep and irreplaceable knowledge of [his] capac-ity for joy" from his sexual experience.[14]

In his *Confessions*, Augustine narrates his own desire from infancy for-ward as a compulsive grasping at every object that crossed his path in the fear that something would be missed—his word for his anxious rapaciousness is concupiscence. From stealing pears from a neighbor's tree, to professional success as a teacher of rhetoric, to sexual experience Augustine energetically pursued sex, power, and possession until he pushed himself to the point of intellectual and emotional collapse.

He did not recount the destructive effects of his aggressions on other people. My curiosity about the woman with whom he lived for thirteen years and who bore their son—a woman whose name he never mentioned—is not satisfied in the *Confessions*. He did give a rather more ample account of his mother, Monica: he described her as focused single-mindedly on himself, his happiness, and his salvation through Catholic Christianity. Though Monica

14. Lorde, *Sister Outsider*, 57.

had a husband and other children, her son pictured her as completely and passionately attached to himself, following him from North Africa to Milan, praying continually for him with tears "which fell streaming and watered the ground beneath her eyes in every place where she prayed." Monica was, according to Augustine's report, a passionate woman, but her passion was confined to her relationship with God and Augustine. Augustine placed her on a pedestal, a model of selfless female desire: "I cannot express how she loved me and how she labored with much greater pain to give me birth in the spirit than she had labored when giving birth to me in the flesh." We learn little of her own subjectivity or of any woman's subjectivity from Augustine's heroic epic. The women of the tale are only there as part of Augustine's support system.

The central moment in Augustine's autobiography, the moment for which the book is famous, is that of Augustine's conversion. Curiously, it was not a moment of intellectual insight, religious ecstasy, or belief or faith. Augustine described this experience quite explicitly as a conversion from compulsive sexual activity to continence.

Prefiguring and mirroring his conversion, Augustine juxtaposed images of himself as alternately distracted or dispersed among pleasures or gathered and collected in a disciplined "return" to himself and to God throughout the *Confessions*. His model of the spiritual life as re-collection has become the dominant model of Western Christian subjectivity and spirituality and has, in the twentieth century, passed into secular culture in the form of numerous varieties of psychotherapy and secular spirituality. The model is one of centering, of arresting the hemorrhage of energy and attention that flows out of the self toward other human beings and objects of all sorts and pulling that energy within, collecting, focusing, centering. This was Augustine's model. It is based on Augustine's sexual experience, and I question its usefulness as a model for women and for late twentieth-century people in general. Augustine's clearest definition of the model occurs in the following passage:

> I have been spilled and scattered among times whose order I do not know; my thoughts, the innermost bowels of my soul, are torn apart with the crowding tumults of variety, and so it will be until all together I can flow into you [God], purified and molten by the fire of your love.

Re-collection, continence was, for Augustine, both a literal practice, a renunciation of sexual activity, and his model of the spiritual life. His image of sin, as "turning away from you, God, toward lower things—casting away, as it were, its own insides, and swelling with desire for what is outside," being "spilled and scattered" are almost embarrassingly direct and literal allusions to male orgasm. Continence, on the other hand was, for Augustine, the pivotal point of change. Again, his model was concrete and explicit, based on retention of seminal fluid:

> The Word calls you to come back . . . you will lose nothing. What is withered in you will flower again, and all your illnesses will be made well, and all that was flowing and wasting from you will regain shape and substance and will form part of you again.[15]

In Augustine's physical and spiritual universe, the hoarding of seminal fluid became both practice and paradigm for an integrated life. My intention in calling attention to the physical model of Augustine's subjectivity is not to discredit or minimize his powerful description of the inner life. It is, however, to help us see that the re-collected life is but one form of interior development; it is not the only or the necessary form. Other models of subjectivity need to be imagined, fleshed out, and embodied.

As his own writings demonstrate, Augustine was well aware of the danger of his construction of desire and subjectivity; he knew that he must keep insisting that he intended no disparagement of the objects of the sensible world in urging detachment from them. Yet his formulation of the inner life as a withdrawal from attachment to the world of senses and objects, from other people and the natural world, has played a role in creating the present condition of the earth and of human society. Alternatives to Augustine's model are desperately needed, models that respond to the crises of our own day by emphasizing attention to, and affection for, the vulnerable and threatened earth, by energizing committed labor for peace and justice, and by illuminating the spiritual discipline of loving relationship and community.

As a "great text of the Western world," the *Confessions* has played a role in the social construction of desire. This powerful statement of desire and fulfillment has formed and informed Western people's amorphous, polymorphous, multiple, and inarticulate longings. But what we have thought of as "human" desire is always marked by the particularities of individual lives, by socially constructed gender assumptions, expectations, and roles, by social location, institutional affiliation, class, and race. If the claim that desire is socially constructed and differentiated according to these factors seems far-fetched, attempt to imagine a female protagonist of the *Confessions*. Could

---

15. Augustine *Confessions* 11.29.

Augustine's demanding, energetic, aggressive passion have occurred—much less been admired and become a classic formulation of physical and spiritual desire—in a woman, in his time or in ours?

I am envious of the social construction and support of Augustine's passion, both his relentless pursuit of worldly satisfaction and his latter passionate love of God, combined with institutional authority. To search frantically, desperately; to long restlessly, lustfully, feverishly; to embody the kind of consuming and complex desire that knows its object when it touches it; few women have sustained such uncompromising desire, at least partly because women have had few literary paradigms, few images, few models. In the societies of the Christian West, women's desire has been constructed to serve male desire as its mirror and counterpart.

The lack of female models does not mean, of course, that no women have managed to formulate and pursue a distinctive desire; it does mean that it is immensely more difficult for women to do so in societies that have no female epic heroes, no models but male models for passionately seeking women. Many—though not most—women have learned to use male models, to adopt, adapt, or rebel against these models of heroic hunger. Educated women have learned to read as men, blind to the biology and socialization, the institutions, and the legal and social arrangements that have *authorized* the author.

A gendered reading of the *Confessions* is attentive to who speaks and who listens; it reveals the myriad ways that the male author's experience informs and gives body to his text. It is certainly significant that Augustine critiqued his society's construction of male sexuality, equating tumescence and the myth of male helplessness in the face of sexual urges with pride and sin. He experienced, he says, a vast relief and freedom in the practice of continence. Later in his career he formulated a model of sexuality based on principles of complementarity and responsibility. This was not a model he had ever lived, and it did not go as far as to imagine equality and mutuality, but it became an enormously influential model. No alternative model could hope to produce the social effects of a model of heterosexual relationship that enjoyed the institutional and personal authority of Augustine himself.

IV

Let us return to the "pleasure of no pleasure." How can a fruitful approach to eating disorders be sketched? Let us first consider briefly two contemporary authors who have addressed the problem. Caroline Walker Bynum, in *Holy*

Feast and Holy Fast,[16] explores the food attitudes and practices of medieval religious women, concluding that they were often able to gather social and religious authority by their abstinence from food. Bynum, who is an insightful and perceptive historian, understands the social and religious context in which these medieval women lived. In an epilogue, however, she argues that there is no connection between medieval women who fasted for religious reasons and contemporary women who fast, she says, simply in order to achieve the slender boyish body that is repetitiously reiterated in fashion magazines, on television, and in films.

I question whether Bynum's medieval women are as unrelated to contemporary fasting women as she claims. Common to both medieval and twentieth-century North American middle-class women is the fact that they lived—and live—in male designed and administered societies. Both groups of women operate in societies that deny them collective power in the public sphere, societies in which they are largely unable to affect the institutions that legislate and enforce the particular social arrangements that shape their lives.

Bynum misses the opportunity of demonstrating that modern anorexics who starve themselves, complaining that their bodies are "too big" might, like medieval women, be describing an unbearable asymmetry between their cultural provisions and support, and their personal yearning. Twentieth-century women are socialized to confine their longings to concern for physical attractiveness—that is, to anxiety regarding their value as commodities in a consumer culture. Like medieval women, twentieth-century women live in a culture that neglects to incite, encourage, and provide support for women's intellectual, psychological, and spiritual development. Eating disorders might be seen as a form of resistance to a society in which the bodies of young women are "too big" a focus of attention in relation to intellectual, psychological, and spiritual aspects of women's lives. By contrast to her society's attention to her body, a young woman experiences her subjectivity as too small, underdeveloped, unable to balance the body whose social significance is so huge. Bynum finds in medieval women's food practices a "resonance and complexity" that emerges only when these practices are placed in their "*full* context."[17] A similar study of twentieth-century anorexics might fruitfully identify the full context of modern women's use of food as tool or weapon, seeking in it the "range and richness" that Bynum finds in medieval women's food practices.

16. Bynum, *Holy Feast and Holy Fast.*
17. Ibid., 298. Bynum's emphasis.

The problems of women who live in societies designed and administered by men have some fundamental similarities, despite enormous differences in particularities. These problems revolve around two foci: first, the cultivation of a subjectivity that is *defined* neither by social conditioning nor by rebellion from the normative male subjectivity, and second, imagining and constructing social roles that are not *assigned* by male projection, language, economics, and pleasure. In my book *Carnal Knowing: Female Nakedness and Religious Meaning in the Christian West*, I proposed three conditions I consider essential for progress toward equitable social arrangements between men and women.[18] Women must have (1) access to public space—in media and institutions—in which to (2) develop a collective voice that will enable them to (3) represent themselves as subjects of their own experience rather than as objects of male projections.

Susan Bordo's article "Anorexia Nervosa: Psychopathology as the Crystallization of Culture"[19] identifies a grid on which the "control axis" and the "gender/power axis" intersect to produce the phenomenon of anorexia nervosa. Bordo's complex analysis enables her to glimpse the dynamic of temptation and resistance in the behavior of fasting women. Anorexic women, she says, "are as obsessed with *hunger* as they are with being thin." She quotes women who describe their *pleasure* in fasting—what I have called "the pleasure of no pleasure." Bordo's analysis suggests that what must be asked is how eating disorders are produced by constraint, that is, by the foreclosure of more directly pleasurable routes.

I will close by suggesting that the primary pleasure of asceticism is the development of a centered, chosen self, built up gradually from the many decisions, the many choices, the many disciplines occurring over a period of time. In eating disorders the issue is not control but the shaping of a self that is nowhere required, supported, or suggested in values circulated in the public sphere of a media culture. The crucial question is this: what feature(s) of human experience does a society designate as symbolic of self, revelatory of the truth of who-one-is?

In Augustine's world, sexuality played this role so that the way to develop subjectivity was to scrutinize and manage sexual activity. That arena of self-expression, however, seems presently to be exhausted, enervated, perhaps, by the public circulation of a hedonistic rhetoric that promotes sex as good, healthy, invigorating, and recreative—even though the reality of many

18. Miles, *Carnal Knowing*.
19. Bordo, "Anorexia Nervosa" in *Unbearable Weight*, 139–64.

people's experience may be otherwise. The early medieval ascetic's imaginative dynamic of sexual temptation and resistance and the later medieval women's abstention from food has been superseded by the anorexic's preoccupation with food. In a consumer society, the arena of struggle and self-definition chosen by many young women is food, a commodity that is everywhere, requiring constant opposition. And this activity of desire, temptation, and resistance can be intensely pleasurable.

This analysis suggests that clinical approaches to treatment must identify more direct, more complex, and polymorphous—more *satisfying*—pleasures that could effectively create, focus, and direct desire around less dangerous self-definition than that achieved by eating disorders. Individual therapy, however, is only part of the solution. Until women can define their distinctive desires and pleasures and gain symbolic representation and support for these desires in the public sphere, the private and privileged reeducation of desire can never hope to help more than a few; it cannot alter the epidemic of fasting women.

5

Celibacy as Sexual Orientation[1]

The 1990 Canadian film *Jesus of Montreal* featured a priest who is *only human.* Unwilling to surrender the social esteem and the political and material benefits of priesthood, he nevertheless maintains a sexual relationship with a much younger woman. His bad-faith representation of church authority while violating his vow of celibacy ultimately—through a series of circumstances—results in the death of "Jesus." This priest is one fictional representative of the actual effects of the ancient tradition of celibacy in the lives of countless Roman Catholic clergy and laypeople.

At the end of the twentieth century the stabilized power of the Catholic Church is more evident to many people than its sensitivity to human pain. Examining the requirement for a celibate priesthood and the church's sexual doctrine, Richard Sipe describes, by examples and figures, the evidence for an appalling amount of suffering, both by priests and by those to whom they relate sexually. Sipe's figures are estimates; they may even be conservative estimates. Whether or not they are exact is not the issue since figures never give an accurate reading of human pain. Sipe estimates that approximately 2 percent of those vowed to celibacy achieve it. Since 1960, twenty thousand priests have left the active priesthood in the United States, the majority to marry. At any one time, 20 percent of priests in good standing are involved in sexual relationships with women; 8 percent are experimenting sexually, approximately evenly divided between heterosexual and homosexual activity; about 30 percent of priests have a homosexual orientation. About 50 percent of both homosexual and heterosexual priests practice celibacy.

In the context of the Roman Church's prohibition on all forms of sexual activity for its ordained priesthood, a conspiracy of secrecy maintains the privilege and social esteem of the priesthood while permitting sexual activity. Moreover, since *any* and *all* sex is forbidden, there is no discussion of crite-

---

1. This chapter originally appeared as the Foreword in Sipe, *Sex, Priests, and Power.*

ria for moral responsibility in sexual behavior. Given this situation, abuses are inevitable. A number of priests use their power and position to seduce women, children, and men who are led to expect from their priest the care of a loving father. Certainly, sexual abuse is not specific to Catholic priests, but its occurrence among a clergy pledged to celibacy and service to others strikes the North American public as a particular travesty when they read of such incidents in the daily newspaper.

How did the *celibate/sexual system* analyzed in the following pages originate? Why did some highly intelligent and resourceful historical people adopt a practice that is the source of the high levels of human pain Richard Sipe describes? Although it is seldom useful—or even accurate—to identify a single historical villain, it *is* instructive to reconstruct the social and institutional circumstances in which a practice originated. When those historical situations have been considered fairly and in sufficient detail, the productivity of the practice in question for its society of origin can be understood. More importantly, it is also possible to see that a practice that made sense in the context of its society of origin can have destructive and painful effects in a vastly changed contemporary society.

A full description of the institutionalization of the Roman Catholic Christianity in the fourth-century Roman Empire is beyond the scope of this brief introduction. Two aspects of the rapid advance of Christianity during the fourth century are, however, important to contemporary discussions of celibacy. These are (1) the centrality of control of sexuality to emerging formations of institutionalized power; and (2) the recognition of the practical usefulness of sexual regulation and/or abstinence for gathering and maintaining spiritual energy.

A groundbreaking book, Samuel Laeuchli's *Power and Sexuality in the Early Church*, explored—when other historians of Christianity were largely treating their field solely as a history of theological ideas—a dramatic preoccupation with issues surrounding sexuality at the beginning of the fourth century. Using as his evidence the *canons*, or rulings on practices, of the 309 AD Council of Elvira, Laeuchli demonstrated that church leaders recognized—whether consciously or unconsciously—that establishing authority in matters of sexuality was intimately connected to establishing and maintaining institutional power. A bit later, the ecumenical Council of Nicaea also legislated both sexual and institutional practices with equal attention. It is remarkable that a church that moved, during the course of one century, from persecuted sect to official religion of the Roman Empire should expend so much attention on regulation of sexuality both among clergy and laity. By the 380s, when Catholic Christianity became the religion of the Empire, the professionalization of a Catholic clergy involved the demand that clergy maintain a practical and symbolic separation from secular society.

The universalization and institutionalization of celibacy testifies to its importance at a particular moment in history when leaders of a recently marginalized and persecuted church felt the need for gathering social power. With the most massive persecution of Christians ever in the West—the Diocletian persecution—still in living memory, the Constantinian Peace of the Church offered the opportunity for the irreversible establishment of Christianity. Toward the end of the fourth century, Christian leaders rejoiced in the establishment of a Christian Empire. For a religious body whose experience in the Roman Empire had been vulnerability and necessary secrecy, power represented, first of all, permanent relief from persecution and execution. Secondly, it is important to remember that in the late-classical world, power was understood not primarily as *power over*, as a modern people tend to think of it, but as *power to* accomplish the fundamental necessities of providing food and protection to unimaginably precarious societies. In this historical context, celibacy took on a very different value than it has in a wealthy and powerful Church that has had, for many centuries, the ability to legislate belief and practice and to punish dissidents. The statements on celibacy of an Augustine or Jerome must be understood in this social context if we are to be fair and sensitive historical interpreters.

Secondly, the first legislation of clerical celibacy occurred in a society enamored with asceticism as a method for achieving what Michel Foucault has called the "care of the self." Fascination with a "self" constructed by disciplined practices—especially of diet and sexuality—crossed religious and philosophical affiliations. In the context of this fascination with asceticism, a monk named Jovinian drew the vitriolic and verbose ire of both Augustine and Jerome by proposing that marriage provided a condition in which spiritual discipline and progress could be achieved equally with celibates. Clearly, asceticism was the ascendant mood of the moment, and not only within the Christian movement. By incorporating the ascetic ideal of philosophers, Roman religions, and the spectrum of religious groups that self-identified with Christianity, Catholic Christianity simultaneously strengthened both its respect in the eyes of secular society and its internal energy. Celibacy also provided the definition of what one historian has called "Christian over-achievement," a way to differentiate between ordinary members and those who sought Christian perfection. Critical as twentieth-century people may be of the fourth-century social consensus on asceticism, it is difficult to see that a more relaxed Christianity would have achieved the institutional power with which the Catholic Church was able to modify some of the social calamities of the fifth century.

St. Augustine, bishop of the North African town of Hippo at the end of the fourth century, is commonly cited as the primary expositor and advocate of clerical celibacy. It is certainly the case that he articulated with remarkable power his own experience of compulsive youthful sexual activity as well as his resolution in celibacy of a sexuality that was destructive both to himself and to others. Augustine undoubtedly found relief and "freedom"—his word—in celibacy, but he was careful to say that this solution was both personal and God-given. He insisted repeatedly that celibacy should neither be universalized for all committed Christians, nor should it be admired as the result of intransigent will power. Augustine's followers, however, did not heed his cautions. Stimulated by the rhetorical beauty of his descriptions of his own conversion to celibacy, they claimed celibacy as the "higher way." Ignoring his insistence that sexual abstinence is a *gift*, not the result of a teeth-gritting willpower, celibacy developed into a requirement for all Catholic clergy.

A more precise understanding of Augustine's analysis of the root of sin may help to demonstrate that contemporary concern over priests who abuse their power and indulge their sexuality are not unique to the twentieth century. Augustine's word for the cause of sin was *concupiscentia*. Although modern interpretations of concupiscence tend to confine the meaning of the term to sexual lust, late-classical authors understood it to entail irreducibly the three lusts endemic to human nature—lust for sex, power, and possession. No single lust—if it were possible to separate them for purposes of analysis—has the destructive potential of the closely woven combination of lusts. It was *concupiscentia*—the interconnected lusts, not sexual lust in isolation—that Augustine labeled "original sin." Strikingly, Augustine understood the whole human race—both perpetrators and abused—as "victims." He insisted that the appropriate reaction to the ubiquitous evidence of original sin is empathy. After discussing children's and adults' compulsive pursuit of the socially designated objects of sex, power, and possession in his *Confessions*, he marveled, "And no one is sorry for the children; no one is sorry for the adults; no one is sorry for both of them" (*Confessions* 1:10). Similarly, Sipe is empathetic with priests as well as with their partners and victims. Yet he deplores the systemic ignorance and—to use the ancient word—concupiscence that creates so much suffering. What he advocates is exposure and discussion of the interconnection of power, sexuality, and secrecy on which the celibate/sexual system is built.

Sipe focuses here on the male priesthood of the Roman Catholic Church. In order to fully understand the operation of the celibate system, a similar study of women celibates needs to be done. Sensitive to both the ideological sexism that maintains the celibate system and to the treatment of actual women who become priests' friends and lovers, Sipe does not presume to generalize his findings to women members of religious orders. A study of female celibacy could be expected to reveal both some similarities with male celibates and some startling differences. It is to be hoped that this book will stimulate and encourage such a study.

Sex, Priests, and Power: Anatomy of a Crisis can be understood as part of a massive contemporary project of revision and reconstruction within Christianity. Many Christians are presently recognizing that some central affirmations of Christian faith have been either ignored or too slenderly developed to merit a place in mainstream Christianity. When one considers the strong affirmations of human bodies implied in the doctrines of creation, the Incarnation of Jesus Christ, and the resurrection of the body, it seems odd that management of one of the human body's most intimate functions, sexuality, has not been considered a crucial part of one's *religious identity*.

It would be simplistic to blame the inclusion of philosophical ideas in Christianity for this. *All* the religious and philosophical movements of the centuries in which Christianity was being formed struggled to define the role of the body and sexuality in religious practice. Moreover, it does not solve the problems of the present merely to identify the historical origin of ideas that live and have their effects in the present. Augustine is frequently and unfairly blamed for distorted sexual doctrine because he worried about and addressed, with the conceptual tools available, issues of sex and the body. The relative silence of Christian authors prior to and contemporary with Augustine and their own inadequacies in addressing sexuality have, ironically, guaranteed their immunity from twentieth-century criticism.

Finally, Sipe admires celibacy, not as legislated and institutionalized, but as a personal "quest of spiritual relationship and religious reality based on unflinching self-knowledge and radical truth about one's innermost desires." As a *sexual orientation*, those who have the gift, and have undertaken the hard work of self-knowledge required for productive celibacy, he says, evidence "an interior freedom and integration that unite their individuality and their service." Those who are gifted with celibacy are, in Sipe's word, "awesome." And, in his studied opinion, they are rare. The goal and spirit of this book, then, is not the overthrow of an institution that damages people, but scrutiny of a destructive strain within a church that *could be so much more powerful for healing and blessing* if it were willing to examine and revise its celibate/sexual system. It is a book that exemplifies and advocates what therapeutic programs call "tough love," the ruthless honesty and relentless analysis that exposes the self-deception of an individual or an institution in order to heal, not to destroy.

6

Religion and Food

The Case of Eating Disorders

Within Christianity, food has frequently been a focus of anxious ambivalence. The most profound ritual mystery of Christianity is one in which the body and blood of an incarnated God are eaten and drunk. Yet the ritually powerful activity of eating was not unambiguous for early Christians. Throughout the Common Era, "safe eating" has been a watchword of committed Christianity. Both the object and the subject of the act of eating were scrutinized. From the perspective of the subject, the practice of fasting was an indispensible tool for disciplining the spirit and for fashioning the Christian body. The object—food—has been regarded as both symbol and site of pleasure and danger, nourishment and prohibition.[1]

Christianity is not the only religion to place emphasis on the intentional use of eating—and refraining from eating. In this issue of *JAAR*, the symbolic uses of food for devotional practices and community-building are discussed in relation to North African Jews in France, and in relation to Sufis in addition to a variety of Christian practices. Food practices are one of the most readily accessible, democratic, and easily manipulable features of everyday life. The management of food has thus, throughout history and across the world, been one of the most consistent means for resisting secular socialization and designing a religious self.

Within Christianity, patristic authors argued that since Eve and Adam brought sin into the world through eating an apple, upwardly mobile Christians must reverse the momentum of that slippery slide by fasting. The great "athletes" of the Egyptian desert taught that attachment to food, the

---

1. I am grateful to Michelle Lelwica for stimulating discussions of eating disorders across several years. Her dissertation, published as *Starving for Salvation: The Spiritual Dimensions of Eating Problems among American Girls and Women* (New York: Oxford University Press, 1999), addresses these issues.

58

original and paradigmatic pleasure of human life, must be broken if the spirit is to be reoriented to food that nourishes eternal life. Christian ascetics worried about eating, for eating is not only a human being's first and foundational delight; it is also possible, they believed, to ingest demons with their food. Thus they sought both to minimize the pleasurable activity of eating and to confine themselves to certain foods.

The earliest Christian ascetics developed a body of quasi-scientific lore about the physical and spiritual effects of particular foods and, more generally, about the amount of food most conducive to a life focused on creating and sustaining a religious self. The literature of Christian asceticism may well be the most detailed, closely analyzed manuals dealing with food and its effects before the present media hyperattention to food.

Although the dangers of literal eating were prominent in the minds of the early shapers of Christian practice, the vocabulary of food—hunger, nourishment, and satisfaction—has apparently been indispensable to the rhetoric of spirituality within the Christian tradition. The power of religious language depends, in fact, on its ability to evoke and reconstruct physical pleasure as spiritual pleasure. Language drawn from eating and sexual union, arguably the two most pleasurable of human activities, has dominated the literature of Christian devotion and mysticism. "What am I at my best," asked Augustine, Bishop of Hippo in North Africa, addressing God in the *Confessions*, "but one suckling the milk you give and feeding upon you, the food that is imperishable"(4.1).

In the literature of Christian spirituality it is the activity of eating, rather than food itself, that assumes symbolic significance for the creation and cultivation of a religious self. Yet there is a connection between literal food practices and spiritual nourishment. The converted Augustine complained that he struggled daily against the temptation of overeating, calling eating and drinking "a dangerous kind of pleasure," one that he explicitly included in his prayer for continence (*Confessions* 10.31).[2] In *Holy Feast, Holy Fast*, Caroline Walker Bynum described medieval women who fasted from material food in order to feast on spiritual food. These women, recognized as saints by their societies, were certainly preoccupied with food as *method* and means of the spiritual and social agency they exercised.

2. Significantly, in the context of describing the difficulty of attempting to "keep a hold which is neither too loose nor too tight on the bridle of my throat," Augustine invoked his famous formula, usually associated only with sexual continence, "Give what you command, and command what you will"(10.31).

The connection between actual eating and spiritual nourishment is desire, hunger, or appetite. Augustine claimed that a human self is called into being and configured by its desire. Whether that desire leaned out in longing toward objects in the world, or toward the source of its being, God, determined who the person *is* in the most profound and fundamental way.[3] To understand a person, then, one had primarily to ask, What does she love? His model of self was one in which the person or self is almost infinitely plastic, *composed* of and articulated by what it loves. He saw the most important task of religion as that of calling forth, shaping, and ordering desire.

The management of desire is also, perennially, a *social* task. Societies must achieve some degree of consensus around values, whether those values include unlimited consumer products or agreement on when a society should go to war. Often there is some continuity between religious values and social desiderata, but there may also be profound conflict. The purpose of this paper is to explore one such conflict around constructions of desire in contemporary North America.

Late twentieth-century North Americans tend to think that desire has a great deal to do with the body. We tend, *unlike* Augustine, to understand the *self* as helpless victim of the *body's* desires. We think of desire as plotted in the genes, born with the body, and knowing its objects when it sees them—irreducible, intractible, and non-negotiable. But this model of the desiring body neglects, perhaps purposely, to investigate the representations that inform and cultivate desire. To know ourselves realistically, not primarily as autonomous individuals but as social beings *to the core*, requires that we examine our society's gendered representations of desire. We are, of course, *both* individual *and* social, but we usually deny, and therefore neglect to acknowledge or examine, the social assumptions and expectations in which we all participate as members of North American society. As individuals we all—to some extent—resist, laugh at, and/or critique media representations of objects of desire. Nevertheless—as a society and as individuals—we do not remain unaffected by repetitiously circulated media images.

I

Preoccupation with food has become media news. A three-page article in the *Boston Globe* on August 1, 1994, described the global "expansion" of fat documented by "obesity specialists." "Obesity has increased sharply in the United

3. Miles, *Desire and Delight.*

States," the article proclaims, "with fully one third of US adults estimated to be significantly overweight in 1991." Researchers document similar increases "nearly everywhere around the world where [obesity] has been studied." Because of glaringly inequitable food distribution, problems of overeating and undereating characterize most of the world's population. Dr. Van S. Hubbard, of the National Institute of Diabetes and Digestive and Kidney Diseases, claims that overeating is a larger problem worldwide than is food deprivation, costing immense amounts in health care. Blaming fat food, inactivity, and television for increasing obesity, researchers agree that "Americans are more fat than most European countries except Germany" (26).

In the same society in which fat is on the rise, voluntary hunger is also at an epidemic level. The phenomenon of voluntary food deprivation is not, however, evenly distributed across the population of North America. Over 90 percent of eating disorders occur in young middle-class women. A recent study at Harvard University showed that one in ten college women suffer from eating disorders. Medical and psychiatric leaders acknowledge their bewilderment about what might be the most effective theoretical and clinical approaches.

A variety of explanations have been proposed as to why young women as a group are more prone—"tempted"—to starve themselves than are other social groups. Yet I am persuaded that explanations that ignore religion, though suggestive and useful, cannot construct an adequate theory of eating disorders, nor can such explanations propose effective clinical treatment. For there are some startling continutities, in practices and in effects, between contemporary eating disorders and the food practices by which medieval women established their religious authority. These continuities provide a basis for diagnosis and prescription that may be more effective than the medical and psychiatric approaches of secular society.

Two main explanatory theses have been proposed for eating disorders. The first is that young women starve themselves in order to look like the model women they see in the media. The second proposed hypothesis is that dangerous, damaging—ultimately even killing—food practices are attempts by powerless people to control *something*—their own bodies, if nothing else. Both of these explanations have some validity, but they only partially explain the phenomenon. I will consider the evidence for both these hypotheses, and then suggest a hypothesis that incorporates both but places them in a broader frame of reference. I will suggest that until eating disorders can be seen as a result of thwarted desire—*eros*, desire in its broadest sense—as simultaneously sexual, social, and spiritual, theoretical and clinical approaches will be largely ineffective.

Contemporary food practices, I will argue, need to be understood as extensions and revisions of the ancient ascetic principle that in order to change consciousness and the psyche, one must alter the daily habits of food intake that stabilize the body and defend the psyche against insight and change. But externally identical practices—food deprivation—in two different societies are effectively different practices. Lacking a publicly recognized religious context for fasting in contemporary North America, eating disorders signal the inadequacy of symbolic provisions. It is to that symbolic repertoire that I now turn.

II

Representations—images—provoke and inspire imitation. Far from being an insight of recent critical theory, this is an ancient knowledge, implied, if not explicitly acknowledged, as early as Psalm 101:3: "I will set no worthless thing before my eyes." Like contemporary North Americans, historical Christians were surrounded by images that informed their self-images and their ideas of relationship and community. They were seen daily in the context of the communal worship and devotion of the community.[4] In a time before technological communication, this verbal and visual "media" included sermons, devotional manuals, sculpture, and painting. Imitation of former practitioners of Christian devotion was the central motif of religious life. And it was by studying the postures, gestures, and—to a lesser extent—the facial expressions of the human beings who surrounded the earthly Christ that one knew how to imitate them.

In contemporary North American media culture, media images masquerade as entertainment and/or information, concealing their ability to provoke imitation. Nevertheless, just as study of the "media" of historical people gives a more accurate sense of their resources for shaping and training desire, so study of contemporary media can reveal the imitative practices of our own society. Why are so many young women in North America preoccupied with slenderizing and shaping their bodies, so that they subject them to debilitating and dangerous shortage of food? What readily accessible resources are provided for "desperately seeking" young women in media culture? How are young women *informed* about how their subjectivity might be shaped, their spirituality or interior life strengthened?

4. Miles, *Image as Insight.*

To begin to answer these questions, we must examine how we—as a society—represent young women. The young female body has been adopted by North American consumer society as a vehicle for selling everything from cars to cigarettes. Young women are frequently represented in advertising and film images as combining danger and delight, as sexual attraction and commodity in the publicly circulated media images in North America. Ancient habits of representation are still with us today. Contemporary images of half-clothed Eves, Judiths, and Susannas appear regularly in newspapers and magazines, on television, and in films. The association of "woman" with body is enjoying a very long shelf life. Today, as formerly, consistent representational strategies lock in place a public gaze that fixes women's bodies as objects of voyeurism: unclothed, or partially clothed, fetishized, often posed in unbalanced postures. The contemporary secular dress (or undress) of media images of women masks the amazing continuity of such representations across the historical societies of the Christian West.

There are, of course, many media-circulated protests and alternatives to the dominant images of women. Yet even within the pages of a single popular magazine, articles addressed to consciousness-raising on issues of gender and representation are juxtaposed to repetitive images of the media's ideal woman. Text and image contradict one another; the editorial content is undermined, and the same old image of the young, slender, light-skinned woman is reiterated. It is neither the occasional consciousness-raising article nor the unusual or exceptional image that circulates ideals of female beauty. Rather, it is the insistently repeated images of pleasure, beautiful people, and happiness that *cumulatively* inform individual and collective desire.

Although women are repeatedly represented in advertising images, something more complex than women's trivialization and reduction to body takes place in these images. The sale of a product is secondary to the primary message that consistently and cumulatively *pictures*, images, a way of life in a consumer society. Media images train a whole population to objects of desire, to particular and concrete objects of sex, power, and possession, to what looks and feels like reward, achievement, *pleasure*. Advertising icons also designate the beautiful people of North American society. Young, apparently wealthy, Anglo-Saxon, heterosexual women and men are overwhelmingly represented as the satisfied users of the products they recommend. And though they consume voraciously, these beautiful people are thin. Thirty years ago the average model in North American advertising weighed 8 percent less than the average woman; five years ago, the average model weighed 23 percent less than the average woman.[5] A disparity between the representations of women we look at as a society and the bodies of actual women is increasing.

It is important to ask about the *effects* of these visual clichés rather than to simply accept them as "genre": "that's just how advertisements *are*." To examine and critique advertising images is to begin to understand a society that prides itself on its "pluralism" but brings multi-million dollar resources to positioning people as more—or less—desirable objects. If we attend to the media's daily supply of images of slender, predominantly white, apparently wealthy, and overwhelmingly *young* women and men, we will see why authors like Carolyn Walker Bynum have suggested that eating disorders occur because young women want to look like the models they look *at* so constantly.

III

Let us now consider the second analysis of epidemic eating disorders, namely that powerless young women practice dangerous and debilitating food practices because they have identified something they *can* control, their own bodies. For this also, we need to recall a long tradition in which Western Christians were urged to take on the project of self-chosen self-shaping.

From the first Christian devotional manuals forward, a rhetoric of choice and change accompanied instructions in the practice of piety. These earliest best-seller, self-help manuals were based on the assumption that one could substantially develop and exercise one's soul, creating a religious self that survived death and determined what came after.

Presently in North American public culture, a similar rhetoric of choice and change relates, not to souls, but to bodies. The idea of the designer body has led to "fantasies of re-arranging, transforming, correcting . . . [of] limitless improvement and change."[6] The postmodern image of the plastic self, the commodified self defined by its multiple objects of desire, seems to have generated a parallel fantasy of a similarly protean body, infinitely plastic, free from bodily determination. Epidemic eating disorders among young North American women are only one of the social effects of imagining bodies as limitlessly malleable.

The present preoccupation of North Americans with altering bodies is well documented. As a society, North Americans are "committed"—the rhetoric is recognizably religious—to myriad forms of physical exercise and

5. Seid, *Never Too Thin*, 15.

6. Bordo, *Unbearable Weight*, 246.

eating regimes. Many also volunteer to undergo painful and expensive surgery to redesign their bodies. In 1989, 681,000 cosmetic procedures were done in the United States. The most frequent of these surgeries were nose jobs, face lifts, tummy tucks, breast augmentations, collagen-plumped lips, and liposuction on ankles, calves, and buttocks. This figure represents an 80 percent increase over cosmetic surgery in 1981.[7] In the United States in 1993, cosmetic surgery was a "$1.75-billion-a-year industry, with nearly 1.5 million people a year undergoing cosmetic surgery of some kind."[8] And preoccupation with the body in our society begins young; a recent survey showed that a shocking 80 percent of suburban nine-year-old girls make dieting and exercise the organizing regimes of their lives.

Advertising for cosmetic "procedures"—the word "surgery" is assiduously avoided—speaks of the "transportation of fat from one part of the body to another."[9] "Procedures" are often compared to hair care and make-up, and described as "play." Yet motivation for undergoing expensive and painful cosmetic surgery is not born but made. It is generated by myriad and ubiquitous efforts in popular literature and advertising to make all women and many men dissatisfied with their bodies. People visually habituated to seeing the "perfect" faces and bodies of models become vulnerable to suggestions that their own features can be dramatically altered. A century ago, devotional best-sellers imaged the soul as the battleground for a mortal struggle over its eternal destiny. Presently, the body is the battleground. The ancient Grail question, "Whom does it serve?" needs to be asked.

Clearly, the commodified body serves the maintenance of a capitalist consumer society. But perhaps there is something more subtle that we are missing if we think only in economic terms. Perhaps an ancient Christian phenomenon is masked by contemporary media jargon. "No pain, no gain"; "Go for the burn!" While these phrases are, as far as I know, peculiar to the later twentieth century, the assumptions they articulate were well known to Christian ascetics. The ancient language of Christian asceticism, used in relation to physical exercise and eating habits, is startling and significant. It gives, I think, an important clue about the covert longings expressed by food and exercise practices. It should also alert us to a connection between ancient and modern asceticisms and desire. If we think of eating disorders

7. Ibid.
8. Ibid., 25.
9. Ibid., 246.

as misplaced asceticisms, then the longing to control or *shape* some part of oneself is prominent.

IV

One of the most counter-productive conceptual habits of North Americans is a predilection for identifying as *individual*, or personal, problems or difficulties that are social. Let me now try to characterize the characteristics of the present moment in our society in a way that enables us to understand young women's eating disorders as a *social* rather than an individual problem.

The present moment in North American society is an awkward one for women and men, for intimate relationships, whether heterosexual or homosexual, and for families. Clearly, young women are not the only focus of struggle and suffering in our society. Some suffer as the result of social change; others suffer because the changes are *not enough*. Racial and sexual minorities feel the pain of a racist, homophobic, and sexist society that has not changed *enough*, while other social groups experience pain because of the changes that *are* occurring.

The "growing pains" of a changing society surface and are characteristically felt and expressed by its vulnerable members. Young women seem to be simultaneously the most *noticed* and the most undernourished members of media society. Although in many pockets of society there have been earnest and effective efforts to adopt inclusive language and to allow women access to institutions (at least at entrance levels), institutions themselves have not changed significantly. The first women to reach positions of authority still spend precious energy and attention on demonstrating that they can do what is perceived, both by themselves and by others, as a "man's job." They frequently do not have time—or do not take time—to confer with others—women and men—about how institutions might change in the direction of becoming as "user-friendly" to women as to men.

Real change, institutional change in the direction of a just society, will not occur, it must be acknowledged, without much individual and social pain. Everything depends on whether we interpret this pain as productive—like a birth—or as threatening the demise of "civilization as 'we' knew it." As privilege is distributed more equitably, those in positions of privilege *will* experience pain.

Social scientists differ in their description and evaluation of the present moment in American society. In her 1990 book, *Slow Motion: Changing Masculinities, Changing Men*, Lynne Segal finds that most men have not changed as much as the mythology of social displacement of men claims. "The cultural expression of misogyny," she writes, is so "naturalized," so taken-for-granted, that it is virtually invisible in public culture. Sexism, classism, and racism are so thoroughly woven into and thoroughly embedded in the assumptions, attitudes, and legal arrangements of North American society, that until recently they have seldom been highlighted for scrutiny, much less for moral judgment.[10] Statistically, women's progress toward more just social arrangements is still minimal, Segal argues. But it has, nevertheless, produced an experienced loss of male privilege in relation to the law, to institutions, and to the attitudes and practices of North American society.

In his book *The Body and Society*, Bryan Turner argues that a culture of unquestioned patriarchy is being dismantled in North America, albeit slowly and with many reverses. This dismantling of male privilege has created what he calls a culture of "patrism." Patrism is characterized, he writes, by male resentment and reprisal in many small but hurtful ways—in the home, in the workplace, in the media.

Segal and Turner disagree over the extent to which change in the direction of more just social arrangements is occurring. Turner is much more confident than Segal that well-established changes in the direction of equality and justice have occurred, while Segal's statistics seem to reveal that to date change is minimal. These cultural analysts agree, however, that the perception, if not the reality, of the distribution of privilege is creating what Susan Faludi has recently labeled "backlash." Yet, just as differences among and between women have been an important discovery for educated white feminists, differences among and between men must be recognized. The extent to which men differ in their committed efforts to create a just society has perhaps not been as carefully acknowledged as it needs to be.

Although most institutions have changed, to date only slightly, there is one institution of North American society that *has* experienced great changes in the last decade. That institution is the family. Less than 30 percent of our population has lived within a traditional household for the past two decades. In the Reagan era, the number of American households headed by single mothers increased by 21 percent. In 1988, 54 percent of mothers with children under three were in the work force. Nor can the home be considered a safe place for women: 42 percent of the women murdered in the United States are killed by a member of their family, usually their husband. Yet "the

---

10. Segal, *Slow Motion*, 178.

family" has become increasingly prominent in public discourse, as it simultaneously diminished as a reality.[11]

Since it really *is* changing, the family presently bears the brunt of a public rhetoric of investigation, discontent, and social anxieties. From the nineteenth century to the 1980s, the American middle-class ideal of female domesticity has been fundamentally unchallenged, even though its class affiliation is so immediately evident. Women have always worked outside the home, but the majority who did so were from the so-called "working class." But today, growing numbers of women of all classes, with and without children, single and married, aspire to full-time careers. In a society that has traditionally defined nurturance as a female responsibility, fears arise that, if women don't spend their live nourishing others, no one will.[12]

Shared wage-earning and shared parenting are only a partial answer. They do not, for example, address issues of the multiple social supports for traditional gendered roles in the family. Unless popular public representations of gender are changed, efforts to equalize private domestic labor are vulnerable. Moreover, shared parenting usually depends on sufficient income to hire household help and thus on the availability of cheap, primarily female, labor. The family is the battleground of social ideologies, because it is more sensitive than other social institutions to changing values, images, and ideals.

In her book *Brave New Families: Domestic Upheaval in Late Twentieth-Century America*, sociologist Judith Stacey questions the "image of the white working class as the last repository of 'modern' family life." Instead of deploring the demise of the nuclear family, however, she sees the present situation as a "democratic opportunity." Because the "modern family script which prescribes nonnegotiable roles for its members has been ruptured, new patterns of intimate interaction are occurring." "The family is not here to stay, nor should we wish it were," Stacey writes at the conclusion of her study:

> Efforts to expand and redefine the definition of family by feminists and gay liberation activists and by many minority rights organizations are responses to this opportunity, seeking to extend social legitimacy and institutional support to the diverse patterns of intimacy that Americans have already forged. . . . There is bad faith in the popular lament over family decline. Family nostalgia deflects social criticism from the social causes of most 'personal troubles.'[13]

11. Armstrong, "Death and Sinister Afterlife," 24.

12. Traube, *Dreaming Identities*, 124

13. Stacey, Brave New Families, 270.

Both within the family and in institutions, young women with eating disorders are among others who feel either the pain of a changing society or the pain of a society that has not changed enough and rapidly enough. Eating disorders do not demonstrate unique suffering, either in amount or kind; neither is this suffering representative of that of others. It has, however, a distinctive relation to the history of Christianity, both in its focus on the body and in its location in a post-Christian society in which ancient attitudes toward women's bodies now appear in secular dress.

V

Let us consider again the primary hypotheses about why eating disorders are prevalent: the first states that young women who fast want to control *something*; the second, that young women feel they must resemble the models they see so continuously. "My body is too big," anorexic and bulimic girls and women say repeatedly. Could this mean that the fetishized female body of media imagery is too important—"too big"—that it too exclusively and insistently designates the value—or lack thereof—of women?

Could it also mean that fasting girls and women experience an imbalance between the body's "size" and the interior life, that the soul—to use traditional language—or the spirituality of young women is too slenderly supported, encouraged, developed? In the media culture of North America, no balance is attempted or achieved between the vast importance of young female bodies and the paucity of symbolic provisions for women's subjectivity and spirituality. The failure and fault does not belong to girls and women with eating disorders but to a society that does not provide adequate resources for the development of young women's subjectivity or inner life while fetishizing their bodies.

Contemporary eating disorders among young women in post-Christian North America are continuous with a long history of food practices as a discipline used to develop and exercise a religious self. Like Augustine, women with eating disorders seek less constraining forms for their desire than those to which they were socialized. Like many medieval women, they use their bodies harshly for purposes of developing an interior life, a will and agency that is not encouraged or supported by secular society. They suffer from what Leon Kass has called "spiritual anorexia."

Yet the differences between similar practices in different societies must be equally marked. Lacking the social context of religious support, interpretation, and respect that a medieval saint could assume, the medicalized food "asceticisms" of the present lack both the cautions and the rewards—social and spiritual—that accompanied historical fasting. Perhaps the authorizing context of a historical, dominantly Christian, society cannot redeem, in our eyes, the sometimes fatal fasting practices of medieval women. But women who fasted for religious purposes *were* regarded as saints in their own societies, making their practices not *merely* self- destructive.

The persistence of eating disorders among young middle-class North American women can be understood only when eating disorders are seen as a response to a lack of symbolic resources that would encourage young women to develop an interior life. Eating disorders have proved resistant both to adequate theorizing and to effective clinical strategies, because, I think, they have not been considered in relation to a social context in which extreme attention is paid to a young woman's body but little attention is paid to her subjectivity. If this analysis is correct, the theoretical and clinical task would then be to help persons with eating disorders to identify and cultivate more direct and fulfilling—and less dangerous—satisfactions.

The proposals I can offer in conclusion are neither satisfyingly optimistic nor reassuring. I began by understanding eating disorders as an expression of desire for an interior life, a subjectivity that is not authorized, encouraged, or supported by the communications media that contribute such a large proportion of most North Americans' daily symbolic "nourishment." Traditional forms of interiority were religious, composed of a spirituality that placed human life in a larger context than that of daily life, a symbolic universe that included time and space, life and death, cosmos and history. Moreover, despite largely misogynist representation of naked female bodies in religious images, a broad visual and verbal vocabulary within Christianity depicted female figures as some of the most dedicated and esteemed followers of Christ. The figures of Mary, Christ's mother, and Mary Magdalen, among others, were figures with whom historical Christian women could identify in exercising and cultivating their own religious identities.

It has traditionally been the responsibility of religion to provide the "food" by which the soul is nourished. Yet the malnutrition of fasting women in a belligerently secular North American public sphere can be only partially compensated by efforts of religious groups endeavoring to do a better job of challenging, supporting, and nourishing young women—though this should certainly become a priority in religious communities. The provision of religious alternatives to media fetishization of young women's bodies will help those girls and women who regularly participate in church, synagogue, mosque, or temple. But they will still live in a media culture.

Ultimately, the answer must lie in a major revision of media images, a revision that is not—realistically, given the present effectiveness of such images in a capitalist society—likely to occur soon. Lacking a dramatic revision of media provisions, young women can be helped to create a critical subjectivity by becoming conscious of the power and effects of media imagery and by resistance to it. Religious groups can develop a critical stance toward secular society, understanding themselves neither as rejecting nor adopting wholesale the values of secular society, but as critically revising secular offerings. They can recognize as *religious duty* the training of all their members to *see* what they look at in media communication, to become conscious of their own complicity in passively absorbing the daily circulation of media messages. Religious groups can also seek and create a repertoire of verbal and visual images that encourage young women to develop an interior life that will support their agency in society. They can seek and create images that inform and nourish young women's endeavors to place their desire in objects worthy of their attention and affection. In so doing, religious groups would more adequately acknowledge two traditional religious responsibilities, the critique of secular society and the strengthening and directing of individual and communal desire.

PART II

Society

7

Voyeurism and Visual Images of Violence

The television film *The Day After*, viewed by 100 million Americans, was rife with images of wounded and suffering bodies, the result of a depicted nuclear holocaust. The film was produced in order to awaken Americans to the present possibility of a nuclear war and to motivate the public to protest the buildup and stockpiling of nuclear weapons. The story begins several days before a missile attack on Kansas City partially destroys the nearby town of Lawrence, Kansas, and follows the lives of several people, from the frustrating but minor problems of ordinary family living to the survival efforts of those who come through the holocaust. A young woman, shown in the early scenes preparing for her wedding, becomes a hairless victim of radiation sickness. A vigorous, skillful physician who survives the blast appears in the final frame as a half-demented figure embracing a stranger in the rubble of his former home. The dramatic suffering of human beings who have been introduced to us as likable, generous, and valuable people is the primary vehicle for the message of the film; namely, that we must not stand by helplessly and allow such nuclear destruction to occur.

Did this intended message, embodied in images of violence and human suffering, actually reach the vast audience? At issue here is the larger question of the effects on viewers of media images of violence. The intended message is not necessarily the one that is received; the conscious intention of a media image's creator is not decisive in determining perceptions of the message. First, we must ask how viewers can relate to such an image; that is, through what personal experience is the image seen, interpreted and responded to?

A historical image will give us a basis for comparison with contemporary media images of violence and human pain: the early sixteenth-century Isenheim altarpiece by the artist Mathias Grünewald. When folded, its outer surface displays one of the most vivid crucifixion scenes ever painted. Here a grotesquely twisted Christ, his body riddled with wounds and a mass of festering sores, hangs dead on the cross; on his left the Virgin swoons, and on his right John the Baptist points calmly to the tortured and broken body. The 16 x 11 ft. altarpiece was commissioned in 1510 by the Anthonite Order of Isenheim, a monastery that had become a hospital caring for victims of plague, leprosy, syphilis, and a disease known as "burning sickness"—described as a sort of gangrenous ergotism, "showing itself in the form of apostems and abcesses, gradually spreading to the arms and legs, and after burning them up, detaching them little by little from the torso."[1]

It was for people afflicted with these diseases and for those who cared for them daily that the altarpiece was painted. The lacerated and infected skin of the crucified Christ mirrors the incurable epidemic diseases suffered by those who looked at this grotesquely depicted body. By a stipulation of 1498, even patients who could not walk were regularly brought to the altar of the monastery chapel to pray for miraculous cure or for the strength to endure their affliction.

This painting of cruel and gratuitous suffering was intended not as a voyeuristic experience, but rather as an image expressive of the physical experience of the sufferers and of those who cared for diseased and tortured bodies. Those first viewers of Grünewald's painting related to that image of violence and human suffering through the pain of their own wounded and diseased bodies. The artist modeled his crucified Christ after those patients, and his treatment was so realistic that the effects of the now-extinct "burning sickness" can be studied from the painting. That Christ shared and gave meaning to the sufferings of the patients who contemplated this image would have been the most immediate message of the altarpiece. However, there is a further aspect of this work of art. When it is opened, there is revealed a scene dramatically different in content, visual impact, and emotional tone. In the center a Madonna who looks like a German peasant girl holds the infant Jesus, while a heavenly orchestra of angels plays viols and a supernatural light streams from the radiant figure of God. On the left panel is an annunciation scene; on the right panel a risen Christ, in an aureole of rainbow-colored light, soars upward from an opened tomb, shedding his shroud and startling the guards into unconsciousness. The crucifixion scene thus gives way to a picture of resurrection and bliss within the horror of human pain and death. A third opening of the altarpiece shows saints who have triumphed over temptation, suffering, and death.

1. Grünewald, *Grünewald: The Paintings.*

These two features of the Isenheim altarpiece are crucial in an evaluation of the effect of this image of violence. Its original viewers related to it through their own immediate and overwhelming experience of sickness and imminent death. Moreover, the image of the crucified Christ is firmly placed in a larger context of the meaning and reward of human suffering. Far from being the final word, the crucifixion is depicted as the opening, the access to participation in the glory of the incarnation and resurrection.

Both of these aspects are conspicuously missing from contemporary images of violence and human suffering. *The Day After* presents images of violence to which most viewers can relate only voyeuristically. The vast majority of Americans who watched the film have not experienced anything remotely like an excruciatingly painful and debilitating disease. Furthermore, since in American society the victims of disease and accident are cared for by trained professionals in the impersonal setting of a hospital rather than by their families, most of us have not witnessed severe suffering at close range. Even the ravages of age are frequently concealed from view in convalescent hospitals and homes for the elderly. Nor do we prepare the bodies of our loved ones for burial. For most Americans, then, violence and human suffering as a visual experience can be only a secondhand experience, not one to which we relate directly. Further, images of suffering in *The Day After* were not placed in a larger context of hope or meaning. The film itself lacked any suggestion of how nuclear holocaust could be either avoided or interpreted (although the network sponsored a panel discussion of these matters immediately after its airing). The weeping preacher's attempt to interpret the event was a caricature of religious meaning:

"We thank you, God, that you have destroyed those who destroyed the earth," he says; only the "good" survive to rebuild. That a nuclear holocaust would be meaningless was one of the most insistent messages of the film.

Were these images of violence and human suffering, "consciousness-raising"? When expression and interpretation of present experience are lacking, is a voyeuristic horror effective in stimulating awareness and action? The potentially horrifying images of human suffering in *The Day After* may have momentarily fascinated and appalled the viewers, but they are accustomed to simultaneous emotional withdrawal from, and titillation by, a steady diet of violent images. A generation of children growing up with media violence and practicing voyeurism daily may assimilate the damaged bodies of *The Day After* into the unreal, emotionally neutral images offered by movies and television. Habituated to the visual experience of both actual and fantasy violence by press photographs and by television news and entertainment, Americans may not be shocked by images of violence.

People who are accustomed to images to which they cannot respond with horror or empathy may simply be further habituated to media violence by films like *The Day After*. Despite its intended message that the events depicted were completely in the realm of possibility, the film as an experience was the same as that of any viewing of media violence about which we can do nothing.

Americans are addicted to a daily supply of violent images. We are accustomed to feeling nothing and doing nothing about the disease, suffering, hunger, and death that we entertain visually every day in the comfort of our own homes. We are titillated by the horror, even while we consciously deplore the suffering and ask helplessly, "What is the world coming to?" Exploiting our voyeuristic addiction, the *New York Times Sunday Magazine* and other periodicals regularly place images of starving, sick, and dead bodies in the same visual field with advertising featuring luxury items: fur coats, alcoholic beverages, cigarettes, and expensive cars. Recognizing that the advertising revenue a periodical can command is what determines its success or failure, we must assume that images of violence and human suffering sell fur coats.

The editorial content of a newspaper or magazine, given the facts of economic survival, must provide an effective setting for the advertising, not the other way around. The visual training received by the public encourages a brief response of fascinated horror to images of violence, but this response is quickly replaced by a sense of emotional distance and the determination to provide for oneself the satisfactions offered by a commercial society.

This comparison of *The Day After's* hard-sell techniques with the messages of the Isenhen Altarpiece's equally violent crucifixion scene raises issues that go beyond the film itself to a consideration of the daily visual manipulation of the American public. A society habituated to images of violence can be gradually trained to accept violence and human pain on a massive scale as inevitable. In a context in which the primary relation of the audience to the image is voyeurism, in which the viewer's own physical experience (or experience of caring for the diseased and dead bodies of loved ones) is not evoked by the image, the violence depicted may not be consciousness-raising, but may result in further visual habituation. And such habituation to images of violence may be one of the primary sources of the lethargy, inertia, and failure to respond to the nuclear threat to all human bodies and to the body of the earth—a pattern that has characterized most Americans for almost forty years.

8

Religion and Values in Contemporary
North American Popular Film

In the 1970s film, *My Dinner with Andre*, Wally remarks to Andre that when he thinks of himself in the context of his immediate relationships and responsibilities, he feels like "a pretty good guy." He pays his rent; he takes out the garbage; he is nice to his friends; he does his job. But if, for a moment, he places himself in the context of a suffering world, a world full of physical hunger, violence, and war, he no longer feels quite so good about himself. He is then forced to recognize that his lifestyle uses more than his fair share of the resources and wealth of the world. He realizes, moreover, that he is oblivious to most of the suffering of the world, and that he has built his own happiness and sense of self-worth on that obliviousness. This is an unsettling and challenging filmic moment.

I am presently writing a book that examines the cumulative impact of popular films' treatments of Christianity, Islam, and Judaism in the decade 1983–1993.[1] In it, I propose a method for identification and analysis of the values imaged in films, especially those related to race, gender, and class. My aim in this study is to demonstrate that popular entertainment films are value-laden and to advocate that critical religious perspectives should be brought to examining the values circulated in this popular medium in the public sphere. The relevance of a study of religion and values in popular film to issues of spirituality may not be immediately evident. Yet I believe that there is a strong, even pressing, relevance. Hollywood films, seen by millions of Americans, are saturated with values. Because they circulate under the guise of "pure entertainment," the values they present are usually not analyzed, nor are decisions made about whether, and to what extent, we want

---

1. *Seeing and Believing: Religion and Values in Contemporary Popular Film.* I will discuss such films as *The Last Temptation of Christ, Jesus of Montreal, The Mission, Romero, The Rapture, Long Walk Home, Daughters of the Dust,* and *Jungle Fever.*

those values to inform us, shape our spirituality, modify our attitudes and the intentional practices by which we shape our religious lives.

The cultivation of a chosen form of spirituality is frequently thought of as a largely verbal enterprise, a matter of finding fruitful religious concepts. Because most of us are not trained to use religious images, we do not think of images as influential. Thus we do not examine the role of media images in orienting Christians, along with others, to our world. A long history of iconoclastic movements within Christianity, however, demonstrates the power of images. People at various times and places have feared the power of images to attract the devotee to the image itself rather than to its prototype. Others, arguing on the same grounds, have believed that images are too powerful a medium of religious communication and training to jettison. Both understood the power of images better than most twentieth-century filmgoers.

Moreover, most Americans like to think of themselves as individuals. We resist acknowledging the extent to which "the big structures of society play through our being all the time, and our only chance of freeing ourselves from them is to catch them at work."[2] Examining the cultural resources that shape us as individuals and as a society is a preliminary step toward knowing ourselves. Knowing ourselves, as individuals and collectively, is itself preliminary, in most spiritual traditions, to creating and exercising a spiritual practice.

As a historian of Christianity I recognize the role played by historical visual images in generating and circulating religious meaning. Studying historical religious communities in the Christian West, I developed a method for examining the religious images of Christian communities as an important part, along with their theological texts, their liturgies, and their devotional practices, of the communication of religious values.[3] If it is important to explore religious art when we study historical Christians, it is even more important to examine one of the most popularly accessible means by which the present North American public receives representations of identity and diversity, relationships, values, and institutions, social arrangements and the natural world. In the present media society we think of film primarily as entertainment, yet film's multiple, cumulative, often repetitive images have concrete effects in the circulation of values and attitudes in North America.

Directors often explicitly deny that films communicate values. Sam Goldwyn, in an often-quoted aphorism, once said that "anyone looking for

2. Inglis, *Media Theory*, 144.

3. See *Image as Insight: Visual Understanding in Western Christianity and Secular Culture*; and *Carnal Knowing: Female Nakedness and Religious Meaning in the Christian West*.

messages should go, not to the movies, but to Western union." Typically, message films bomb at the box office. Clearly, if they are to be successful, films must entertain. But Roland Barthes taught that one "gets" the cultural message at the same instant that one gets the pleasure; the greater the pleasure, the less one notices and examines the cultural message.

• • •

My own relation to "the movies" is one that may not be shared by many readers. My immigrant fundamentalist parents forbade movie-going. My childhood was spent visualizing the scriptural stories I read and acted out with my sisters. In an iconoclastic branch of Christianity, one in which "graven images" were feared as idolatrous, the only images I saw were on the Sunday School papers I received weekly. I remember two of these images vividly. One Sunday, a small girl with chubby arms leaned on a windowsill gazing out into the starry night. The text beneath the image read, "There is no God beside me." Unaware of the secondary meaning of "beside" as "except," I was puzzled. I had thought that every effort was being made, at home and in Sunday School, to remind me that there is a God beside me. That illustration failed to communicate its intended message. Another memorable series of Sunday School papers carried colorful cover pictures each week illustrating the breaking of one of the Ten Commandments. Being ten years old by then, I eagerly anticipated the seventh week. It was a disappointment. It pictured a milkman pouring a pail of water into a large vat of milk. The caption read, "Thou shalt not commit adultery."

My childhood repertoire of images largely failed to stimulate and challenge my psyche. I turned to words and soon learned to scorn any book that had pictures. But I could not walk by the movie marquee without devouring with my eyes the fascinating pictures they carried. From those guilty glances I learned a great deal. I learned that great passion occurs only to young beautiful heterosexual people, though I certainly had neither the word nor the concept until much later. I learned from those marquees that war is noble because the enemy is evil and must be slaughtered. I learned that fat people were laughable, and that people of color were either servants or "comical side-kicks." I learned to yearn to be or at least to resemble those beautiful women on the posters. I learned all of this, and more, in the split second before the parent or grandparent walking with me noticed that I was looking and reprimanded me. "The movies" assumed for me an intense fascination, augmented, no doubt, by the family prohibitions around them.

I saw my first movie, without my parents' knowledge or approval, when I was seventeen; it was *The Glenn Miller Story*. What a riveting experience. A new world was opened to me. In the world of the movies people did and said daring things, looking beautiful all the while, and confident, somehow, that everything would come out right in the end. It has taken me forty years to put the movies in perspective. I needed and could not, until recently, find a way of considering popular films that acknowledged their tremendous quasi-religious power but did not overrate the extent of that power or assume its malevolence.

• • •

The literature I found on religion and film divided neatly into two approaches. The first approach, characteristic of conservative religious groups, deplored "Hollywood" and its influence, finding it the "Whore of Babylon," the quintessential American problem. Many reviewers, on the other hand, found religious themes—alienation, grace, forgiveness, or redemption in most films; in fact, a film became substantial when a reviewer could identify a religious theme or two in it. Thus, it seemed imperative to find a way to assess the influence and the nature of that influence on the popular audiences that consume it. Yet the crabbiness that characterized the warier approaches seemed solipsistic and not likely to attract thoughtful adherents.

Recently, I have found in the emerging interdisciplinary field of cultural studies some useful suggestions for thinking about film.[4] Cultural studies approaches consider a film as one voice in a complex social conversation, situated in a particular historical moment. Since every film is produced and circulated within a particular climate of public events, conversation, and concerns, it is only in relation to that "moment" that a film's communications may be adequately examined. Reconstructing the framework within which one thinks about a film helps to minimize impressionistic and idiosyncratic readings. It limits the unacknowledged perspective of critics who confidently address their readers as "we"; "we feel," "we know," "we almost gasp," "we wonder"—all these phrases appeared in a single film review.[5]

I examine a film in relation to the social conversation, contestations, tensions, and struggles of its time and society of origin. The film is understood as one voice in the complex conversation by which societies continuously define and represent themselves. In concrete terms, then, a cultural studies approach

---

4. See R. Johnson, "What is Cultural Studies Anyway?"; Miller, *Illustration*.

5. Quoted by Bywater and Sobchak, *Introduction to Film Criticism*, 15.

requires compiling information about a film's funding and production, distribution to first-run or art theaters, the director's intended communications (as described in interviews), the box office earnings, and reviews from diverse critical perspectives, as well as analysis of the film's screenplay, camerawork, narrative, and soundtrack.

The point of my study is not to identify films that treat Christianity and/or other religions "positively," nor is it to praise or deplore the values represented in films. It is, rather, to acknowledge that the representation and examination of values and moral commitments does not presently occur most pointedly in churches, synagogues, or mosques, but as visualized for "congregations" in movie theaters. Increasingly, it seems to me, North Americans, including those with religious affiliations, are gathering about cinema and television screens rather than in churches to ponder the moral quandaries of American life. Religion and film share an interest in, and attention to, values. Looking at religion and values in the movies through the lens of a cultural studies methodology can demonstrate the importance of bringing critical religious perspectives to popular public discourse.

I have implied thus far that scrutiny of one's entertainment is an individual task, a task whose fruits are personal self-knowledge and flourishing. This may, indeed, be a rewarding by-product of a greater sophistication and degree of activity in relation to films. Providing direction for personal growth is not, however, the primary purpose of my inquiry. In fact, I hope it will contribute to a collapse of the dualism of personal and social. One of the most damaging mistakes made by a society fascinated with therapies of all sorts is to understand social problems as personal problems. Ultimately, individual flourishing requires a just society. And a just society will entail—along with the revision of public institutions—change in the consistent, cumulative verbal and visual representations of people, attitudes, and social arrangements circulating widely in the communication media of that society.

Change, of course, is inevitable—in ourselves and in society. If we would like to contribute to shaping the changes that will occur, we will first need close and accurate analyses of the present state of North American popular culture. And the pulse of a society—its interests and longings, its fears and anxieties—can be taken by examining its repetitive self-representations. Accurate and insightful analysis is only one of the myriad contributions needed for social change; it is not sufficient, but it is necessary.

I am often alarmed to find that others who worry about the social and personal effects on North Americans of filmic representations of religion and values are often political and religious conservatives. While I too would like to see the present violence, poverty, and insanity of American society overcome, I do not imagine that this could result from a backward step into some earlier version of our society. The inequities and the prejudices of earlier times are too evident to encourage me to think that a return to a society unaware of its glaring injustice, its chauvinism and racial intolerance, would be a step in the right direction. Rather, we must go forward to a society of equality and mutuality that we have never known and for which we have no blueprint. I hope, then, to provoke thought, to propose questions, and to suggest a method for exploring a film's "voice" in public discourse surrounding issues that press American society with their urgency.

It is important to identify what popular films, aimed primarily at entertaining a broad spectrum of the American population, can and cannot do. What films do best is to represent values negotiations. Cinema is an accessible medium in which competing issues of public life in a pluralistic society are formulated and represented for consideration and for interpretation. Films articulate a range of emotionally-toned values, fleshing out these values in characters, and narrating the conflicts that arise as characters endeavor to live out their commitments. They explore what happens, in particular contexts, when one character's values meet, question, contest, or resist those of another. Films represent the most intimate and private confrontations of values—the lovemaking—as well as the most public moments in which values come out into the open, clash, and are violently or peacefully negotiated. They are successful at the box office when they accurately identify and explore a current area of discomfort and anxiety and visualize a possible resolution.

In the decade 1983–1993, issues related to race, age, ecology, family, education, addiction, abortion, violence, gender, class, United States foreign policy, fundamentalist Christianity, the New Right, "family values," reproductive technologies, AIDS—to name only a few—permeated popular films. In short, popular films are a rich resource for identifying the problems and issues of American public life. At the same time, the values and images repetitiously represented in popular film also have social effects.

Although films frequently comment on religious life in the United States, they cannot take the place of religion. Films are neither icons to be emulated, nor are they distillations of evil. They are cultural products, deeply informed by the perspectives, values, and aspirations of their makers. They beg for creative discussion, not merely in terms of the emotions they stimulate in diverse viewers, nor in whether the images they present of various characters are positive or negative, but in relation to the particular anxieties and interests of the social moment in which they circulate.

In a society in which functional illiteracy is high, film images are an important source of information and socialization. The function of a society's art is to educate the emotions, to train the sensibilities to a rich range of feeling, to a perceptual life that excludes nothing of importance. To the extent that the arts we live with supply stimulation, articulation, and perceptive delicacy to our relational lives, we are well-served. If, however, we find that the media arts with which most Americans live on a daily basis are governed by a narrow emotional repertoire, by conventions of representation, and by genre films with minimal elements of surprise, we are not well served. A media diet is not sufficient emotional nourishment for anyone, yet millions of Americans live on such a diet. Ultimately, stocking one's imagination with the rich and varied images that are capable of criticizing and enhancing relationship, community, and society will require more than the movies.

Fundamental to my study is the contention that religion has centrally to do with the articulation of a sense of relatedness among individuals, within families, communities, and societies, and with the natural world. Religions also provide a picture of the greater whole in which all living beings are related. Religious beliefs, narratives, and institutions emerge from and specify organized and stabilized understandings of relatedness. Defining religion in this way means that relationships between people in faith communities, as well as attitudes and practices in relation to those outside the group require scrutiny. Thus, understandings of race, gender, class, and sexual orientation are not accidental or incidental to religious perspectives but, as a concrete way religious perspectives are articulated, are central to religious values. Spiritual hunger arises from relationships that lack equality and mutuality and from unjust institutions and social arrangements as surely as it comes from inadequate theology or belief. It also arises from impoverished symbolic resources for imagining our relational lives.

If religion is about relationships, about a network of connections— human beings to God and to one another, to the natural world, to history and the universe—then religion is also centrally and essentially about the values according to which people design their relationships. To recognize that religious communities are centrally concerned with the formulation, exploration, and practical application of values is also to recover one of religion's public functions, that of critically examining secular values and of providing alternatives.

9

Film Talk

An Approach to Moviegoing

In *Love's Knowledge*, Martha Nussbaum points out that drama for the Greeks served a purpose that went beyond mere entertainment. "To attend a tragic drama was not to go to a distraction or a fantasy, in the course of which one suspended one's anxious practical questions. It was instead to engage in a communal process of inquiry, reflection, and feeling with respect to important civic and personal ends." Theater provided a way to explore a central question: How should human beings live?

> To respond to [the performance of a tragedy] was to acknowledge and participate in a way of life—a way of life . . . that prominently included reflection and public debate about ethical and civic matters. . . . To respond well to a tragic performance involved both feeling and critical reflection; and these were closely linked with one another.

Film can serve a similar purpose. In its often nuanced exploration of emotions, and in its representation of behavior and social class, films implicitly if not explicitly address the question of how human beings should live.

Someone will object that the Greek tragedies, because they depict epic heroic struggle, are far more worthy of thoughtful analysis than are popular films. We have that impression, I believe, primarily because Greek tragedies have been treated with seriousness not only by their society of origin but also by a long line of respected intellectuals, reaching into our own time. But if the narrative content of a Greek tragedy were summarized as if it were a film plot, it might be difficult to see its profundity. *Medea*, for example, is the story of a woman who loses her husband to a younger woman and in vengeance kills her children; in the end, a chariot swoops down out of the sky and carries her away. If our attention were solely on the "action" in Greek tragic drama, the play could be reduced to such a description.

On the other hand, if popular films were understood as responses to the question, How should we live?, we might notice that they propose diverse answers—some highly dubious and others rather profound—to that important question. Is not the behavior glamorized by a film (implicitly) proposed as a partial answer? Greek audiences may have recognized more communally and consistently than do late twentieth-century moviegoers that the serious question of how one should live lies beneath the surface of drama. But popular films from *Witness* to *Alien* 3 can certainly be seen as addressing that question in myriad ways.

Nussbaum also suggests that Greek spectators attended a public drama *expecting* to identify and discuss its proposal about "how we should live." Similarly, for many filmgoers one of the most prominent pleasures of moviegoing is that of thinking and talking about the film they have seen. If theater was not entertaininent for ancient Greeks, neither is film "pure"—that is to say, mindless—entertainment for many Americans.

Nussbaum's description of Greek audiences helps us imagine twentieth-century spectators who want to think deeply and talk intensely about a popular film. But spectators who enjoy serious discussions of films are among the few who do not merely take in but also critically evaluate a film's depiction of life. One can choose whether to accept, reject, or adopt in part a film's proposed values only when the question of how to live is consciously brought to watching and thinking about a film. Failing that, image is simply heaped upon image, proposal upon proposal, without clarification of the potential choices of "how we should live."

Of course, there are also enormous differences between fifth-century BCE Greek audiences and twentieth-century Americans, two of which are instructive. First, an important aspect of Greek tragedy was its setting. Ancient theater "took place during a solemn civic/religious festival, whose trappings made spectators conscious that the values of the community were being examined and communicated." Nothing signals to modern spectators that questions concerning how to live their lives are to be engaged in the film they attend.

Second, Americans do not think of filmgoing as an especially social or communal activity. Each person is effectively isolated, in the darkened theater. We are next to each other but cannot make eye contact, and we are requested not to talk during the show. By contrast, says Nussbaum, ancient audiences, "sitting in the common daylight, saw across the staged action the faces of fellow citizens on the other side of the orchestra." They simultaneously saw the dramatic action, felt in themselves the emotions elicited by the action, and observed their fellow citizens reactions.

Clearly, moviegoers today lack the communal religious setting that signaled the fundamental seriousness of drama to Greek audiences. Can we, who love to be entertained but who also insist on thinking "how we should live," gather material for considering our lives from the movies? I think we can, and already do. Can we consider the question of how to live to be a question about the common good as well as one about individual flourishing? I think we must.

Conversation is the medium that changes one's idiosyncratic, subjective perceptions of a film to social criticism. Just as the ancient philosopher Socrates needed interlocutors—friends—in order to explore the dimensions and implications of an idea, so too do filmgoers need friends with whom to discuss, to disagree and argue, with whom to negotiate the multiple meanings of a film. Even before interpretations can be proposed, friends are needed to reconstruct the film, to point out details one has missed, the tone of voice, the camera angle, the arrangement of actors on the screen, the soundtrack, the framing, the facial expressions. Friends are also needed to help reconstruct the context in which the film was produced and distributed and to discern how the film might relate to it.

Discussions about film are valuable for another reason: they compensate for the inevitable blind spots everyone has. Most Americans have watched films with attention and delight all their lives. Each person has a film repertoire of information and associations that no one else exactly shares. This means that, although each person has intensive preparation and a store of knowledge, none "controls," "commands" or has "mastered" this voluminous body of work.

Moreover, at the same time that we have a great deal of personal knowledge of films, we are also well trained to respond to filmic conventions in predictable ways. The serious discussion of films should unsettle, challenge, even disassemble these socialized reactions. As one learns to question, to investigate and to make explicit the strategies by which a film produces—or at least directs—our responses, the pleasure of watching a film changes subtly but profoundly from that of passive spectatorship to that of active critical engagement.

A spectator's impressions of a film, then, are simultaneously informed by her education and life experiences and trained by film conventions and viewing habits. This does not mean that the strong feeling a film may elicit should be discarded or overlooked. Rather, the emotion a film evokes should be acknowledged and understood as the starting point for an exploration of the filmic strategies that elicited it. The purpose of paying serious attention to film is twofold. On the one hand, the ability to analyze filmic representations develops an individual's critical subjectivity. On the other hand, films reveal how a society represents itself to itself.

If we want to think about a film not primarily as "entertaining" but as communicating social roles and expectations, values, and constructions of desire and the desirable, then we need to consider the role of pleasure. In her 1975 essay "Visual Pleasure and Narrative Cinema," Laura Mulvey makes the rather startling statement that in order to challenge the "basic assumptions of mainstream film," one must first "destroy" the pleasure produced by the film. This seems to me a particularly problematic approach. It reproduces, in secular language, an ancient Christian mistrust of pleasure, calling for a sort of visual asceticism that assumes that one can work and learn only when pleasure is absent.

I would put it differently. Our task is neither to deny nor to destroy visual pleasure in order to do the sober work of analysis, but to trust our pleasure as a primary tool of interpretation. Certainly a film's implicit claim either to entertain or to mirror reality needs to be examined. Yet to assume that visual pleasure serves only to seduce viewers into mindlessly accepting the film's values distorts a spectator's experience and eliminates the primary motivation for analyzing the film. Visual pleasure is the place to begin because by producing visual pleasure, a film communicates values. Roland Barthes once remarked that one "gets" the cultural message at the same moment one gets the pleasure.

Spectatorial pleasure, far from being jettisoned, must be noticed and examined. Pleasure can be examined by identifying the filmic strategies or devices that produce it and by developing a critical method, an ability to articulate the assumptions and values underlying and informing one's reactions to a film. For the film does not contain and determine its own meaning; meaning is negotiated between the spectator and the film.

This does not mean, however, that a film permits an infinite number of interpretations. Films certainly endeavor to make viewers see what the director wants communicated. The primary tool governing the communication of meaning is film conventions, repeated stylized interactions between the actors that viewers have come to expect from watching countless other films of the same genre. In romantic narrative film, for example, we expect closure, an ending. Trained by Hollywood conventions, we may even expect a "happy ending," by which is usually meant one in which heterosexual partners find each other. If such an ending is denied us, we are likely to feel dissatisfied.

Filmmakers outside the mainstream often subvert film conventions in order to make them evident. In Joan Micklin Silver's *Chilly Scenes of Winter*, the couple separates in the end, which caused several reviewers to complain that the film had no ending. It had an ending; it even had—in the circumstances depicted in the film—a happy ending, but because of the expectation that only the reuniting of the couple would make a happy ending, the film was perceived as unfinished. Similarly, in Claudia Weil's *Girlfriends*, a film convention in which marriage constitutes a happy ending is overturned. A woman's marriage is presented as interrupting her work and confining her character development, as well as undermining her relationship with an important woman friend. Spectators' displeasure is often the first signal that a film convention has been disrupted.

Although religion is hardly a preoccupation of contemporary film, images of religion and religious commitment circulate in the public sphere through this popular medium. Hollywood films generate and maintain attitudes toward religion that have far-reaching effects in American social and political life. That the effects of representations of religion in film are difficult or impossible to define with precision makes them no less important to study.

10

Larry Flynt in Real Life

In *The People vs. Larry Flynt* Miloš Forman explores an American phenomenon: the career of a pornographer who, in the pages of *Hustler* and other magazines, took the representation of sex and violence against women to new lows while fighting in the courts for his right to do so. Since coming to the US from Czechoslovakia several decades ago, Forman has been fascinated by the oddities flourishing in American democracy. His movie makes Flynt a hero, despite—or perhaps by—representing him as lowlife, blasphemous, and aggressively nasty. In conventional martyr style, Flynt suffered for his "belief" in his right to publish pornography, political satire, and images of violence against women.

In real life, the Houston trial that is ridiculed as a right-wing orgy in *Larry Flynt* was "a suit for damages brought by the mother of a 12-year-old [girl] whose strangled body was found next to a copy of *Hustler*" (see letter from Lawrence Cranberg in the *New York Times*, February 8, 1997). The movie positions the viewer to laugh at women's bodies in grotesque positions and situations and at caricatured, self-righteous up-tightness, and to feel relief when the US Supreme Court decides Flynt's violent pornography is constitutionally protected.

Commentators on the movie can be divided into two camps: those who appreciate the high moral tone of the movie and those who focus on the way Forman glides over *Hustler's* seamy content. "The film celebrates not Mr. Flynt but the First Amendment and its role in protecting free speech, particularly political satire," wrote one correspondent in the *New York Times*. One reviewer called *Larry Flynt* "the most timely and patriotic movie of the year," and another spoke of "a delicious dissonance between high principles and low motives."

Bob Herbert's op-ed piece in the *New York Times* (February 3, 1997) took a different perspective. Herbert accused the movie of "fundamental dishonesty" in ignoring the reality of *Hustler's* preoccupation with violence against women. Herbert listed some examples: African American women portrayed with grotesquely enlarged sexual organs; women in various stages of torture, mutilation, and decapitation; and little girls "naked, sometimes blind, and available for sex." Like Herbert, feminist commentators pointed out that the movie makes a hero of a man whose magazines consistently degrade women. Gloria Steinem's commentary (*New York Times*, January 7) prompted demonstrations at many local openings of the film.

Did Herbert's review place him "in the ranks of people who have allowed their self-righteousness to overpower their sense of freedom and justice," as one reviewer alleged? Is *Larry Flynt* really good clean fun, simply entertainment? After all, it incorporates few violent images. Yet in making a hero of Flynt, the film supports—even glorifies—the circulation of violent images.

Movies are cultural products, located in a particular society at a particular moment. Movies succeed at the box office because they have accurately identified popular interests, preoccupations, or concerns. *Larry Flynt* has not been as successful as its producers hoped, but by mid-February it had grossed $19 million, a figure that places it among the largest grossing films of the year.

Larry Flynt should not be viewed as if it were a self-enclosed world unrelated to the society it addresses. The film explicitly represents a real man, a real magazine with a huge circulation, and real events of public life. Though *Larry Flynt* takes some liberties with the facts, it connects its narrative to the real world not only by remaining close to the notoriously raunchy character it portrays, but also by showing portions of the content of *Hustler*.

A recent survey of more than one thousand studies over a thirty-year period has shown decisively that exposure to violent images is associated with antisocial and aggressive behavior. This relationship works in several different ways. Though statistically rare, copycat crime is well documented. Violent images also have broad social effects. They normalize violence and encourage some viewers to emulate violent images.

On an even broader scale, images of violence desensitize viewers, eroding their empathy with victims' pain, helping to create a society in which violence is at epidemic proportions. An estimated 4 million American women are abused by intimate partners each year; a quarter of all American women will be abused sometime in their lives.[1] Between 25 percent and 35 percent of women who go to emergency rooms have medical complaints stemming from domestic violence; 2.5 million women are victims of rape, assault, or robbery

1. See Bell, "Violence Against Women in the U.S."

each year; and the Bureau of Justice Statistics estimates (based on data collected from 1974 to 1991) that approximately 8 percent of American women will be raped in their lifetimes (see "Diagnostic and Treatment Guidelines of Domestic Violence," American Medical Association, 1992).

Women are not the only victims of violent crime, of course. The US is one of the most dangerous countries in the world. "The national homicide rate, corrected for population, increased almost exactly 100% from 1950 to 1990." In large cities, the increase has been much higher: in Los Angeles County, with a population that doubled in the last forty years, homicides have increased over 1,000 percent since 1953.[2]

It is in relation to the violence of American society that *Larry Flynt* should be assessed. Can Americans afford to dismiss the role of violent pornography when it grosses more each year than the film and recording industries combined? *Larry Flynt* is indeed a uniquely American story, not in its support of the First Amendment but in its support of violence, especially violence against women.

2. See Barry, "Screen Violence: It's Killing Us."

11

What You See Is What You Get

Religion in Prime Time Fiction Television

The 1995 Conference on Religion and Prime Time Television focused on two primary complaints about television representation of religion. The first complaint was that the frequency with which prime time fiction television represents religion does not reflect Americans' present engagement with religion. The second complaint was that religion (especially Christianity) was represented too often as a negative or dangerous aspect of American culture, at best a partisan politics that constantly threatens to subvert loyalty to impartial public discourse. Prime time television was charged with depicting religion as inevitably partisan, self-promoting, and subversive of the common good of an increasingly pluralistic nation.[1] I will explore these complaints, endeavoring to identify the contribution of each as well as their ultimate inadequacy as cultural criticism. After discussing my approach to media analysis and exploring why these complaints do not, in my view, attend to the crucial issues surrounding media representations of religion, I will raise a different complaint. I will then make several suggestions for enhancing prime time programming's contribution to the public representation of religion in America.

At the risk of appearing to be the academic that I in fact am, I would like to begin by suggesting that a thorough analysis of media communications on the subject of religion requires the selective use of critical theories. Marxist, psychoanalytic, feminist, cultural studies, ideology critique, contextualist, representation theory: any of these could be useful for analysis of particular media communications. Although critical theory seems initially to be far removed from the practical concerns of television programming, its function is "to help individuals see and interpret phenomena and events."[2]

1. Sheler, "Spiritual America," 49.
2. Kellner, *Media Culture*, 24.

Moreover, everybody has theories; expectations and assumptions direct what we notice and what we fail to see. But most of us, most of the time, do not acknowledge and examine our theories.

We are suspicious of theoretical approaches because we have seen them enslave and blind their adherents, rendering invisible anything not directly focused by the theory. Indeed, the capacity of theories to dominate vision is precisely the reason why theories must be used critically and interchangeably. Each theory illuminates a different segment of social reality, but must be jettisoned when it has reached its limits. Theories can best be thought of as a toolkit, as Michel Foucault suggested of his own theories.

Theory specifies what a reviewer assumes when he or she evaluates a cultural product so that the adequacy of those assumptions can be evaluated as well as the reviewer's conclusions. Only by the use of articulated and examined critical theories can we escape a positivist approach to the television "text." Positivist approaches rely on citing segments or episodes in a cultural product as evidence that topics such as religion have been represented, ignoring the complex medium, the cultural moment, and the economic arrangements through which the meaning of those represented incidents is mediated. Positivist analysis, in addition, denies that analysis is conducted in order to intervene, to change the objects of analysis.[3] In short, a more sophisticated analysis is needed than one that contends, from an undefined and falsely universal perspective, that a movie or television show produces "positive" or "negative" images of certain people or institutions.

Marxist analysis is needed for scrutinizing the economic arrangements surrounding particular depictions. Do advertising agencies have the final word in the content of prime time fiction television? Or do studio executives exercise power to determine what Americans should and should not see? Feminist or gender analysis is needed to expose the assumptions about gender roles and expectations operating in narrative programming. A theory of the way media representations function in American culture will direct us to analyze, not only a producer's intentions, but also the effects of media representations. An adequate theory of representation would, for example, overcome the naiveté of the media worker who claimed, in one of the Conference panels, that merely showing a scene in a gay bar for thirty seconds did not imply approval of homosexuality but simply acknowledged its existence.[4]

3. Agger, *Cultural Studies as Critical Theory*, 135.

4. Media representations of sexual, religious, and racial minorities begin to weave minority people into the mainstream of American society. People unused to seeing

Finally, a contextualized cultural theory is required that places a television program or film in the cultural moment in which it was produced in order to detect its resonant images, that is, images that resonate to a timely cultural experience, making them vibrant beyond their placement within the narrative.[5] In this essay I will endeavor to illustrate the usefulness only of the last of these critical theories.

The cultural studies approach I enlist as a critical lens understands media neither as a vehicle for deception and domination, nor as guileless entertainment, but as an arena of contested, negotiated, resisted, and appropriated meaning, a "contested terrain reproducing on the cultural level the fundamental conflicts within society."[6] Discussion of media's representation of religion, then, like discussion of any other topic, must be contextualized within the social and cultural "moment" in which it occurs.

RELIGION ON PRIME TIME AS REFLECTION OF AMERICAN SOCIETY

The first complaint about prime time fiction television's representation of religion assumes that media programming should reflect social conditions and interests more or less quantitatively. In the case of religion, the diverse forms of religion existing in American society should be represented in frequencies proportionate to the numbers of people they attract. While the simplistic version of this assumption is both impractical and mechanistic, there is, in my view, a kernel of insight within it that should not be lost. What the reflection theory brings to focus is that media entertainment, if it is to contribute to—as contrasted to escape from—discussion of the common social interests

---

representatives of their group in media's reality-creating discourse are validated by such representations. In my view, this is one of the reasons it is important to represent a more inclusive range of our pluralistic society in prime time fiction television. On the other hand, those who object to the representation of sexual orientation minorities do so because they understand the validating power of the media.

5. The term "resonant images" is Kellner's (*Media Culture*, 107). One example of a resonant image might be "Thelma and Louise." In its conclusion, the film condemned those female outlaw buddies by outnumbering and outmaneuvering them with police cars (representative of patriarchal culture) that literally drove them into the Grand Canyon. But in the body of the film, the image of Louise shooting the oil truck whose driver had made obscene gestures and used obscene language was a resonant image for millions of American women who suffer a high and constant level of daily public sexual harassment. Women who loved the movie loved it not for its ending but for such images of female outlaw freedom.

6. Kellner, *Media Culture*, 101–2.

and anxieties of a broad range of Americans, must provide dramatizations that identify those interests and make proposals about them. The media fiction Americans watch is useful to the extent that it localizes and examines the perennial question of human life: How should we live?[7]

If some version of reflection theory were to become a criterion for prime time fiction programming's representation of religion, what could Americans expect to see? Critics of prime time programming often point to the increasing visibility of evangelical Protestants and Roman Catholics in America, urging more representation of evangelical Christians. But the picture of American religiousness they sketch is partial and therefore distorted. Demographic studies of religion in America show that Americans are becoming more religious, but in different configurations than formerly. According to statistics compiled from various sources, the largest religious populations other than Christianity in the United States are the following:[8]

Judaism	6 million
Islam	between 1 and 7 million
Buddhism	between 1 and 3 million
Hare Krishna	500,000
Hinduism	500,000
Christian Science	400,000
Neo-paganism	40,000

According to an extensive study of religious affiliation in the United States, only 9 percent of Americans profess no religion at all.[9] The figures I have cited are educated estimates; no one has yet counted these populations in a systematic way. However, approximate as these figures are, they reveal two important characteristics of contemporary American religiousness. First, that it is changing rapidly, and second, that it is changing in the direction of becoming more diverse. Religious pluralism is one important factor in any attempt to assess the reflective adequacy of representations of religion in America. This means that representations of minority religions occur in a volatile and, for many, anxiety-provoking religious social context, a context

7. Martha Nussbaum has described the origin of this question in ancient Greek public "entertainment" in *Love's Knowledge*, 4 and passim.

8. See Melton, *Encyclopedia of American Religion*; also his *Religious Bodies in the United States*; Lippy and Williams, *Encyclopedia of the American Religious Experience*; and Eck, *On Common Ground*.

9. Sheler, "Spiritual America," 50.

in which media representations can both inform and influence attitudes toward religious groups.

Within Christianity—still, in terms of numbers, clearly the predominant religion in the United States—there is also increasing diversity and change. The *Yearbook of American and Canadian Churches*, which documents trends within Christianity, modestly designates itself a "snapshot of religious activity," since religious organizations are "in constant flux."[10] Mainstream Protestant denominations are declining: the Episcopal Church, the Evangelical Lutheran Church in America, the Presbyterian Church USA, the United Church of Christ, and the United Methodist Church.[11] On the other hand, considerable increases are occurring in the Roman Catholic Church, the Southern Baptist Convention, the Church of Jesus Christ of Latter-day Saints, and the Assemblies of God. The Pentecostal Church is presently the fifth-largest denomination in the United States. Moreover, many members participate simultaneously in more than one church organization.

Christianity in the United States is also becoming less white. Two largely African American denominations are in the top seven in terms of membership size: the National Baptist Convention and the Church of God in Christ. Of the fourteen largest denominations, six have largely African American membership. Moreover, African Americans are apparently more religious than white Americans. By adding membership figures of predominantly African American denominations and estimates of African American participation in denominations with predominantly white membership, together with the one million plus African American Muslims, almost a hundred percent of the total. African American population in the United States is accounted for.[12]

If a reflection theory of representation were adopted, it would need to present something resembling this religious picture. Although media workers object that it is impossible to please everyone with media representations of religion, programming that endeavored both to support those engaged in diverse religious groups by acknowledging their existence, and to inform Americans about the range of religious options presently available in the United States would seemingly rectify the purported problem of religion being underrepresented on prime time fiction television. But is this what those who complain of underrepresentation want? And would such carefully

---

10. Bedell, *Yearbook of American and Canadian Churches*, "Introduction."

11. Ibid., 12.

12. Ibid., "Introduction."

proportioned depictions of religion across network television be an adequate representation of religion in America?[13]

Before I address these questions another consideration deserves attention in relation to the complaint that prime time television does not reflect the numbers of Americans loyal to religion. The charge that religious commitment and motivation is excluded from prime time fiction broadcasting is becoming increasingly difficult to support. An analysis of almost two thousand hours of prime time programming conducted by the Media Research Center of Alexandria, Virginia, showed that in 1993 there were 116 portrayals of religion.[14] In 1994, the same group identified 253 portrayals of religion, more than twice the frequency of 1993 programming.[15] However, even cursory analysis of the Media Research Center's evaluations of prime time programming reveals the conservative religious perspective from which judgments were made.

Apparently, television programming has been affected by the conservative swing in the nation's mood. But when evangelical Christians say that they want to see favorable prime time fictional treatments of religion, it is "positive," or at least "neutral," treatments of conservative Christianity they want to see. They are not eager to entertain depictions of liberal Christianity; nor are they asking for increased fictional representations of the other religious groups presently attracting adherents in the United States. Conservative Christians seem also to assume that a broader discussion and negotiation of values—those "goods" of common life that people would like to be able to assume—can occur only under the rubric of religion, an assumption I will shortly question.

---

13. I assume that the criterion of balance between or among depictions of various religions within a single program is impossible to achieve. Such a criterion would also effectively prevent representation of any religion in any depth or complexity.

14. According to the Media Research Center of Alexandria, Virginia, 42.2 percent of the representations of religion were negative, while 30.2 percent were neutral portrayals, and 27.6 percent were positive representations. However, depictions rated (by whom?) as "negative," "neutral," or "positive" do not specify the criteria by which these evaluations are reached, thereby masking the assumed universal perspective engaged in such judgments. It is likely that a representation of Christianity that a fundamentalist Christian might find "positive" might appear to be highly "negative" to a liberal Christian. Thomas Johnson and Sandra Crawford, "Faith in a Box: Entertainment Television on Religion, 1994," 1.

15. Moreover, in the estimation of this conservative organization, in 1994, "friendly" depictions of religion outnumbered negative ones by almost 2 to 1, the reverse of 1993. "Faith in a Box, 1994," 1.

What do conservative Christians like to see in the entertainment media? The Christian Film and Television Commission's 1994 awards for the best films in the categories of "family picture" and "mature audiences" give an indication of the values that directed their choices. The best family picture was Walt Disney's *Homeward Bound: The Incredible Journey*, "a movie starring two dogs and a cat." The best film for mature audiences was *The Remains of the Day*. *The Age of Innocence* and *Much Ado About Nothing* were runners-up. The Commission denounced *Mrs. Doubtfire*; it was unacceptable because it "flaunts the admonition in Deuteronomy 22:5 that men not wear women's clothes."[16]

If the Christian Film and Television Commission accurately represents the Christian right, its approval and disapproval reveal a lack of recognition of the role of media in North American public life. The Commission awarded films that avoid offense—"nice" movies—rather than films that represent and explore the pressing problems of society. In other words, the Commission subscribes to the film industry's self-stylization as "entertainment," ignoring popular films' ability to represent conflicts of values for consideration, discussion, and negotiation.

The second complaint about prime time fiction television's representation of religion is that fiction media too often represent religion as dangerous and threatening to American public life and the common good. This contention, I believe, fails to acknowledge that such representations occur in a cultural moment in which religious extremists, fanatics, and zealots are both prominent in news media and frightening. That religious "lunatic fringes" exist and are dangerous to the common good has been documented too recently in living memory to be ignored. A society that has not forgotten Jonestown, and for whom images of the Branch Davidians' burning compound are still vivid, needs to explore, through media representation, the damage that can occur when powerful and totalitarian religious leaders are uncritically obeyed. Seen in relation to the cultural moment, representations of religion as dangerous are not difficult to understand. At such a moment, however, media might also contribute by providing images of forms of religion that remind secular America that religion is not monolithic, images that challenge religious people to cultivate their thoughtful exercise of moral responsibility

---

16. "The Envelope, Please," *The New York Times*, March 12, 1994. Religious News Service reports that 72 percent of the top 25 box office movies were "acceptable" to the Christian Film and Television Commission headed by Ted Baehr.

in private and public spheres. This brings me to my complaint about depictions of religion and religious people on prime time fiction television.

RELIGION AS MONOLITHIC ON PRIME TIME TELEVISION

The two complaints against prime time television's representation of religion that I have discussed do not, in my view, go to the heart of the contradiction between Americans' various religious commitments and our commitment to secular public discourse. My complaint is rather that in endeavoring to pacify the Christian right by increasing depictions of conservative Christianity, entertainment media does not help Americans to recognize the complexity of religious commitment. Nor does it help them to discriminate between different religious perspectives in relation to issues concerning the common good. In fact, the label "Christian" has become synonymous with the Christian right.

It is exceedingly difficult for Christians who believe in the literal meaning of the King James Version of the Bible to talk with Christians who do not accept prooftexts, and who consider Biblical texts to be always in need of careful and contextual interpretation. But in relinquishing "Christian" as a description of their concerns and loyalties, liberal Christians permit the category to become monolithic in public usage. Prime time television largely reflects—and supports—the constriction of "Christian" to conservative, countercultural Christianity.

Liberal Christians and minority religious groups who find the religious right dangerously united on some crucial issues must define thoughtful positions on the same issues and thus demonstrate the variety of approaches consonant with Christian belief and practice. In my view, it is important to press on the public agenda religion that holds at its core commitment to social and institutional change on behalf of those who are impoverished, marginalized, and oppressed. This gospel stands in dramatic contrast to a gospel of the "straight and narrow way" that insists on adherence to particular social and sexual arrangements and behaviors. To date, conservative Christians have had a higher profile in pressing so-called "family values" in the name of their religious commitment than have liberal Christians. It would, of course, be helpful to see the complexity of diverse religious commitments examined in prime time programming.

Religions other than Christianity are similarly diverse. Islam, which is rapidly becoming the second most populous religion in America, is perhaps the most extreme example of monolithic representation of religion in

American media.[17] While numerous examples of the abuse of religious ideas can be cited from every world religion, Muslims have become the suspects of choice in the 1990s. Muslims are currently represented in the communication media primarily as intolerant and monomaniachal terrorists. Many examples could be given; I will confine myself to one. In the first CBS news reports of the Oklahoma City federal building bombing, Middle Easterners were identified as the likely perpetrators. Their religion was immediately implicated in these suspicions: film clips were shown of Muslims praying at a convention in Oklahoma City the summer before, implying without stating that the bombing was related to Muslims' religious commitments. Such racial and religious media scapegoating has real effects: in the aftermath of the bombing, Middle Eastern Americans in many different cities suffered harassment and persecution.

I will conclude by suggesting briefly some directions prime time fiction television might explore in order to address more effectively the role of religion in America.

1.   In the context of change and increasing diversity in Americans' religious commitments, accurate and sympathetic information about religions in America is of great importance. Lacking studies of the ratio of representations of Christianity to those of other religions, my informal observation suggests that conservative Christianity receives most of the prime time cultural space devoted to religion. Presumably this occurs both because the Christian right has been the most active of any religious group in protesting television's representation of religion, and because of the numerical dominance of conservative Christianity. However, the very fact that Christianity is numerically dominant indicates that many Americans may have little information about the beliefs, practices, lifestyles, rituals, and values of those of other religions. Without such information, prejudice and stereotype all too easily fill the gap. Moreover, if media representations are to be accurate and nuanced, practitioners of Buddhism, Islam, and Judaism, as well as Native American and other less populous religions, will be needed as consultants.

2.   Prime time fiction television could increase and diversify representations of people who are endeavoring to live lives informed by religious and/or value commitments. Such programs would not focus on religious

17. See Kellner, "Reading the Gulf War: Production/Text/Reception," chapter 6 in *Media Culture.*

aspects of characters' lives but would depict these characters as ordinary Americans for whom religious commitment plays a role in decisions and relationships. One of the media's most prominent capacities is that of "naturalizing" certain behaviors by depicting them casually as part of daily life. The media that regularly naturalizes violence and other irresponsible and destructive behavior might contribute to American society by naturalizing the resources of religious faith.

3. Although the Christian right seems to assume that discussion and negotiation of values must occur in the context of depictions of religion, it is important, in a society that considers itself privately religious but commitedly secular in the public sphere, to recognize that value conflicts do not always occur in the context of religion. Traditionally, in societies of the like-minded, religion has defined, imposed, or attracted people to common values; but American society can no longer assume religious like-mindedness. For many Americans, a secular public sphere guarantees an arena of public discussion free from parochial interests.[18] It is important, then, frequently to depict confrontations of values as occurring outside the sponsoring arena of religion, as prime time fiction programming already regularly does.

4. Finally, there can be no substitute for training Americans in the skills of critical viewing. Although academic statements of critical theories can be relatively inaccessible, critical viewing is not necessarily so esoteric. A four-year-old can grasp the concept that the narrative of a television program or a movie has been made up by someone, and could be imagined differently. An older child can easily detect the race, class, or gender perspective from which a particular program is presented and can learn to question the relationship of advertising segments to the program. Because, as Roland Barthes once said, audiences "get" the cultural message when they get the pleasure, analysis of one's viewing pleasure can be the starting place for such analysis.

18. See Suman, "Do We Really Need More Religion on Fiction Television?" for an argument that "television is not about mirroring reality," and that religion is best understood and practiced in the private sphere. Suman fears that public exposure of religion could eventuate in a resurgence of the intolerance and bigotry that the Constitution seeks to forestall by separating religious and state powers. His argument assumes, however, that the loudest voices in support of public depictions of religion, the Christian right, would achieve hegemony over public broadcasting if more religion were to be televised. If the goal were to present a variety of living and accessible religious options rather than to permit conservative Christianity to dominate, Suman's argument founders.

Children are usually willing to think both more profoundly and more playfully about entertainment than are adults, who often claim that a favorite program is "spoiled" by analysis. Adults are so oriented to entertainment as a feature of their lives that it is, by definition, not to be thought about that they are typically more resistant to learning the considerable pleasures of critical analysis than are children. Moreover, since the media is presently such a large part of Americans' leisure activity, media literacy should he taught in public schools. For people who have developed critical attention to media, prime time fiction television programming can become the occasion for an exercise in considering proposals addressed to the essentially religious question, "How should we live?"

For facilitating consideration of this question, television dramas that present diverse characters in complex situations, working with various religious and values commitments, are a richer resource than are shows that feature conventional characters in simplified dilemmas. That complex dramas are more difficult to produce, more likely to draw attacks from the Christian right, and probably also find it more difficult to attract advertisers should also be acknowledged. Media workers' focus on offending as few people as possible is understandable, but it is also a fundamentally weak position from which to create drama. Prime time fiction television would serve religion well if, instead of fearing to offend, it represented religion in America as diverse, complex, and, like other aspects of life in the United States at the end of the twentieth century, always in need of critical examination.

12

Fashioning the Self

"Have you re-invented yourself lately? If not, maybe it's time for a change."
—advertisement for a women's magazine

"Fashion? Well, here's the main thing: it's fun."
—*New Yorker* (November 7, 1994)

What has fashion to do with religion? Fashion is play, religion is serious. Fashion lives for the moment, religion for a lifetime and whatever is beyond a lifetime. The world of fashion didn't concern itself with religion until recently and briefly when, influenced by Madonna, runway models started wearing large crosses. Yet Christianity has perennially been concerned with fashion.

Two attitudes toward dress have characterized Western Christianity. Augustine argued in *City of God* that dress belongs to culture, differs according to culture, and has no significance in a Christian life. But Clement in Alexandria and Tertullian in Carthage both gave detailed advice to women on appropriate Christian dress.

Clement addressed both men and women, advising them to avoid ostentation, along with faddish hairstyles and makeup. Tertullian's advice to women is more notorious. Concerned about men's—his own, he acknowledges—vulnerability to seduction, he urged women to make themselves ugly through neglect and to veil themselves for good measure. Devotional manuals through the Christian West also offered counsel on Christian dress. It would be too extreme to say that dress—especially women's dress—has been an obsession of Christian male authors; it has been pervasive concern, however.

Robert Altman's film *Ready-to-Wear* brings to mind several underlying relationships between fashion and religion. First, neither religion nor fashion exists in the abstract; each exists in a concrete world of political, institutional, and social arrangements. Fashion relates more explicitly to a particular historical moment and society; the word "fad," a near-synonym for fashion, is an acronym: "for a day." But religion also must continuously maintain and articulate itself in relation to particular needs and interests if it is to retain its ability to address people. Moreover, the cultural tasks of each are similar in some respects: both seek to provide resources for shaping the desires and identities of individuals and communities.

Ready-to-Wear is a send-up of fashion's most glamorous event, the *Prêt-a-Porter* runway show in Paris at which fashion designers show their current collections. The press release states that the film is about clothing "as disguise, as revealing identity, as tools of power, and as keys to a mystery." Although women's clothing is showcased in the Paris collections, men in the film are as concerned with clothing as women. As a black taxi driver remarks, "All white guys look alike to me. The clothes, that's how I tell everyone apart."

The plot is slim. The apparent murder of the unpopular head of the fashion council is being investigated. The audience already knows he has choked to death on a ham sandwich, so no attention is taken away from fashion and the people who live for it—journalists, models, designers, and hangers-on. Their various encounters create the dramas surrounding the shows. Even the laughs are minimalist. After about six different people step in dog excrement, the joke wears thin.

Altman's docudrama was filmed at the 1994 spring collection. Taking roles patterned on actual fashion-world figures, Sophia Loren, Julia Roberts, Marcello Mastroianni, Anouk Aimée, Tim Robbins, Stephen Rea, Forest Whittaker, and Kim Basinger star in the stories-within-the-story. As in Altman's *The Player*, many famous faces make cameo appearances—fashion designers and models as well as such actors as Danny Aiello, Lili Taylor and (playing themselves) Harry Belafonte and Cher.

Cher makes one of the film's few references to a world outside the Paris shows. When asked, "What do you think of ready-to-wear?" Cher replies: "I think it's sad. It's about the loneliness of women. I'm a victim as well as a perpetrator. I think it's not about what you put on your body, but what you are inside." Altman comments in a press release that Cher's speech "cut to the heart of what the film is trying to say." The other reference to a larger world occurs when Lili Taylor, playing a *New York Times* photojournalist, asks Anouk Aimée a routine question; Aimee protests, "Why doesn't anyone ask real questions?" "All right," Taylor replies, "How do you feel about the fact that 50 percent of the world's pollution is caused by textile mills?"

Good filmmaker that he is, Altman doesn't preach. He spoofs the fashion world by showing its preoccupations as vacuous, trendy, and mean-spirited. But the fashion world Altman shows is suspiciously one-dimensional. No one in Altman's fashion industry is talented and hard-working. No one cares about other people apart from their professional or sexual utility. And behavior has no physical or moral repercussions.

Laughingly confessing that she has "a little problem with alcohol," Julia Roberts (who wears a shirt that says "the world's greatest mom") falls into bed with a stranger and stays there throughout the shows on which she is supposed to be reporting. Nothing in the film questions this behavior. After days during which champagne arrives every time they are on-camera, the lovers part, thanking each other politely for a "great time"—and looking gorgeous.

Altman makes his point. Despite his professed reticence to criticize fashion, he has drawn an all too familiar picture of Vanity Fair. Like John Bunyan's *Pilgrim's Progress* (in which the term Vanity Fair first appeared), *Ready-to-Wear* is a morality tale.

What does not appear onscreen in this "exposé" of fashion? Anything that might have humanized these shallow people. No one has pain. There is no mention of the way AIDS has wreaked havoc in the fashion world. Sex occurs frequently and with little provocation, but safe sex has apparently never been heard of. Similarly, there is no mention of the eating disorders that are a routine part of many models' lives.

Even the death of a husband, lover, and colleague cannot stop the show. Isn't it a bit too convenient that no one was saddened about the death of the "murdered" man? He just wasn't a "nice guy." It is also frightening to realize that the people represented as arguably the least talented and articulate are a black designer and two black models.

Is the fact that Altman was permitted to film the spring 1994 collections supposed to be taken as further evidence of the fashion industry's lack of integrity—it thinks any publicity good publicity? There is an irreducible contradiction in Altman's claim that the "reality level of the film is very high" (it was shot "like a documentary") and his derisive representation of high fashion. Documentary sticks as close as possible to reporting Altman's film is an acknowledged caricature.

It's a cheap shot to ridicule people that most Americans—Altman's target audience—already think of as superficial and vacuous. If the film *were* a documentary rather than a send-up, it would let film audiences see that, in the highly stressed world of high fashion, as with any other collection of human beings, there are some deeply felt, enduring friendships, some people honor their committed relationships, many feel pain, and at least some people are generous.

Ready-to-Wear is a farce, but Altman has decided that the fashion world is a farce as well, and he uses an old motif to rub it in—the emperor's new clothes. In the last show of the event, Simone Lowenthal (Anouk Aimée) sends her models onto the runway naked, with little makeup and no gimmicks. Within the film, this scene is supposed to exhibit humorously the bankruptcy of fashion. The audience within the film gets the joke and laughs, after the first shock. Then they stand up and applaud. But the models—real runway models, young women not accustomed to exhibiting their naked bodies—take it seriously.

Neither ashamed nor strutting, they are simply there, walking the runway in their bodies rather than in the clothing they usually exhibit. Even after the film's tedious and often adolescent satire, this is an amazing moment. There—after all the strenuous endeavors of fashion to embellish, conceal and deny it—is the body.

No matter how unclothed it may be on television, in movies and in advertising, the female body is always "dressed," posed and presented for a reason—to sell cars or alcohol or sex. In the eye of this beholder, the shocking beauty of those unadorned young bodies transcended Altman's use of them. While I deplore the filmmaker's use of young women's bodies to communicate his message, I nevertheless saw them as quite astonishing and wonderful.

It struck me that fashion and Christian theology both have a penchant for hiding, disclaiming, and silencing bodies. Both, in different ways, seek to ignore the fact that bodies—not ideas or ideals—inform a large part of people's diverse perspectives, needs, and interests. Race, class, gender, sexual orientation, age, degree of health: each of these factors contributes strongly to the way a person sees and experiences the world. Yet both religion and fashion endeavor to establish an ideal body as normative.

Liberation theologies have repeatedly opposed traditional Christianity's indifference about the oppressive political and social conditions that do harm to bodies. For Christianity, the actual body has all too often been less important than the fully redeemed body, which can only exist outside present experience. And even when fashion proclaims, "The body is back!" (as did the cover of *Vogue* this past November) it quickly becomes evident that the body that has "returned" is a very particular and seldom-seen body—an ideal body. If bodies—and who has ever seen "the body," an ideal body unmarked by biology, gender, or race—were indeed "back" we could expect to see big changes in both fashion and theology.

Fashion is "play," we are repeatedly told. To take it seriously is to ruin the fun. But for whom can today's high fashion—or even getting dressed every morning—be fun? Fashion exists in the context of a culture that repeatedly reminds all women and most men of their physical and sartorial inadequacy, evoking anxiety even in those young, white, thin, wealthy, heterosexual people who embody the ideal body of current fashion. Those who cannot aspire to that ideal because of age, race, sexual orientation, or class still find it difficult to ignore our culture's ideal body. Furthermore, all clothing gives intended or unintended messages, helping people to categorize strangers and acquaintances alike. In this context, can fashion be play for anyone?

High fashion is about money and power, even when it borrows fashions from the street. As is true of every human enterprise, fashion is inevitably invested in issues of power. Fashion exercises what Michel Foucault called "strong power" in the way it attracts (it doesn't have to coerce) large numbers of people to want the current look. Yet the media-driven fashion industry, equipped with nothing but the possibility of attracting, can be resisted. In fact, it is particularly vulnerable to widespread, sometimes near-unanimous resistance. The more desperately some designers endeavor to attract, the more resistant their public becomes.

In short, a sympathetic—or even fair—look at the fashion world would reveal not only (or even primarily) a dictatorial power that exerts its force on an intimate part of everyone's life, but also a creative, temperamental, and hard-working group of people who have suffered disproportionately from the contemporary plague. The fashion world as a thoroughly debased Vanity Fair exists only in caricature—and in farce.

Nothing approximating the fashion industry of the twentieth-century existed throughout the history of Christianity. But religious leaders have long recognized that in its capacity to shape desire and create identities, fashion can compete with religion, which takes those tasks as its essence. A long look at the amount of cultural space taken up by proposals for redesigning bodies and clothing reveals intense attention to appearance. Fashion becomes constricting—even demonic—when it encompasses a disproportionate amount of attention, when it is used to define and design who one is. But then, of course, it is not "high fashion" or "the fashion industry" that is the problem, but the person—man or woman—who seeks identity in a "look."

Finally, however, the "slave of fashion" must be seen as representing a religious and social failure—a failure to provide resources and nourishment more capable than fashion of bearing the weight of identity, relatedness, and responsibility. Rather than blaming fashion's individual "victims and perpetrators," we should scrutinize the culture's symbolic resources.

Ready-to-Wear, like many other popular films, is better at raising issues than it is at identifying culprits or offering alternatives. Nevertheless, Altman's film offers an opportunity to reflect on and explore some of our culture's dominant and dominating values.

13

Disney Spirituality

An Oxymoron?

Roland Barthes once said that a person "gets" the cultural message at the same instant that s/he gets the pleasure. The pleasure masks the message; the greater the pleasure, the more effectively the cultural message is communicated. Or, as Walt Disney put it, "Just a spoonful of sugar makes the medicine go down." These statements define the theme of this essay. I will return to them.

In April 1998 I went to Disney World to attend a meeting. The trip was also an opportunity to do some on-location research and reflection on the topic of Disney and its effects. I had, I acknowledge, a strong sense that I was receiving just retribution for never having taken my children to Disneyland or Disney World and for thinking that by not doing so I had escaped the Disney experience forever!

I should acknowledge that I am, in some ways, an odd person to be writing about Disney because I have not had much of the Disney cultural experience. I was raised (mostly) in Canada by fundamentalist parents who did not permit me to attend movies and who, long after television had become common, did not own a set. I have not, as it were, taken the rides! This gives me simultaneously a privileged and a limited perspective on the Disney phenomenon.

Some initial observations: There is no death here. Everything is crisp, clean, and new. There is no tragedy. Colors are sharp and bright. Tinned music comes from every lamppost and authoritative male voices instruct by recordings from the moment you drive in and as you sample the "attractions" of Disney World. Huge pink dolphins or swans perch atop our hotels, the giant relatives of the pink flamingos my father insists on placing in his garden. There are no panoramic vistas; the scenery is all "background," on the theory that, as one Disney commentator said, "Spectacles excite, landscapes do not."[1] After all, Walt Disney was not a painter but a cartoonist. Disney World is intended to be a "good and happy place" that celebrates work—both the labor of machines and of people.

I walked and watched. A wedding party strolled along. Instead of holding hands with each other, the groom held Minnie Mouse's hand, and the bride held Mickey's. What can it possibly mean, I asked myself, to intentionally place the notoriously fragile, and necessarily developing and changing relationship of marriage in the never-never land of Disney? Until I saw six or seven other wedding parties that same weekend, I thought it a strange choice of location for a wedding. I have learned since that, despite the utter sexlessness of Disney World, it is presently the number-one honeymoon destination in the country and may soon be the number-one wedding site.

I had thought of Disney World as a place for children, yet in addition to the omnipresent nuclear families, I also saw many adults, young and old, who came to Disney World without the excuse of children. What do they see in it? I wondered. Certainly it is a white, English-speaking world in which people of color appear, and even then rarely, as servants.[2] It is a world that is designed to feel safe to white, middle-class people like myself. And the impression of safety is nice, of course. The biggest thrill I got at Disney World last April was the unaccustomed luxury of strolling alone in the evening. Most women have habituated so thoroughly to caution that we no longer even register the ways our lives are curtailed by these adjustments. Does Disney represent escape from reality, or a much-needed respite from the rigors of twentieth-century life? Is it a place "free-floating between a nostalgic past and an endless future of 'progress'—though never quite touching base in the present"?[3]

Ironically, in such an atmosphere discordant notes are amplified: irritated parents, annoyed that they had saved, and are now spending, so much money for a vacation that their overstimulated and exhausted children do not seem to appreciate. Even the harsh strong colors, the rigidly controlled grass and shrubbery, the constant noise (music, to some ears) and the visual distraction of mechanical movement, grated.

Disney is the heart of consumer capitalism, its seductions aimed at children of all ages. It is a Garden of Eden, a place of mythical attraction. Piero

1. Marling, *Designing Disney's Theme Parks*, 196.

2. Professor Emilie Townes told me that black people who work for Disney call Disney World "the plantation."

3. Kuenz, "It's a Small World After All," 66.

Camporesi wrote about the role of the Garden of Eden in medieval fantasy life. Its similarity to the myth of Disney is striking:

> The garden of Eden was above all an orchard of health, a mild place sheltered from illness and decay, a general clinic in the open air . . . a place immune to putrefaction, where neither human beings nor the fruits of the earth suffer degeneration. . . . Both body and fruit are as though fixed in eternity; time stands still forever.[4]

An Edenic place must have animals. Disney features the so-called "natural world" but Nature is heavily managed here, humans first: an oddly mixed dress code forbids makeup, nail polish, and facial hair on theme park employees.[5] Non-human nature is less tractable. Disney World's Animal Kingdom is spread over five hundred acres and contains over one thousand animals.[6] But Disney has learned, on several nearly disastrous occasions, as Carl Hiassen said, that "nature is nothing but trouble. Wild creatures don't get with the program. They've got their own agenda."[7] For example, in 1997 Nala, a full-grown African lioness, namesake of the lion king's playmate, escaped from JungleLand Zoo, eluding searchers for three days.[8]

DISNEY IDEOLOGY

Walt Disney has been called "the most influential American of the twentieth century."[9] His influence is profound, for, as a fair-minded biographer put it, he "operated not only as an entertainer but as a historical mediator. His creations helped Americans come to terms with the unsettling transformations of the twentieth century."[10] Economic depression, global wars, rapid rates of technological and social change—all are reflected and responded to in Disney films.

Disney had the genius to grasp, better than anyone else of his time, the role and the power that the twin gods of twentieth-century entertainment and consumerism, might have in American public life. He once said of mass

---

4. Camporesi, *Incorruptible Flesh*, 149.

5. Hiaasen, *Team Rodent*, 19.

6. Ibid., 68.

7. Ibid., 72.

8. Ibid., 36.

9. Watts, *Magic Kingdom*, xv.

10. Ibid., xvi.

entertainment that it is "a public necessity—as important as food, shelter, and a job."[11]

In the emerging American popular-culture industry, Disney was a key player. Born in 1901, he grew up with the twentieth century from an "intensely religious" childhood in small-town America to the mega-corporation he headed at the time of his death in 1966. The issues of the century were grist for his mill. Steven Watts, in his book, *The Magic Kingdom: Walt Disney and the American Way of Life*, remarks that Disney

> shaped into a synthetic, compelling form the diverse bundle of images, values, and sensibilities that many twentieth-century Americans struggled with—individualism and community, fantasy and technology, populism and corporate authority, modernism and sentimentalism, consumerism and producerism, progress and nostalgia.[12]

While Americans thought they were being entertained, they were also being more-or-less painlessly injected with attitudes and values. For example, a quick survey of some prominent Disney films reveals the following social messages.

Snow White (1937) exemplified the triumph of the (literally and figuratively) little person or underdog, the value of hard work, and the "virtues of communication among common people."[13] *Pinocchio* (1940) and *Bambi* (1942) both had strong populist themes; they featured the "quest for stability, self-definition, and humanity within a threatening social environment."[14] In *Fantasia* (1940) Disney questioned the separation of high art and popular art in a media culture. It was also his "attempt to democratize culture" by caricaturing or satirizing "stiff-necked, elitist elements of high culture."[15] *Dumbo* (1941) stirred in its viewers a sense of justice.[16] Fighting commercial exploitation and tribulations of various sorts, Dumbo becomes the star of the circus.

Disney movie themes have generally taken the form described by Steven Watts:

---

11. Ibid., 363.
12. Ibid., 452–53.
13. Ibid., 86.
14. Ibid., 87.
15. Ibid., 89–90.
16. Ibid., 90.

> The virtuous defenseless underdog . . . struggles against arbitrary forces, bucks up his courage, finds his way to productive work, and ultimately joins with other marginalized figures to overcome their oppressors.

Watts adds that this story was a social and political allegory for Depression-era America, endeavoring to instill in the American public a sense of optimism even in the worst of circumstances.[17] "The little fellow, through a combination of luck, courage, and cunning, can always overcome in the end the big bad person in his numerous guises, all of which signify Power and its abuses."[18]

The Disney industry boomed during cultural moments in which painful adjustment was called for. He "eased his audience from one cultural milieu to another."[19] One of the main tenets of "Disney doctrine," according to Watts, revolved around the conviction that "the nuclear family, with its attendant rituals of marriage, parenthood, emotional and spiritual instruction, and consumption, was the centerpiece of the American way of life."[20] Disney values, cultural critic Jane Kuenz writes, support "excruciatingly normative heterosexuality, unexamined nationalism and a system of social relations based on consumption."[21]

John Hench, "one of the most intensely creative figures in the history of the Disney enterprise,"[22] has described the Disney aesthetic as: "not deception but conception."[23] Hench writes: "Beneath the fantasy and the sentimentality, and supporting the environmental controls and the purified expressions of Disneyland, surges a profound primordial instinct to regenerate life. . . . We strive for . . . the experience of being alive."[24]

THE DISNEY EMPIRE

I will return to this description of Disney ideology, but first, some further description: Disney should not be considered entirely in terms of cultural

---

17. Ibid., 90.

18. Marling, *Designing Disney's Theme Parks*, 198.

19. Watts, *Magic Kingdom*, 41.

20. Ibid., 326.

21. Kuenz, "It's a Small World After All," 65.

22. Marling, *Designing Disney's Theme Parks*, 14.

23. Watts, *Magic Kingdom*, 435.

24. Ibid., 438.

communications within the United States. It is also a global empire. Some statistics will help us to picture the extent of its influence and thus, by the way, the reason that students and practitioners of religion should take seriously its cultural messages.

Films are only part of Disney's annual revenues. In 1996 The Walt Disney Company reported $18.7 billion, a 54 percent jump from the previous year. In 1997, Disney revenues exceeded $20 billion.[25] Carl Hiaasen, author of the book, *Team Rodent*, a journalistic description of the Disney empire, comments, "Disney touches virtually every human being in America for a profit. That is rapidly becoming true as well in France, Spain, Germany, Japan, Great Britain, Australia, China, Mexico, Brazil, and Canada."[26]

Disney is far and away the most important interpreter of the American way of life to an international audience. For example, *The Lion King*, originally an animation feature that grossed $772 million worldwide, has now become a stage show, which promises to become "the most successful production in Broadway history."[27] And Disney entertainment is more diversified than you might expect: the same company that brought you 101 *Dalmatians* brought you *Pulp Fiction* and the television shows *Home Improvement* and *Ellen*.[28]

There are also scores of Disney products—from Mickey Mouse caps to Mickey and Minnie garden statues, to a $400 Disney chess set—that retail in more than 550 Disney retail stores (like the Disney Store on 42nd Street in New York) in eleven countries. "Disney is the most trusted brand name in the history of marketing."[29] Disney is emblematic of capitalism itself.

There are also the theme parks. Disney World, the most popular vacation destination on the planet, is visited annually by over 40 million tourists (augmented in November 1998 by about 9,000 members of the American Academy of Religion, whose annual meeting was held there). Twenty-seven thousand acres were purchased secretly in 1965 for $5.5 million for the development of Disney World. Like the Vatican, Disney World is a state within a state. It has its own utilities, its own building codes, administers

25. Hiaasen, *Team Rodent*, 10.

26. Ibid.

27. Ibid., 2.

28. *Ellen* signals a curious anomaly in Disney's otherwise predictable "American way" values: Disney was one of the first huge corporations to extend health care to partners of gay employees, and it holds an annual Gay Day at Orlando. Presently 15 million Southern Baptists claim to boycott Disney to protest these policies.

29. Hiaasen, *Team Rodent*, 13.

its own planning and zoning, employs its own inspectors, maintains its own fire department, has the authority to levy taxes, and maintains its own eight hundred member security force. Again, this is not solely an American phenomenon. "The number of visitors to Tokyo Disneyland in the first 10 years of its existence was nearly equal to the entire population of Japan"[30]

Let's remind ourselves that despite its huge popular dissemination, Disney is a class-based phenomenon. The "Mickey Mouse Club" may have been relatively accessible to children on television, but the theme parks are expensive. A parent spends roughly $125 for each child for entrance fees and rides at Disney World; that figure does not include food or lodging.

DISNEY SPIRITUALITY?

So much, for the moment, for Disney facts and figures. John Hench's statement that I quoted earlier, "We strive for . . . the experience of being alive" segues nicely into the question of spirituality. I begin with my definition. Spirituality is a consciously chosen set of beliefs, attitudes, values, and practices that the person selecting them anticipates will serve the purpose of more life by providing orientation and specifying responsibility to the human community and all living beings. John Hench's statement—"We strive for the experience of being alive"—paraphrases that of a fourth-century monk and bishop, Serapion of Thmuis, who put this succinctly in a liturgical prayer: "We beg you, make us truly alive." Spirituality is a "way of life," a discipline that endeavors to work with "whatever happens" (chance) in such a way as to learn from it and create with it a rich human life. It is about choice, but not about control. It is about understanding one's own life as a gift to be actively appropriated, not passively endured, about seeing oneself in the context of one's whole life and seeing one's life as both an art and a way. One's spiritual discipline should provide—at different moments—challenge and comfort. Spirituality is about living fully in the present moment, and living in the moment irreducibly references the fact of death. For no matter what we believe about life after death, it is rather clear that we will not live *here* forever.

Questions about spirituality must be, at least in part, examinations of two crucial words, desire and pleasure. One must ask: What desires are intentionally constructed and cultivated within a particular spirituality? And what pleasures are promised and delivered? To look at this issue, and to place our thinking about Disney in historical context, we need some background to the ways we presently conceptualize spirituality.

30. Isozaki, "Theme Park," 179.

AUGUSTINE ON THE SELF

Approximately fifteen hundred years ago a Roman citizen from North Africa made a quiet but ground breaking claim about what it is to be human. Illustrating his proposal by narrating his own experience, Augustine of Hippo claimed that a human self is called into being and configured by its desire. Let me say that again in order to emphasize the radicality of his claim. The self is *defined*, Augustine said, by the objects of its desire. To understand a person, then, one had primarily to ask, "What does she love?"

Because Augustine thought of the individual soul as created and shaped by the objects of its attention and affection, by its desire and delight, he understood desire as a matter of survival. His model of self was one in which the person or self is almost infinitely plastic, *composed* and articulated by what it loves. One of Augustine's favorite authors, Plotinus, had said, "We *are* what we look upon and what we desire." For Augustine, to love the fragile fleeting objects and people in the world as *if* they could provide a total stimulus, a reason for being, is to make (literally), a deadening choice. When the objects a person loves vanish into thin air, so does the self defined by them. It is, then, in the most literal sense, a matter of survival for the soul to attach itself with desire and delight to a trustworthy object, an object that can neither be relativized nor vanish.[31]

THE POSTMODERN SELF

Today, Augustine's idea of the self integrated by its desire is questioned. Postmodern philosophers call the integrated self a self-deceiving fantasy and rejoice in its demise. Thomas Traherne, a seventeenth-century author, might have been defining postmodernism when he wrote: "We love we know not what, and so everything allures us."[32] The documented ability of an entertainment culture to produce multiple overlapping and conflicting desires has led to cynicism over the possibility of a unified self. Objects and representations

---

31. In the twentieth century, a new secular language of the psyche/soul has largely replaced ancient religious language. Yet the model is similar: "The ego is the cumulative effect of its formative identifications. . . . Identifications not only *precede* the ego, but the identificatory relation to the image establishes the ego. . . . As a result the ego is not a self-identical substance, but a sedimented history of relations which locate the center of the ego outside itself, in the externalized *imago* which confers and produces bodily contours." Butler, "Lesbian Phallus and the Morphological Imaginary," 148.

32. Traherne, *Centuries of Meditation*.

create desire. A postmodern perspective finds the unified self a fiction, albeit one with a long history of use.

The term "postmodern" embraces widely divergent phenomena in the arts and architecture, in literature and philosophy, even in theology. In its loosest sense, "postmodern" merely specifies a historical time—the present—"characterized by an explosion of technologies and the acceleration of information, mass media access, and cultural change." "Postmodern" refers to "the death of the 'master narratives' in culture, the 'death of the author' as a category of inquiry, and an endless play of surfaces and meanings." Postmodernism applauds confusions of distinctions and boundaries; it recognizes simply a proliferation of values and styles, and is concerned with violating boundaries rather than with defining them in new ways.

Yet postmodernism should not be presented as an unrelieved counsel of despair. Its instinct to de-stabilize the socialized self and to question every claim for a personal or social center has begun to redistribute access to institutions and the authority of self-definition to people formerly on the margins of social power. Moreover, postmodernism places the self integrated by socialized desire under scrutiny and critique. I want to be clear that postmodernism is very valuable on these counts. I do not share the conservative reaction, which deplores the postmodern world as "the end of civilization as we knew it." If I inquire who the "we" is in that complaint, it is immediately evident that it was not women or racial, ethnic, or sexual orientation minorities. I do want, however, to question the postmodernism that acquiesces to a hopelessly fragmented self—a self, in fact, that "matches," and responds to, and is the product of consumer culture's kaleidoscope of desirable objects. Today the postmodern, infinitely fragmented, commodified self appears to bring to a close the long historical claim that the self can be integrated by a strong organizing desire. Yet I notice that the postmodern "self" is still defined by its desire and delight even though these are now multiple, incoherent, "a dizzying accumulation" of identities.[33]

Exploration of what it means to be human in the postmodern world is not easy. The individual "real self" in this scenario is impossible to identify and therefore difficult to study. Dispersed among its multiple representations, its parts can only be reassembled by examining those representations. In examining Disney enterprises, then, we question a dominant purveyor of the images and representations that inform desire.

33. Suleiman, "(Re)Writing the Body," 25.

The West presently has greater technological capacity to shape individuals and society than any earlier society ever had. In the US there are more television sets than indoor toilets. Why have we not noticed, or perhaps, not wanted to notice, that a society in which a very high majority of the population walks around with the same news stories and photojournalism in our heads, we also have a strong rhetoric of individual choice? We must place Disney's attention to the individual, the little guy marginalized and abused in an indifferent society, in *this* social context. Disney's most famous characters—"individuals"—developed at the same time as did the media's technological ability to create a population who have the same images, the same cultural narratives, and the same so-called "news" stories in our heads. In other words, media with the ability—as never before in the history of humankind—to homogenize a society.

What is freedom in this situation? The constant reminders in Disney's EPCOT "American Adventure" of how free we are has what Theodor Adorno called "the embarrassingly quality of impotent reassurance." Moreover, the unity of the American people has been reduced to our common status as consumers. "The point is not that differences no longer exist, but that under global capitalism they no longer *matter*."[34]

SPIRITUALITY FOR THE PRESENT

Where did American society get our rhetoric of, and our desire for, individual and collective choice? There are, I believe, some strong roots in historical spirituality. A strong rhetoric of choice and the possibility of change has characterized popular devotional manuals from the sixteenth century forward. These earliest self-help manuals were based on the assumption that one *can* change, can substantially develop, shape, and strengthen one's soul. In devotional manuals of the sixteenth and seventeenth centuries this advocacy of developing the soul was accompanied by a rhetoric of "denying," disparaging, the biodegradable body. A similar rhetoric of choice and change presently is related to our bodies rather than to our psyches or souls. It is fascinating to me that different individuals and societies take charge aggressively of different aspects of human life. Some attend to souls, others to society, yet others to politics or to body. Each ignores (beyond belief) other aspects of human life in relation to which they feel helpless, burned out, or ineffective. In short, if one attends to media culture, the designated site of change, control, and

34. Kuenz, "It's a Small World."

individual shaping in contemporary North American society is not souls but bodies. But the rhetoric is remarkably similar.

Does desire integrate the self—as Augustine thought and taught—or is the postmodern chameleon self, infinitely multiple, trying on and casting off identities, the most accurate and heuristic model for our time? The postmodern image of the plastic self (it's not fake anything; it's real styrofoam!), the commodified self defined by its multiple objects of desire seems to have generated a parallel fantasy of a similarly protean body, infinitely plastic, free from bodily determination. This image of bodies has led to "fantasies of re-arranging, transforming, correcting . . . limitless improvement and change."[35] Epidemic eating disorders among young North American women are only one of the social effects of imagining bodies as limitlessly plastic.

"No pain, no gain;" "go for the burn!" While these phrases are, as far as I know, peculiar to the later twentieth century, the assumptions they articulate were well known to medieval ascetics. The language of asceticism, used in relation to physical exercise and eating habits in fact is startling and significant. It gives, I think, an important clue about the covert desires expressed by food and exercise practices.

Augustine pictured the body as the helpless victim of the desiring soul, not responsible for, but suffering—or benefiting from—the soul's desires. Late twentieth-century North Americans tend, I think, to understand the *self* as helpless victim of the *body's* desires, desires we imagine as plotted in the genes, born with the body, and knowing its objects when it sees them— irreducible, non-negotiable, "natural," built-in desires. But this model of the desiring body neglects, perhaps purposely, to investigate the representations that inform and cultivate desire.

What about pleasure? Does Disney World enable the millions of children and grownups who visit each year to play? Cultural critic Susan Willis would rather speak of "amusement" than "play." She writes,

> Amusement is the commodified negation of play. . . . "Play is all but eliminated by the absolute domination of program over spontaneity. . . . To get your money's worth you have to do everything and do it in the prescribed manner. . . .

She describes the "erasure of spontaneity" in which, she says, spontaneity itself has been programmed."[36]

35. Bordo, "'Material Girl,'" 258.
36. Willis, "Disney World," 122–26.

Are there criteria by which we might rank pleasures? In the *Nichomachean Ethics*, Aristotle evaluated pleasure on the basis of whether it is intrinsic to a whole life, or whether life is accessorized by pleasures "as if by a necklace."[37] I don't think all pleasures are equal. Jane Kuenz has studied the nature of Disney pleasure. Her article "It's a Small World After All: Disney and the Pleasures of Identification," she writes: "No one is compelled at Disney to become anything, nor necessarily and definitively inscribed in one identity or another. While most of the pleasures to be had there require these identifications from us, the pleasure itself is something we produce in ourselves as we learn or recognize the nature of these roles and how to perform them adequately."[38] She is careful to say that this *is*, in some sense, pleasurable. However, she sees this as a real but nevertheless deficit pleasure: "Identifying with a dominant ideology and the role it assigns us has long been the source of a lot of happiness for many people."[39] The pleasure at Disney theme parks comes from "the repeated validation of choices already made."[40]

In sum, Disney spirituality—according to my definition of spirituality as focusing on more life and my investigation of the Disney proposal for more life—is an oxymoron, a contradiction in terms. Disney is about entertainment, amusement, safety, and comfort. "Control has been the signature ingredient of all the company's phenomenally successful theme parks."[41] Disney theme parks place visitors in the past and the future, never in the present.[42] They aim at "overcoming time" by placing visitors either in small town America of a hundred years ago or in EPCOT (Experimental Community of Tomorrow). The present disappears in this "atemporal world." Moreover, spirituality is *located*; at Disney World even place is absent. Carl Hiaasen, author of *Team Rodent*, wrote: "You can spend a solid month at Disney World and never see evidence of the *real* Florida."

Life is about risk, faith, and struggle. By contrast, everybody who comes to Disney World will have a "virtually identical experience—"not at all unpleasant, just fake."[43] Tom Carson, in the *Los Angeles Weekly*, said that Disney theme parks are a "control freak's paradise." It can't be experienced in any

---

37. Aristotle *Nichomachean Ethics* 10.7 (Thomson, 303).
38. Kuenz, "It's a Small World," 66.
39. Ibid., 83.
40. Ibid., 80.
41. Hiaasen, *Team Rodent*, 69.
42. Marling, *Designing Disney*, 195.
43. Hiaasen, *Team Rodent*, 80.

way, or yield any meanings other than those Walt meant it to. "If Walt had really wanted our imagination to soar, he would have given us wings, not mouse ears."[44] Walt Disney wanted to bubble Disney World at one point, so that even the air could be managed and bird droppings eliminated. Far from stimulating the visitor's imagination, the Disney imagination is the only allowable imagination. Jean Baudrillard wrote:

> In both Disneyland and Disneyworld, it is clear that everything that can be derived from the imaginary has been caught, represented, made representable, put on display, made visual. Literally putting it on show for consumption without any metaphors is obviously a radical deterrent to the imaginary. That is, to the stimulation and exercise of one's *own* imagination.[45]

If the Disney experience is such a deficit pleasure, what is the point of bringing cultural analysis to it? I have wondered this many times as I thought about Disney, and I still wonder. It seems, on the one hand, too trivial to bother analyzing. On the other hand, it's too large and successful to have any illusions that one's criticism might generate further thought or cultural change. Yet in her article, "Critical Vantage Points on Disney's World," Susan Willis asks why there is so little serious criticism of Disney. "What's at stake in mass culture and what critical analysis must always strive to redeem is the desire every one of us has to experience in culture both the gratification of social bonding and the affirmation of self in creativity and imagination."[46]

I close with two observations:

1. When we evaluate the adequacy of a cultural phenomenon like Disney, taste is not at issue. The issue is not a disjunction between elite versus popular tastes or on what "we" (whoever "we" is) like or do not like. Rather, analysis of both what is communicated and the *effects* of that communication is the issue. The apparent innocence of entertainment must be analyzed in the light of Roland Barthes' statement to the effect that one gets the cultural message at the same instant as one gets the pleasure; the pleasure masks the message; the greater the pleasure, the more effectively the cultural message is communicated.

   Suzanne Langer's argument in her book of essays, *Philosophical Sketches*, is relevant here: Langer believed that the arts with which individuals and

44. Tom Carson, "To Disneyland," *Los Angeles Weekly* (March 27–April 2, 1992) 246.

45. Baudrillard, "Hyperreal America," 246.

46. Willis, "Disney World," 4.

societies live *educate* the emotions, either articulating and eliciting a broad range of emotional responses or constricting and flattening emotions to a narrow and predictable repertoire. In a media culture, the arts with which we grow up and continue to live are communicated through media and consumer products. The function of cultural criticism is to examine, from explicitly acknowledged perspectives, the adequacy of the arts that inform who we are.

2. It is as true now as when Marshall McLuhan said it thirty years ago that "the medium is the message." In a society in which commodification rules, the commodification of spirituality is, I believe, to be resisted whether that commodification takes the form of secular preoccupations, religious gurus, or even academic disciplines. Our spiritualities should challenge the idolatries to which we are socialized. A person's spirituality should give her a place to stand, a perspective from which to question, evaluate, and choose or reject her cultural provisions. I do not advise an automatically adversarial attitude toward these provisions, but rather one of active questioning and scrutiny. As scholars of religion and as religious people we dare not abdicate this responsibility, because, like children, we long for entertainment. Dorothy Dinnerstein, author of *The Mermaid and the Minotaur*, said, "We never feel as grown up as we expected to feel when we were children."[47] Yet the challenge of an intentionally developed and exercised spirituality is precisely the challenge to grow up, to value serious play over amusements, and to take pleasure in developing the ability to choose what shapes us.

---

47. Dinnerstein, *Mermaid and the Minotaur*, 190.

14

Bonhoeffer (the Film) and Bonhoeffer (the Theologian)

The 2003 film *Bonhoeffer*, directed by Martin Doblmeier, relates the influences of the historical circumstances in which Bonhoeffer lived on the direction and development of his thought. The film also exemplifies the historical moment in the development of documentary film in which *Bonhoeffer* was produced. My topic is primarily *Bonhoeffer* (the film) rather than Bonhoeffer (the theologian), but I will also suggest several interesting correspondences between several of the film's strategies and Bonhoeffer's theology.

DOCUMENTARY FILM AT THE BEGINNING OF THE TWENTY-FIRST CENTURY

The 1950s initiated the idea of modernist documentary film as "a plotless, commentary-less, vérité-style record of life-as-it-is—the notion of the documentarian as a fly on the wall."[1] Synchronized sound shooting, high-speed film, and lighter and more mobile cameras helped to create the illusion of the absent camera. Frederick Wiseman has been called the "Mozart of the form," but even in his films, which contain no voice-overs, no interviews, and no direction of the film's subjects, the director communicates a message. Wiseman acknowledged in an interview, "All the material is manipulated so that the final film is totally fictional in form although it is based on real events."[2] Wiseman's films preach about "dehumanization—what happens to individuals when they get caught in a system." His neutral style, then, does not result in neutrality. In fact, documentary filmmakers have usually (like Wiseman and Michael Moore) been advocates.[3]

---

1. Menand, "Nanook and Me," 92.
2. Ibid., 93.
3. Ibid., 90.

Modernist biographical documentary film sought to present the essential truth of an individual. But this goal has progressively eroded since the 1950s. Two conditions fatally undermine any claim to an objective account: "one is that the number of details identifiable in any singular event is potentially infinite; and the other is that the context of any singular event is infinitely extensive or at least is not objectively determinable."[4] Despite undermining claims of objectivity, however, postmodern biographical documentary film is still interested in the individual, an individual differently imagined. The subject of biographical documentary is presently viewed "not as a coherent site of knowledge or creativity to be understood, but as an 'effect' of the larger play of signification of which it was a part."[5] The subject of postmodern documentary film is a thoroughly *social* individual. It is assumed that "self entails other; the other refracts self."[6] This understanding of individuals also has implications for the viewer. Because people are social beings, self-knowledge and knowledge of another human being are always dialectally related so that peering into the soul of another yields self-knowledge.

FILM AS BIOGRAPHY

Donna Haraway has said, "We are responsible for what we learn how to see."[7] *Bonhoeffer* invites us to learn how to see differently than modernist documentary had trained us to see, to revise our habits of seeing and our expectations of documentary film. It resists a singular, and therefore reductive, answer to the question we are likely to bring to it, namely, did Bonhoeffer "do the right thing," in participating in a plot to assassinate Hitler, presenting instead an ambiguous, complex, and bewildering human dilemma.

It is not only the great events of world historical moments that shape and direct loyalties. *Bonhoeffer* positions Bonhoeffer within his relationships with his "large and closely-knit" family and his friends, not as a "humanizing" gesture (as modernist film might do), but as central to his vision and his choices.[8] The viewer is invited to notice that family members were involved in the plot. Filmed interviews with people who knew Bonhoeffer and his

---

4. Renov, *Subject of Documentary*, 131.

5. Ibid., 109.

6. Ibid., xiii.

7. Haraway, "Persistence of Vision," 286.

8. Bonhoeffer, *Letters and Papers from Prison*, 57.

work also flesh out the conviction that a self is formed, not only by world-historical events, but also by family, friends, and social location.

Emmanuel Levinas has said, "Nonindifference to the other is the precondition of Subjectivity."[9] Levinas's interest in the foregrounding of ethics over knowing is reflected in the film. Bonhoeffer became sensitized to the suffering of an oppressed and marginalized people—Jews in Germany—by listening carefully to African Americans in New York City. From them he learned that socialized prejudice is invisible. Transferring what he learned from African Americans to German Jews, he challenged the German Church to stand with the Jews: "Only he who cries out for the Jews can sing Gregorian chant," he said. Personal experience as well as world events contributed strongly to the many realizations that eventuated in Bonhoeffer's decision.

Christians pray, "Save us from the time of trial." *Bonhoeffer* presents a man who was not spared the time of trial, but was forced to an excruciating and questionable decision. The film's purpose was not to enable spectators to judge whether—or not—Bonhoeffer's decision was right or wrong. Rather, the question addressed by the film is: What factors were involved in Bonhoeffer's decision? In short, the film moves away from the modernist interest in streamlining vision "toward a singular truth to the embrace of ambivalence, multiple, even contradictory" evidence.[10]

THE FILM AS FILM

How does the film produce these effects? First, as already discussed, Bonhoeffer is presented as a social individual, formed by being part of a generation defined by "worldwide economic crisis and social upheaval."[11] Film clips throughout remind viewers of the larger historical events, but Bonhoeffer is not presented as a "lone ranger" who responds to a massive social evil. Rather, "history and subjectivity are mutually defining categories."[12] In short, the film reconstructs Bonhoeffer as a thoroughly historical self. At certain critical points, fast editing gives a sense of rapidly escalating events, events that left little time for thoughtful assessment of a range of possible responses to the situation. Bonhoeffer's constant and passionate references to Jesus Christ *collect*, condense, and

---

9. Renov, *Subject of Documentary*, 159.

10. Ibid., 144.

11. Ibid., xix.

12. Ibid., 109.

reference his much more complex theology, revealing a particularly urgent situation demanding response.

Consider the film's use of voice-over. In many modernist documentaries, voice-over was used to create an authorial omniscience that firmly directed viewers to particular conclusions. But voice-over need not necessarily play this role. It can also function as testimonial presence, inviting viewers not primarily to knowledge, but to meditation on the ambiguity inherent in Bonhoeffer's actions. The narrator acknowledges, for example, that although the plot to assassinate Hitler failed, several others were killed when the bomb exploded. Issues surrounding violence become part of the viewer's meditation. A gap opens between intentions and effects. Presumably, Bonhoeffer's actions were read differently in their original context than in the present context of societies in which violent "counter-terrorism" is terrorism, generating more terrorism.

A final filmic strategy encourages the viewer to meditate on complexity rather than placing the viewer in a passive role before the director's omniscience. Throughout, point of view is distributed among Bonhoeffer's family members and colleagues, film clips of historical events, and footage in which Bonhoeffer himself speaks. The film ends with a curious shot in which these diverse points of view are collected. The viewer looks out at an ocean scene from just behind Bonhoeffer's head, sharing his point of view. As the concluding shot in the film, it has significance. It suggests that each of the various points of view engaged throughout the film actually *constitute* Bonhoeffer in the only way we have access to him.

BONHOEFFER'S THEOLOGY

The film mirrors Bonhoeffer's theology in several interesting ways. First, its focus on his relationships and communities reflects Bonhoeffer's insistence on the centrality of community to the Christian life. In reaction to 1920s and 30s German Christianity, in which emphasis was placed on the individual Christian and her relationship to God, Bonhoeffer (at the age of twenty-one), wrote in his doctoral dissertation, "Sanctorum Communion," "Christ is really only present in the community." This theme strengthened as he matured. In his *Ethics*, written between 1940–1943 (two years before his death in 1945), he wrote: "It is, to say the least, very questionable whether one can at all regard as ethically relevant the notion of an isolated individual in detachment from his historical circumstances and historical influences; such a notion is unreal and is therefore, in any case, a theoretical and peripheral matter which is entirely lacking in interest."

Bonhoeffer also acknowledged the ambiguity of all human action. Ironically, in order to gather information and preclude suspicion, Bonhoeffer became a civilian employed by the Military Intelligence Service, an "integrated part of the Himmler S. S. organization." His friend and editor, Eberhard Bethge, speculates that had Bonhoeffer survived to the end of the war, he, like several others in his position, "would have been imprisoned for years by the Americans in one of the special camps provided for the reeducation of S. S. men."[13] Denying that a human being is ever faced with a simple choice between "a clearly known good and a clearly known evil," Bonhoeffer sought instead "that authentic decision in which the whole man, complete with his knowledge and his will, seeks and finds the good in the equivocal complexity of a historical situation solely through the venture of the deed."[14] The absolute concept of a "good that is good in itself," he said, "fails to make contact with life."[15] Bonhoeffer's last writings, *Letters and Papers from Prison*, emphasize that "it is only by living completely in this world that one learns to have faith."[16] Regretting nothing he wrote, "To renounce a full life and its real joys in order to avoid pain is neither Christian nor human."[17] *Bonhoeffer* reiterates the painful ambiguity of Bonhoeffer's decision to become a double agent in the plot to kill Hitler.

Bonhoeffer's emphasis on community, on self as constituted by attentiveness to the other, and on the ambiguity of all human good is represented in *Bonhoeffer* by the filmic strategies I have mentioned. The film offers a case study in a complex human situation, inviting its viewer, not to a certain knowledge, but to recognition, from within her own experience, that we all, always, must somehow act with conviction in the dark, in uncertainty. We do not know what is generously responsible in particular situations. We see with clarity only our own intensions. We do not know the good; we pursue the human good without assurances of its realization. Because of the difficulty of living in and with such ambiguity, we design principles to provide us with guidance that we hope will limit the damages of our actions. But finally, whether we recognize and acknowledge it or not, like Bonhoeffer, we live by faith.

13. Bethge, "Challenge of Dietrich Bonhoeffer's Life and Tehology," 27.

14. Boheoffer, *Ethics*, 215.

15. Ibid., 216.

16. Bonheoffer, *Letters and Papers*, 201–2.

17. Ibid., 119.

15

The Passion for Social Justice and
The Passion of the Christ

Popular movies, measured by their box-office success, should be examined not only for their narrative content and cinematography, but also for historical antecedents and for their relation to the cultural "moment" of their production and first-run circulation. After considering the history of instructions on meditating on the passion, I will explore the messages sent, or "effects," of *The Passion of the Christ* in the context of a dramatically growing gap between haves and have-nots in American society. Within the culture of fear created by this gap, *The Passion* can be seen as "misdirection"—a magicians' term for gestures that attract attention away from what is actually occurring. In this context I suggest that attention to what the Gospels report Jesus as saying and doing would be more fruitful than attention to what was done to him.

Let us begin with the obvious: *The Passion of the Christ* is a movie. It is neither a window on nor a mirror of reality. And we, watching it, are spectators. As spectators, we do not see a movie as if for the first time. We are *trained* by our many viewing experiences to expect and respond to a number of film conventions. A series of learned responses is activated as soon as the lights go down in the theater. The first of these is detachment. You are not there; you are in the comfortable anonymity of a darkened theater, perhaps eating popcorn. In other words, movies are entertainment, and entertainment places the viewer in a position of distance and passivity.

Some spectators report that *The Passion of the Christ* provided a vivid stimulus for increased Christian commitment. In what follows I consider this claim in relation to film conventions in contemporary American entertainment culture. On the one hand, viewers' reports of their own experience are to be respected. On the other hand, there are reasons to doubt that the movie ultimately enhances understanding of, and empathy with, Christianity's founder.

Two contexts help to focus *The Passion of the Christ.* The first is a long history of Western devotion to Jesus's Passion (from the Latin *patior*, to suffer). The second is the historical moment and social context in which the movie was produced and had its first run. Both contexts reveal a gap between the director's much-publicized intentions in making the film and the film's effects.

Until the fifth century of the Common Era, Christians did not use the cross as a symbol of their commitment. Not a single cross can be found in the large number of extant catacomb paintings of the second and third centuries. As depicted in *The Passion*, crucifixion was a Roman form of painful and ignominious execution used for slaves and noncitizens. Constantine (r. 313–37 CE), the emperor under whom Christianity was legitimized, discontinued its use. Its association with criminal punishment had faded from living memory by the fifth century, when the first cross in Christian art appeared on the carved wooden door of Santa Sabina, Rome. In short, the earliest Christians did not consider the cross an acceptable emblem of their faith.

After this, however, the history of Western devotion to the Passion reveals increasingly realistic Crucifixion scenes in the form of paintings and tableaux. The popular devotion to the cross first arose in Western Europe in the fourteenth century. Franciscan preachers urged their listeners to place themselves imaginatively in the emotions of spectators at the foot of the cross, empathetically sharing their devotion and grief. Frescoes in churches facilitated viewers' imagination, and devotional manuals provided detailed instructions on how to place oneself emotionally within the sacred scene. In northern Italy several *sacra monti*, or sacred hills, presented tableaux from the life and Passion of Jesus, featuring lifelike figures with real clothing and hair. Pilgrims paused at each scene to meditate on the narratives and to experience the emotions represented. Some tableaux are still in use today: for example, the one at Ste. Anne de Beaupre, outside Quebec City in Canada, attracts tens of thousands of visitors annually.

The devotional instructions that accompany exercises in contemplation of the Passion encourage devotees to imitate its first viewers' love and grief, and prompt them to detailed imaginative reconstruction of the smells, sounds, temperature, physical fatigue, and spiritual anguish around the Crucifixion. Viewers were instructed to imagine themselves in the body and emotions of one of the spectators, so as not to presume identification with

Christ's suffering. In Renaissance paintings, Saint John, the Virgin, and the hysterically weeping Mary Magdalene are the figures whose postures and gestures communicate their emotions and invite the viewer's identification. In *The Passion of the Christ*, however, there was little inducement to identify with those who watched the Crucifixion. Both Marys weep helplessly, while John is an incidental character with little substance. Rather, spectators are asked to identify with the suffering Christ, and little or nothing of this suffering is left to the viewer's imagination. There is a contradiction between entertainment (passivity)—the condition in which movies are viewed—and religious engagement that requires viewers' imaginative participation (activity).

Early Christians' rejection of the cross as a symbol of their faith prompts further examination of the value of this symbol. Every religion must, if it is to be effective in orienting people's lives, "explain" suffering, and the message of the cross is that, contrary to most human experience, suffering can be productive. Christians believe that the salvation of the world was achieved through Christ's death and Resurrection. Moreover, suffering people can identify with Christ's suffering, believing that Christ shares their suffering.

In its contemporary context, *The Passion of the Christ* might find its visual precedents in the grotesquely suffering Crucifixion images of the Spanish-influenced southwestern United States. Contorted bodies, blood, and anguished expressions are featured in this art, for which the suffering of oppressed and marginalized people provides the context. Similarly, Matthias Grünewald's early-sixteenth-century Isenheim Altarpiece, one of the most gruesome Crucifixions ever painted, was commissioned by a monastery hospital that served patients with the "burning sickness," which ate into their skin and eventually caused them to lose limbs. Patients were regularly brought to contemplate the grisly Crucifixion scene that matched so accurately their own disease in order to identify with Christ's suffering and pray for either healing or the grace to bear their torment. The context is different for a Hollywood movie marketed primarily to comfortably middle-class Americans who are shielded in every possible way from seeing and/or experiencing extreme physical suffering.

Was the real achievement of Christ's Crucifixion a physical event in which a human being suffered and died? Or was it, as Eastern Orthodox Christians believe, a spiritual event? In Orthodox icons Christ is shown reigning triumphantly from the cross, his eyes open, his body erect. The answer must be that the Crucifixion entailed both physical suffering and spiritual triumph. Jesus's real suffering was the point of the earliest theological debate in the Christian church: Gnostic Christians claimed that his suffering was only in appearance, not in reality. Other Christians said that the doctrine of the Incarnation depends on the fact that Jesus shared the human condition in every respect—birth, vulnerability to suffering, and death. By the end of the second century, "orthodoxy" (literally, "right belief") was defined by belief in the Incarnation of Jesus in a real human body. By the mid-fourth century, Jesus's full divinity was acknowledged at the Council of Nicaea, along with his full humanity. To deny one or the other became heretical. The only brief reference to Christ's divinity in *The Passion* was the moment in which Christ healed the soldier's ear, struck off by Peter in anger. Despite the director's stated intention of making a movie faithful to the Gospels and Christian belief, Jesus's physical nature dominates the film to the near-exclusion of his divine nature.

The second context important to interpretation of *The Passion of the Christ* is the culture and society in which it was produced and shown in first-run theaters. Even when a director contributes his own money toward financing a film, it will not be made unless there is a reasonable expectation that it will be successful at the box office. Box-office success is at least partly predicated on attracting the largest social group that determines box-office success, namely, male teenagers. Rated R, *The Passion* was the top moneymaker at the box office for three weeks after its release on February 25, 2004. A week after it opened it had grossed almost $224 million, a figure that climbed past the $370 million mark in the nineteen weeks it remained on the top-ten list. During Holy Week of 2004 alone, *The Passion* earned an estimated $17 million, passing the top-grossing movie of the weekend before, *Hellboy*. While *The Passion* was in the top ten of VHS rentals, it was rented 3,220,000 times. A reedited version, *The Passion Recut*, which eliminated some of the most violent footage, was released in March 2005.

Although the audience for *The Passion* was increased by intensive marketing to conservative churches, many spectators were attracted by the movie's violence. Can violence effectively convey a religious message in the context of a society in which violence is no longer shocking, but entertainment? Desensitized by screen violence, the American public takes a high level of street violence for granted. Considering it deplorable but inevitable, we are unwilling to take measures that could significantly reduce it.

Multiple film conventions besides violence ensured the popularity of *The Passion*. Traditional Hollywood gender roles and expectations were reiterated. For example, though some reviewers claimed to see an androgynous devil, the devil, played by a female actor, is a woman. The familiar bad woman/good woman dichotomy was evident: while the bad woman instigates and enjoys Jesus's torture and crucifixion, the good women weep passively. Moreover, Hollywood movies often use beautiful music to accompany and romanticize violence. The soundtrack of *The Passion* has, at the time of this writing, gone gold (selling 500,000 CDs) and is expected to hit platinum soon. The director, Mel Gibson, commented that the musical score "propels the brutal image to a higher, almost lyrical, plane." In short, recognition of the film conventions that contributed to the box-office success of *The Passion* makes it necessary to question whether these are conducive to religious inspiration.

The broader context of American society must also be considered when we seek to understand the possible cultural effects of a movie. The United States does not lack suffering people who might identify with Christ's suffering, but these people probably lack the price of admission to the movie. It is striking that the wealthiest society in the world does not adequately feed its needy young, care for the old and the sick, and assist the poor to earn a living wage. In their 1999 book, *The Social Health of the Nation: How America Is Really Doing*, Marc and Marque-Luisa Miringoff argue that while Americans receive constant reports on the nation's economic health, reports on the nation's social health are few and episodic. Reports on such factors as "the well-being of America's children and youth, the accessibility of health care, the quality of education, the adequacy of housing, the security and satisfaction of work, and the nation's sense of community, citizenship, and diversity" are not publicly and regularly available as part of "how we're doing." If social data were regularly reported, the Miringoffs say,

> Americans would have to acknowledge that despite a booming economy, several key social factors have worsened significantly over time and are currently performing at levels far below what was achieved in previous decades. Suicide rates among the young are 36% higher than they were in 1970. . . . Income inequality is at its worst level in fifty years. . . . More than 41 million Americans are without health insurance, the worst performance since records have been kept. Violent crime remains almost double what it was in 1970. . . . Average wages for American workers have fallen sharply since the 1970s, despite the strong economy. Child abuse has increased dramatically. . . . Approximately one in five children in America lives in poverty, a 33% increase since 1970.

In a cultural context in which American society is slipping dramatically from levels of support achieved more than thirty years ago, becoming meaner and meaner, often in the name of Christian values, *The Passion* implies that contemplation of the sufferings of Christ is the sole duty of a (still dominantly) Christian society. When Christians' attention is exclusively on Jesus's suffering and death, they are not likely to understand their religious duty to be the alleviation of present suffering. Whether or not the director intended it, the movie supports the short-sighted cruelty of our society.

Focus on the last hours of Jesus's life effectively erases most of his life and teachings. Isn't Christ's life normative for Christians? Yet his ministry is given brief attention, and that only in a few flashbacks. A very different picture of the mission of the Christ would emerge if attention were focused away from what was done to him and onto his own words and actions. For, according to the Gospels, Jesus spent his adult life ministering to bodies as well as souls. He fed and healed those who were hungry and sick. But Jesus's message of loving concern for the people he encountered is not a message that American society wants to hear. The very name "Christian" has been usurped by those who advocate fewer provisions for the indigent, the sick, the young, and the old. Tax cuts that ensure the riches of the rich and the poverty of the poor are supported by leaders who identify themselves as Christian. Yet Jesus's life and work stood for the kind of compassion that would include a more equitable distribution of resources, both within the United States and across the globe. In this context, *The Passion's* tacit encouragement to neglect the pressing needs that surround us in favor of passive engagement with a visual representation of Christ's suffering is, to many, a welcome cultural message.

Because movies are distributed internationally, they must be discussed not only in the context of American society, but also in a global context. In a world in which ethnic conflicts create wars, *The Passion* depicts caricatured and stereotypical Jews as responsible for Jesus's death. Pontius Pilate, described by historians of his time (Philo and Josephus) as a bloodthirsty thug who liked to crucify Jews without trials, was portrayed as sensitive and reluctant to kill Jesus. In Western history, every period of increased attention to Christ's Passion has been accompanied by increased persecution of Jews. The First Crusade (1096), preached as vindication for Jesus's crucifixion, included the first pogroms against European Jews. Persecution of Jews also accompanied renewed devotion to the Passion in the fourteenth century. The domestic screening of *The Passion* has created an uncomfortable public ambience for Jews. We can predict that its international distribution will encourage further harassment and persecution. Indeed, during Holy Week of 2004, Palestinians sold thousands of copies of the video of *The Passion* in order to spread the negative image of Jews it contains. One American reviewer wrote, "Hitler would have loved this movie."

I suggest that Christians could become better Christians, not by viewing a Hollywood director's interpretation of Christ's sufferings, but by participating in Christ's teachings and ministry. A present-day imitation of Christ might take the form of supporting social programs that feed the hungry and provide people with health care. And the Christ who drove the moneychangers from the temple would be likely to protest corporate greed. The active, compassionate Christ of the ministry years has much to teach American society. But it is not likely that a movie about that Christ would be successful at the box office.

16

Love in a Culture of Fear

God was in Christ reconciling the world to himself.
(2 Corinthians 5:19)

The most Reverend Frank T. Griswold, Presiding Bishop and Primate of the Episcopal Church, USA, whose work we honor in this volume, has said that "the mission of the church is to participate in God's mission." That mission is reconciliation of the world God *so loved*. Often, reconciliation is thought of as abolishing differences. Indeed, urgent injunctions to unity throughout the history of Christianity have resulted repeatedly in the exclusion of differences of belief and practice. Yet God's work in the world cannot be the eradication of difference, but rather the extension of God's love to and within the world's full complexity and particularity.

There are, however, energies at work in our society that can block our participation in God's rich and generous love. One of the most prominent of these is fear. People, whose vulnerable bodies are always subject to disease and accident, have always had much to fear. But we have not always lived in societies in which fear was actively cultivated and often exaggerated. And living in a culture of fear makes it difficult to live in passionate, generous, and loving engagement in our needy world.

Several Western authors have suggested that human beings and societies can be *defined* by their love or their fear. In his *Enchiridion*, the fifth-century African, Augustine of Hippo, said, "If you wish to know who a person is, ask what he loves." Centuries later, Sigmund Freud suggested that to understand a person, one must ask what she fears. Two thousand years before Franklin D. Roosevelt asserted that "fear itself" should be feared for its capacity to undermine human well-being, the author of the New Testament book of First John described the relationship of love and fear. "Perfect love," he said, "casts out fear" (1 John 4:16). Interpreting this text for his congregation, Augustine said that God is love and when Christians love generously, freely, and without self-interest, we *are* God's body in the world. I will first describe some features of the culture of fear in which we live and its effects; then I will offer some suggestions for living lovingly, as God's body, in this context.

A CULTURE OF FEAR

In the last several years American daily newspapers, newscasts, and news magazines have featured many causes for fear, some of them grossly exaggerated in terms of the actual danger they represent. Isolated incidents are regularly characterized as trends, and anecdotes are substituted for facts. Moreover, since fear factors do not capture our imaginations for long, new reasons to fear are continually discovered. Remember Y2K? Killer bees, razor blades in Halloween candy, killer kids, road rage, anthrax, mad cow disease, homelessness, computer viruses, homicide rates, and even AIDS have now largely yielded front-page space to terrorism.

In his book *The Culture of Fear*, Barry Glassner pointed out that Americans fear the wrong things. For example, in 2001, over 42,000 Americans were killed in motor vehicle accidents, while 3,547 people were killed *worldwide* in terrorist attacks, 3,000 of them on September 11.[1] But traffic deaths are not news, except when celebrities are involved. More subtle anxieties are also a part of the steady diet of fear we consume every day: fear of flying, harmful foods, fat, aging . . . the list could go on and on. The point is *not* that there is no reason to fear, but that the *culture* of fear in which we live takes our attentions and energies away from creatively addressing the pressing problems of American society, instead encouraging attitudes of helplessness—or worse, aggression.

Who benefits from the culture of fear? The most obvious beneficiaries are TV stations, news magazines and news programs, advocacy groups that sell memberships, lawyers selling class-action lawsuits, and elected officials. According to political commentator Joseba Zulaika, the tragic events of September 11, 2001, "transformed a president whose election had been the most questioned ever into a president with the highest popularity ever."[2] And Jonathan Alter wrote in *Newsweek* that the subtext of President Bush's advertising campaign for the 2004 election was very clear, namely that "We

---

1. Glassner, *Culture of Fear*, xvii.
2. Zulaika, "Self-Fulfilling Prophecies of Counterterrorism," 194.

should be afraid, very afraid, for our physical safety should he lose."[3] More generally, fear prompts consumption. As Michael Moore observed, "Keep everyone afraid, and they'll consume," in order to feel better temporarily.

We must also ask, who suffers from a culture of fear? The answer is, everyone, but some more than others. Fear is hard on bodies. According to Glassner, anxiety is the number one health problem in the country, leading to epidemic depression, alcoholism, eating disorders, and prescription drug addiction. In a culture of contagious insecurity, psychological vulnerability makes Americans willing to live in gated communities and to lose civil liberties and privacy in exchange for security measures.[4]

Moreover, American society is violent because it is fearful.[5] Americans incarcerate at 14 times the rate of Japan, 8 times the rate of France, and 6 times the rate of Canada.[6] The Bureau of Justice Statistics reports that executions in the United States rose from zero in 1969 to ninety-eight in 1999. On the global level, evidence suggesting that counterterrorism activities provoke more terrorism has not been taken seriously, and Americans have become willing to accept proposals for pre-emptive strikes. It is startling that the wealthiest society in the world does not feed its needy young, care for the old and the sick, and assist the poor to earn a living wage. In fact, collective neglect of those who are vulnerable is the norm.

Marc and Marque-Luisa Miringoff's 1999 book, *The Social Health of the Nation: How America Is Really Doing*, argues that while Americans receive constant reports on the nation's economic health, reports on the nation's social health are few and episodic. Social health is measured by assessing such factors as "the well-being of America's children and youth, the accessibility of health care, the quality of education, the adequacy of housing, the security and satisfaction of work, and the nation's sense of community, citizenship, and diversity."[7] Yet reports on these factors are not publicly and regularly available as part of our picture of "how we're doing" as a society. If social data were regularly reported, the Miringoffs say, Americans would have to acknowledge that despite a booming economy, several key social indicators

3. Alter, "Fight for High Ground."

4. Glassner, *Culture of Fear*, 162; see also Rosen, *Naked Crowd*.

5. MacFarquhar, "Populist: Michael Moore's Art and Anger," 138.

6. Brent Staples, review of *Life on the Outside*, by Jennifer Gonnerman, *New York Times Book Review*, March 21, 2004.

7. Miringoff, et al., *Social Report*, 23–49.

have worsened significantly over time and are currently performing at levels far below what was achieved in previous decades.

> Suicide rates among the young are 36% higher than they were in 1970. . . . Income inequality is at its third worst level in 50 years. More than 41 million Americans are without health insurance, the worst performance since records have been kept. Violent crime remains almost double what it was in 1970. . . . Average wages for American workers have fallen sharply since the early 1970s, despite the strong economy. Child abuse has increased dramatically. . . . Approximately one in every five children in America today lives in poverty, a 33% increase since 1970.[8]

Since 1970, the gross domestic product has risen 140 percent, but America's social health has decreased by 38 percent. When these figures are compared in the same categories with other industrialized nations, it is evident that Americans are not doing all we can to improve our social health. For example, although the infant mortality rate improved steadily throughout the twentieth century, twenty industrial nations have fewer infant deaths (per 1,000 live births) than the United States. Moreover, infant mortality rates vary significantly by race; the rate among African Americans is "more than twice as high as the white rates, a proportional gap that is higher than the one in 1970."[9]

A constructed culture of fear paralyzes Americans' ability to address systemically the evils of poverty, hunger, desperation, and violent aggression in our homes, on our streets, and across the globe, persuading us that any effort is doomed to failure. We must discover practical ways to confront the rhetoric by which fear is established as a way of life. I suggest that the passive, "helpless victim" mentality and aggression resulting from fear can be challenged by a committed practice of love.

MAKING A LOVING SOCIETY

"Love," in North American media culture, is a much overused and abused word. Romantic love is the subject of most of our television and movie dramas. And we employ the word for even our most trivial fondnesses: "I love animals," one wit has said, "I think they're delicious." Rather than attempting to define love, let us for the moment accept Augustine's insistence that love

8. Miringoff and Miringoff, *Social Health of the Nation*, 5.

9. Ibid., 50.

is not primarily a state of mind or emotions, but an activity. He said: "Love has feet . . . love has hands, which give to the poor, love has eyes, which give information about who is in need, love has ears. . . . To see love's activity is to see God."[10] Love is not a state one falls into passively, as usually represented in American media. It is something individuals and societies actively make. Christians are exhorted to make love. Love is not, in the words of the twentieth-century poet e. e. cummings, "Words, words, as if all worlds were there." In short, love is not rhetoric, but a practice of daily life.

If love has the potential of eliminating fear, however, fear can also disable love. I suggest that the rhetoric of romantic love in our entertainment culture effectively functions as "misdirection," a magician's term for the dramatic gesture that attracts attention in order to prevent spectators from noticing what the magician is doing with his other hand. Our society's preoccupation with romantic love takes our attention away from noticing that loving treatment of needy human beings, in the form of social services, health care, and support for education, is disappearing.

The 2004 Mel Gibson movie, *The Passion of the Christ*, can be seen as another example of misdirection. In the context of a society that is becoming meaner and meaner to the vulnerable, the movie invites spectators to contemplate the sufferings of Christ. Its focus on the last hours of Jesus's life erases most of his life and teachings. If attention were directed to his life and actions, instead of on what was done to him, a very different picture of Christ's mission would appear. For, according to the Gospels, Jesus spent his adult life healing sick bodies and feeding people, as well as teaching them. In the context of a society in which tax cuts ensure the wealth of the rich and the poverty of the poor, however, to claim that Jesus's life and work stood for the kind of compassion that would establish a more equitable distribution of resources may not be the basis for a box office success.

Living lovingly in a culture of fear requires attention and intention. If Americans are effectively to confront our culture of fear with a practice of love, we must have resources. Many Americans of diverse religious commitments find in their religious convictions motivation and energy for working for social justice, ecological responsibility, and political engagement. A disciplined attentiveness to beauty in its myriad forms is also a vast resource. But it must be acknowledged that spirituality, the secular religion of our time, can also be used to escape these tasks.

10. Augustine *Homily* 7.6.

The daily practice of love requires that we live with our uncertainties rather than catering to them. As human beings with limited knowledge and perspectives, we are always uncertain, even about the most crucial matters. We do not know the generously responsible way to address particular situations. We always pursue the common good in the dark by faith, not knowing for sure what it looks like or feels like; sometimes we do not even recognize it when we see it. However, fear that we do not possess certain knowledge of the humanly good must not be allowed to prevent our passionate commitment to it.[11]

The dominant religious and intellectual traditions of the West seem to have neglected the urgencies of this world in favor of attention to another world, of ideas or values. Until the second half of the twentieth century, it was not possible to identify and map with scientific precision the interconnectedness of living beings. A few Western and Eastern philosophers intuited an interdependent web of sentient beings, but those intuitions could not be documented, so those who subscribed to them were labeled "romantic," "soft," or "nature-worshipers" by "hard-headed" philosophers. But now, the tangible effects of environmental crises such as the disappearance of the rain forests, the extinction of animal species, and pollution of air, food, and water can be measured. The fundamental fact of life is that the universe is utterly interdependent. This knowledge is no longer intuited or romantic, but factual and concrete. As the novelist Maxine Hong Kingston put it, "There is already an amazing gold ring connecting every living being as surely as if we held hands, flippers and paws, feelers and wings."[12]

Christianity, like other world religions, has traditionally been very concerned about the danger of attachment to power and possessions, but the equal dangers of resignation, passivity, cynicism, and indifference to the suffering and struggling of other living beings have not been articulated as frequently or as forcefully. Similarly, Christians often emphasize the power and greatness of God in ways that de-emphasize human responsibility. Theologies that focus on humans' child-like dependence on God can fail to challenge Christians to mature activity and accountability. The feminist philosopher Dorothy Dinnerstein wrote, "We never feel as grown-up as we expected to feel when we were children."[13] Because we do not always, or perhaps often, feel confident and capable, we evade responsibility. Yet we are the grownups.

11. Miles, *Reading for Life*, 202.

12. Kingston, *China Men*, 92.

13. Dinnerstein, *Mermaid and the Minotaur*, 190.

No spirituality should help us transcend the needy world in which we live, a world that requires our attention, affection, and most of all, our work.

A practice of love for the twenty-first century can be exercised in many arenas—in politics, from voting to running for public office—in ecological activity, from recycling to advocacy—in social justice, from awareness of who suffers to support for proposals for relief. We must resist being overwhelmed by the multiplicity of dangers facing us. Since one individual cannot work effectively on all urgent matters, each of us must take the risk and responsibility of deciding how to focus our efforts without requiring that everyone focus on the same projects. Indeed, I must be grateful that others are correcting the one-sidedness of my vision by addressing problems and dangers that my experience has not prepared me to detect.[14]

Finally, as Augustine said, "We are the times; if we are good, the times are good," or, in contemporary parlance, "the times R us."[15] We can resist the rhetoric of fear that surrounds us, intentionally and actively replacing it with a practice of love. We can insist on defining ourselves not by our fear, but by our loving active concern for the beautiful world in which we live and for the consummate, irreducible, and irreplaceable worth of all living beings. The 1983 Peace Ribbon project took a similar approach. Rather than focus on the horrific effects of nuclear war, panels of the banner depicted what its creators valued most dearly. The fifteen-mile-long banner, wound several times around the Pentagon and the Capitol Building in Washington DC, bore images of fruit and flowers, trees, ocean, loved faces, dancing figures, and lines of poetry and scripture.

The effects of fear are today more evident than ever in history, but to work to create a loving society is to participate in God's mission of reconciling the world to Godself. It is to be God's body in the world. Let us resolve to place our attention and energies not on the rhetoric of fear that surrounds us, but on the practices of love.

14. Miles, *Practicing Christianity: Critical Perspectives for an Embodied Christianity*, 183.
15. Augustine *Sermon* 80.8.

PART III

Christianity in
North American Society

17

Pilgrimage as Metaphor in a Nuclear Age

In order to live a Christian life, one must first imagine such a life, must visualize what it might look like and feel like. In the history of Christianity, metaphors have been a primary device for providing a setting and lending vividness to the ideas and practices by which a person incorporates and embodies a practice of Christianity. Metaphors govern understanding by suggesting that an unknown and ineffable entity, life, can best be understood as an activity that one knows something about—pilgrimage, ascent, battle, or imitation of Christ, for example.

In the twentieth century, the metaphor of revolutionary struggle informs the Christian practice of thousands of base communities in Central and South America. In Christianity understood as revolutionary struggle, people worship, pray, study Scripture, and participate in sacraments in order to achieve the communal solidarity and empowerment necessary for achieving political, economic, and social change. A generation ago, the metaphor of exodus, God's leading of an oppressed people to freedom and justice, informed the deeply religious civil rights movement in the United States. Both of these metaphors—revolutionary struggle and exodus—highlight engagement and action, vigorous participation in the public world of politics and society.

Before the twentieth century, metaphors for Christian life usually focused less on struggle against unjust social and political arrangements than on individual renunciation of "the world." What the author meant by "the world" differs in the devotional manuals, sermons, hymns, and visual images by which metaphors were circulated, but the function of the chosen metaphor was similar: to provide a conceptual framework within which a consciously chosen religious self could be created and cultivated. As an alternative to socialization in the values, interests, and pleasures of one's culture, the formation of a religious self offered the possibility of a critical perspective and the choice of values not available in secular society. The power, richness, and polyvalence of metaphors—Christian life as athletic contest, perhaps, or as piloting one's fragile vessel across a stormy sea—made them an indispensable tool for the exercise of self-construction.

Yet the metaphors that have carried the most energy for historical Christians have also carried implicit or explicit assumptions and values that need contemporary reexamination. While metaphors from the Christian past are certainly not the only historical factor that has contributed to the creation of a nuclear world, their tremendous popular interest in early modern European and North American culture insures that they had an influence in the construction of the collective psyche of the West and therefore in the social and political arena. The nuclear world is only the most vivid presenting symptom of a complex of world problems such as hunger, overpopulation, ecology, disease, exploitation, oppression, and unjust distribution of wealth. These conditions should prompt Christian people to examine the history and the present practice and teachings of Christianity for resources with which to address these problems, as well as for detailed understanding of how we have come to the present crisis. This article will explore one metaphor from the Christian past. I will endeavor to identify why this metaphor, along with its assumptions and values, was attractive—even compelling—to historical individuals and communities, and to examine the assumptions and values entailed in the metaphor from the perspective of the contemporary global crisis.

I

Pilgrimage—moving through the world of human society as through a strange and alien place—has been perhaps the most popular metaphor of Christian life for laypeople. But pilgrimage was not only a metaphor; it was also a practice. Christians went on extended journeys to holy places, and—especially after the Protestant reformations of the sixteenth century—they stayed at home, but conceived of their practice of Christianity as a long sojourn toward heaven, their native land. The theology of Christian life as pilgrimage was first formulated by St. Augustine. In *The City of God*, Augustine pictured the human race as divided into two cities, "for the present mixed together in body, but in heart separated."[1] Human beings participate in the "city of this world" or the "City of God" according to the objects of their love and longing. If a person's love flows toward the possession of objects in the sensible world, he

---

1. Augustine *Enn. in Psalmos* 136.1.

is a citizen of this world; if her love flows in the direction of God, she is a member of the city of God. A citizen of the heavenly city, however,

> as long as he is in this mortal body, is a pilgrim in a foreign land, away from God; therefore he walks by faith and not by sight. . . . While this Heavenly City is on pilgrimage in this world, she calls out citizens from all nations and so collects a society of aliens, speaking all languages.[2]

Augustine's idea of Christian life as pilgrimage provided the framework within which this metaphor was developed for the next fifteen hundred years.

Contemporaneously with Augustine's metaphorical use of the image of Christian life as pilgrimage, the practice of pilgrimage became popular. The first famous pilgrim to Jerusalem was Helena, mother of the emperor Constantine, who claimed to have discovered there a piece of the true cross. It was she who initiated popular interest in pilgrimage to the holy places. By AD 380, Christians in large numbers began to travel to the "Holy Land" to express and renew their devotion to Christ by placing themselves at the locations of the major events of Christ's life. In addition to pilgrims who went on one or several long pilgrimages in a lifetime, some pilgrims adopted the life of continuous pilgrimage as a protest against a Christianity that had become socially acceptable, and even, by the end of the fourth century, a convenient affiliation for the upwardly mobile. Many fourth-century pilgrims found pilgrimage exciting as well as edifying. In writings by and about them, the note of thirst for experience is strong. For example, Jerome writes of the wealthy pilgrim, Paula, and her entourage:

> Though they [pilgrims] deprived their bodies of material comforts, they delighted their souls with pilgrimage. They wanted to see everything with their own eyes and experience everything for themselves. . . . In visiting the holy places so great was the passion and enthusiasm she [Paula] felt for each, that she could never have torn herself away from one had she not been eager to visit the rest. Before the cross she threw herself down in adoration as though she beheld the Lord hanging on it; and when she entered the tomb which was the scene of the resurrection she kissed the stone which the angel had rolled away from the door. Indeed, so ardent was her faith that she kissed the very spot on which the Lord's body had lain, like one athirst for the river which she has longed for.[3]

---

2. Augustine *City of God* 19.14, 17.

3. Jerome *Ep.* 108.9.

Paula's eagerness for visual and tactile contact with the places and objects that had touched the body of her incarnated God comes through strongly in Jerome's account.

The development of the Christian practice of pilgrimage from its origins in the fourth century to its peak of popularity in the later Middle Ages cannot be told here. It had become, by the fifteenth century, a frequently questioned practice; by then its widespread popularity had led to abuses in which pilgrimage had sometimes lost its religious austerity and had become, on occasion, the sort of lark recounted in Chaucer's *Canterbury Tales*. In Protestant lands, largely under the influence of one devotional manual, *The Pilgrim's Progress*, pilgrimage became, by the seventeenth century, a popular metaphor for Christian life. Literal pilgrimage has continued to be practiced for inspiration and renewal in most Roman Catholic countries, and many Protestants are presently discovering that pilgrimage can be a profound religious experience.

Even the most uneventful medieval pilgrimage resulted in physical and emotional change of the most thoroughgoing sort; the pilgrim was completely removed from accustomed environment and relationships, work, nourishment, and behavior. In addition, pilgrimage was a strong experiential reminder that the unpredictability of human life is not adequately represented by a sedentary lifestyle. Travel over dusty countrysides, steep and slippery mountain passes, through woods, and over hills and valleys was a more accurate representation of human life. Different geography created awareness of the diverse landscapes of the soul, the rocks, sunlight, green growth, and the dust of emotional life. Twentieth-century people who keep appointment books, plan for retirement, and nourish the life of the imagination on media images are able to maintain illusions of immortality very alien to the medieval pilgrim. Life as pilgrimage can be acknowledged intellectually but not grasped emotionally and psychologically without the experiences that make evident and immediate the brevity and unpredictability of human life.

In the sixteenth century, when pilgrimage began to be practiced less, some gains and losses occurred as practice became metaphor. Before we can evaluate these, however, we must consider the metaphor of Christian life as pilgrimage as it was mapped in what has been called "the most popular work of Christian spirituality ever written in English,"[4] John Bunyan's *The Pilgrim's Progress*. Translated into over one hundred languages in subsequent centuries, it has appeared in hundreds of editions, most of them illustrated.

4. Wakefield, *Westminster Dictionary of Christian Spirituality*, 63.

II

John Bunyan (1628–1688) was born in a family he described as "being of that rank which is meanest and most despised."[5] He was an itinerant tinker, or mender of pots, when he became a member of the Particular Baptists, one of the myriad religious sects in seventeenth-century England. After years of spiritual torment over whether his attention to religion had occurred "too late" for efficacious repentance and redemption,[6] and anxiety that perhaps the "day of grace" was "past and gone,"[7] Bunyan at last experienced conversion and began to preach. He was elected minister, without training or formal ordination, of a congregation in Bedford. Imprisoned in 1660 for religious dissent, he was released in 1672.

While he was in prison, under conditions of filth and undernourishment, Bunyan wrote *The Pilgrim's Progress*, an extended allegory of the journey of the protagonist, Christian, through the terrors and trials of the world to the Celestial City. Leaving the City of Destruction in order to "escape from the wrath to come,"[8] as well as from the "lusts, pleasures, and profits of this world,"[9] Christian journeys through the Slough of Despond, Vanity Fair, Doubting Castle, and other places named for their capacity either to encourage or to prevent his progress. He also meets many people along the way who either aid or impede him: Evangelist, Mr. Facing-both-ways, Worldly Wiseman, the Interpreter, Greatheart, Ignorance, Mr. Talkative, Madame Bubble, Vain-hope, Mrs. Know-nothing, and others. The end or goal of Christian's pilgrimage occurs when, passing through the Valley of the Shadow of Death, he and his companion, Hopeful, come at last to the gates of the Celestial City, where they are met by shining angels and ushered into heaven. Accompanied by "melodious noise," they are escorted into the presence of the King.[10]

The vivid images of *The Pilgrim's Progress*, in which the natural world, cities, and humans are externalizations of the pilgrim's inner struggles, temptations, comforts, and assistance, informed all future use of the metaphor of Christian

5. Bunyan, *Grace Abounding to the Chief of Sinners*, 9.

6. Ibid., 10.

7. Ibid., 22; see also Haskin, "Pilgrim's Progress in the Context or Bunyan's Dialogue with the Radicals."

8. Bunyan, *Pilgrim's Progress*, 30.

9. Ibid., 50.

10. Ibid., 174.

life as pilgrimage in the English-speaking world. In the transformation from practice to metaphor, however, some fundamental changes occurred.

In the practice of pilgrimage, dehabituation is a means to the end of a renewed and intensified religious experience. Removing the context and habits of daily living results in the revivification of experience. Altered physical conditions produce an altered—a more alert and sensitive—consciousness. Pilgrimage as metaphor features, instead of an experience, an intellectual reinterpretation of human life as a dangerous "trip." When pilgrimage became metaphor, there was no longer a physical dehabituation; none of the habits of daily life was altered. Rather, the metaphor's effectiveness depends on imaginatively producing a sense of distance from the ordinary world. The medieval pilgrim's physical vulnerability and discomfort in unfamiliar surroundings is translated into seeing the world as a "wilderness," a place of "many mountains, rocks, and rough places," as Jonathan Edwards, the eighteenth-century New England Puritan preacher, said in his sermon, "The Christian Pilgrim." Edwards' conclusion about "the world" was the result of extending the metaphor of pilgrimage to its logical conclusion: "It was never designed by God that this world should be our home."[11]

Thus, the metaphor stipulates a separation of the spiritual world, the goal and reward, from the world of everyday experience, the arena of preparation and struggle. Anything valued in the visible world must be valued primarily, if not solely, for its capability to move one forward on one's journey to "the Celestial City." "Let us not love the world," Augustine wrote. "We must rather labor in it that it seduce us not, than fear it lest it perish."[12] Only what stimulates increased longing for our destination is to be valued; other "goods" are to he used, but not enjoyed for their own beauty or goodness. "We should set our *hearts* [italics his] on heaven," Jonathan Edwards said.

Separation of the *process* from the *goal* or completion of human life, together with the assignment of asymmetrical value to each can, and often did in devotional manuals like *The Pilgrim's Progress*, result in a devaluing of other people, one's "fellow pilgrims" in life. And it was inevitably one's nearest and dearest who were seen to represent the greatest impediment to "pilgrimage." Christian, determined to set out from the doomed City of Destruction, is detained by his wife and children, who, on learning that he was leaving,

---

11. Edwards, "Christian Pilgrim."

12. Augustine *Sermon* 157.4.

began to cry after him to return; but the man put his fingers in his ears, and ran on, crying, Life! life! eternal life! So he looked not behind him, but fled towards the middle of the plain.[13]

If we look beneath the surface of instructions to regard others as "mere shadows," however, we may be able to detect a practical reason for this advice. Jonathan Edwards said that it is important to think of others as on their own pilgrimage, a pilgrimage that has reached its goal and reward when they die, for purposes of "moderation in mourning." The deaths of loved ones, a potential cause of cataclysmic grief and disorientation, are somewhat more manageable if others are thought of as pursuing their own trajectory rather than as appendages of one's own life. The metaphor of pilgrimage, when applied to others' lives as well as to one's own, helps to make the transience of life more bearable; finitude can be accepted as a meaningful condition of human life rather than as outrage and injury. "This is the way to have death comfortable to us," Edwards wrote.[14] Rhetoric that sounds to us like a denial of death and a disparagement of loved ones may rather encourage attitudes toward death that render it a bit less overwhelming. Authors of devotional texts often maximized the difficulties and pains of human life in order to minimize the terror of death—one's own death, or the deaths of loved ones.

This strategy for managing death might seem more attractive to twentieth-century people who have, after all, similar anxieties and griefs, if we did not have technologies that make death seem less continually threatening. Modern medical ability to keep death at bay is somewhat greater than that of historical people; at least most twentieth-century North Americans do not die from small injuries or from formerly fatal diseases that can now be cured by antibiotics. Moreover, when death occurs, we keep it out of sight much more than could people of the past.

III

In spite of these considerations, treatments of death in devotional manuals like *The Pilgrim's Progress* need to be reevaluated in the nuclear world. The instinct to minimize the pain of an unavoidable certainty, we may feel, has gone too far when it is not content with minimizing, but actually glorifies death. Bunyan's description of the death of Christian and his companion, for example, is rhetorically inverted to present death as precisely its opposite, a triumph instead

13. Bunyan, *Pilgrim's Progress*, 27.
14. Edwards, "Christian Pilgrim," 147.

of a painful defeat. Reading Bunyan's exuberant description of the entry of the pilgrim and his companion into the Celestial City, a modern reader may find it difficult to remember that death is the subject of the passage:

> These two men went in at the gate; and lo! as they entered, they were transfigured; and they had raiment put on that shone like gold. There were also [people] that met them with harps and crowns and gave them to them. . . . Then I heard that all the bells in the city rang for joy. . . . I looked in after them and behold the city shone like the sun; the streets also were paved with gold; and in them walked many men with crowns on their heads, palms in their hands, and golden harps, to sing praises withal. . . . And after that they shut up the gates; which, when I had seen, I wished myself among them.[15]

For the vast majority of historical Christians, a future existence in heaven or hell was a vivid reality. As Edwards wrote: "if our lives be not a journey towards heaven, they will be a journey to hell."[16]

Reminders of death in devotional treatises are also related to another major theme. Jonathan Edwards's first practical "direction" for understanding one's life as pilgrimage is: "Labor to get a sense of the vanity of this world; on account of the little satisfaction that is to be enjoyed here: its short continuance, and unserviceableness when we most stand in need of help, *viz.* on a death-bed."[17] The absolute ontological priority of eternity over time in devotional manuals was ultimately supported by consideration of the relative lengths of the present and future lives:

> The future world was designed to be our settled and everlasting abode. There it was intended that we should be fixed; and there alone is a lasting habitation and a lasting inheritance. The present state is short and transitory, but our state in the other world is everlasting. And as we are there at first, so we must be without change. Our state in the future world, therefore, being eternal, is of so much greater importance than our state here, that all our concerns in this world should be wholly subordinated to it.[18]

---

15. Bunyan, *Pilgrim's Progress*, 174; see also Rowe, "Roll faster on, ye lingering minutes: the nearer my joys the more impatient I am to seize them: after these painful agonies, how greedily shall I drink in immortal ease and pleasure." From "A Joyful View of Approaching Death," in Kepler, *An Anthology of Devotional Literature*, 471.

16. Edwards, "Christian Pilgrim," 118.

17. Ibid., 148.

18. Ibid., 141.

The assumption underlying evaluations of the world as worthless is that only what is permanent has value. Unless the "goods of this world" can become reminders of eternity, temporary things, no matter how delightful, nourishing, and stimulating, have little or no value in relation to eternal things. Happiness is presented as illusory at best and, at worst, as distracting from the pilgrim's goal. "All the world," Christian tells his companions, "is in a state of condemnation,"[19] a sentiment that echoes, more than a thousand years later, Augustine's bitter statement, "The world is an enemy to the Christian."[20]

Even though Augustine did not pursue his notion of the world's transience to the point of glorifying death,[21] his postponement of the perfection and completion of human nature until the next life effectively diminished the value of present life in order to stimulate and sustain longing for eternal life. The pleasures and delights of this world inevitably suffer by contrast with the permanent joys of paradise; in comparison with heaven, this world's rewards seem puny and fragile. The metaphor of pilgrimage effectively highlights the transience of human life and the urgency of using it well. But transience is often exalted on the grounds that the world is worthless, or worse than worthless, filled with nothing but evils and temptations. The glorification of transience and death by historical texts is clearly a dangerous teaching in the nuclear world.

When we look at the social and political contexts of world-renouncing rhetoric, it is possible to find other incentives for speaking disparagingly of a frightening world. For example, Augustine certainly inhabited such a world. *The City of God* was written in the decade following the conquest and sack of Rome, in a society without effective internal police, without secure food supply, and in constant peril of invasion. John Bunyan's situation was jeopardous to a similar degree, though in different particulars. The volatile political and religious situation in seventeenth-century England was especially dangerous to a radical dissenter like Bunyan, who spent at least seventeen of his sixty years in prison.

---

19. Bunyan, *Pilgrim's Progress*, 155.

20. Augustine *Enn. in Psalmos* 55.4.

21. We should note, however, that Augustine did not promote the usual correlate of this position—denial or glorification of death. To his own rhetorical question, "Is death, which separates soul and body, really a good thing for the good?" he answers, "The death of the body, the separation of the soul from the body is not good for anyone. . . . it is a harsh and unnatural experience" (*City of God* 13.6).

The lives of most of the people of the past have been heavily burdened—in Hobbes's famous phrase, "solitary, poor, nasty, brutish, and short."[22] Until recently, however, no matter how personally or communally threatened people or nations were, no one could seriously contemplate the disappearance, not only of the world of human affairs, but of all forms of life. Whatever else was perilously slippery, the natural world seemed indestructible to historical people. It did not seem in need of any defense or protection, and they gave it none.[23] Policies of "conquering and subduing" the natural world seemed appropriate under conditions of the presumed stability and inexhaustible supply of natural resources.

IV

We no longer live in such a world. And therefore the rhetoric of Christian tradition, its metaphors and images, must be examined and reevaluated in the light of the fragile and threatened world of twentieth-century experience. Although belittling the inherent value of the world has been a time-honored strategy for psychological survival in situations of threat and insecurity, it is not the only possible strategy to adopt in dangerous times. "Everything terrifying," the German poet, Rainer Maria Rilke wrote, "is, in its deepest being, something helpless that wants our help."[24] Instead of permitting ourselves the self-protecting device of finding the joys of human life worthless in contrast to fantasized heavenly delights, we must find the ideas and images that help us to risk intense love and gratitude for the beauty and goodness of the earth. And we must work hard to preserve it, even if we have no assurance of success. Our efforts may be too feeble and too late to save the world from nuclear destruction. Nevertheless, "love is not inactive in a lover," Augustine said.[25] Our love for human life and for the vulnerable earth can stimulate us to work for its preservation.

A feeling of powerlessness and passivity in regard to political, social, and economic change seems to have informed most historical Christian authors, a deep pessimism, perhaps based partly on their own discouraging experiences and partly on a strong doctrine of original sin. The doctrine of original

22. Hobbes, *Leviathan*, 1.13.

23. For detailed studies of environmental exploitation and the rationales that supported it, see Cronin, *Changes in the Land*; Merchant, *Death of Nature*; K. Thomas, *Man and the Natural World*.

24. Rilke, *Letters to a Young Poet*, 69.

25. Augustine *Enn. in Psalmos* 121.

sin posits the pervasive and inevitable element of sin in every human choice and act, the dark undertow of all human life that leads irreversibly to death. Every human effort to change the world for the better is, according to this doctrine, ultimately doomed to failure. Attitudes of passivity and escapism were the result of such pessimism. If "this world is not my home," if nothing can be done to alleviate suffering, or to feed the hungry, or to avert natural catastrophe, then, historical Christians often reasoned, let us lay up our treasures "somewhere beyond the blue."

A further result of the separation and asymmetrical valuing of this world and the next is frequently encountered in devotional manuals that picture Christian life as pilgrimage. Well-being in this life was frequently described as inversely correlated with spiritual health:

> When it is well with you, when all earthly things smile on you, none of your dear ones has died, no drought nor hail nor bitterness has assailed your vineyard, your cask has not turned sour, your cattle have not failed to give increase, you have not been dishonored in any high dignity of this world in which you were placed, your friends all around you live and keep their friendship for you, your children obey you, your slaves tremble before you, your wife lives in harmony with you, your house is called happy—then find affliction, if in any way you can, that, having found affliction, you may call upon the name of the Lord.[26]

From a twentieth-century perspective, historical manuals seem to overstate the point when they insist on the desirability of trouble as a "learning experience."[27] But there is a coherent and cogent rationale in devotional literature for regarding trouble as trustworthy. Troubles are simply "trials," sent by God, who knows "what we are able to bear," and will send only the afflictions that ultimately strengthen a Christian. Scriptural passages state that God's overruling providence of Christians includes sending troubles when these are necessary for reformation, punishment, or "pruning." The advantage of this explanation is twofold: it encourages a sense of God's de-

---

26. Augustine *Enn. in Psalmos* 136.

27. See, for example, Thomas á Kempis, *Imitation of Christ*:

"When you reach a state in which troubles become sweet and satisfying to you for Christ's sake, then you may think that all is well with you because you have found a paradise on earth. As long as you find suffering a burden and try to escape it, things will go badly with you, and you will always be running away from trouble; but if you once accept that suffering . . . your state will soon improve, and you will find peace" (107).

tailed and discerning engagement in a Christian's personal life, and it pictures troubles as intended, not to overwhelm, but to strengthen. An attitude of active learning can alter the effect of situations that seem at first to be nothing but human waste and loss.

Problems with belief in a God that sends adversity on Christians, however, are somewhat more complex. The image of God as a father who "chastens those he loves" can encourage, not only trust, but also helpless dependence on an all-powerful God who will ultimately save human beings from themselves and the nuclear world we have created, even if only in some millennium that will occur after a nuclear holocaust. The image of God as simultaneously "loving," punishing, and, in the end, redeeming tends to minimize the dramatic need for discernment and responsibility in the nuclear world. We can acknowledge some advantages in regarding personal and communal "troubles" as God-sent without finding the idea of God as a powerful and wise Parent an ideal image for twentieth-century Christians.

The nuclear world desperately needs images, metaphors, and models that underscore and strengthen a sense of gratitude and responsibility—gratitude for the fragile and threatened natural world, and responsibility in working for its perpetuation. Thus, this scriptural image—one that has had a strong attraction in Christian tradition—appears to entail risks in the context of the nuclear world. In the late twentieth-century, adulthood, not infancy and dependency, needs to be created and cultivated. Moreover, in a social world in which domestic violence has reached epidemic proportions, an image of God as all-powerful father connotes to many people a battering God rather than a God who protects and shields us from the effects of our childish irresponsibility.[28]

Another common feature of historical devotional manuals is illustrated by *The Pilgrim's Progress*, although it is not unique to the metaphor of Christian life as pilgrimage. The gender assumptions of the Christian West are reinforced—rather than questioned—in these texts. Part II of *The Pilgrim's Progress*, published eight years after Part I, describes the journey of Christiana, Christian's wife, and her children, over the same route that Christian had taken earlier to the Celestial City. Bunyan's account of Christian's and Christiana's experiences as they crossed the same terrain at different times reveals some interesting variations. For example, when the Interpreter describes to Christian what to expect on the road he will travel,

28. For a discussion of the effect of child-rearing on adult personality, see A. Miller, *For Your Own Good*.

he characterizes the pilgrimage in the vigorous metaphor of a fight.[29] When Christiana meets the Interpreter, he instructs her about her journey with the following object lesson:

> So he [took] them into a slaughter-house where was the butcher killing a sheep: and behold, the sheep was quiet, and took her death patiently. Then said the Interpreter, You must learn of this sheep to suffer, and to put up with wrongs without murmurings or complaints. Behold how quietly she takes her death, and, without objecting, she suffereth her skin to be pulled over her ears.[30]

The example seems an odd one for illustrating the necessary attitudinal stance for Christian life, but it makes evident the unfortunate flexibility of the metaphor of pilgrimage for adapting to—rather than questioning—existing gender roles. Although Christiana's choice to undertake the strenuous pilgrimage might have been used to challenge women to take responsibility for developing an individuated life, a centered self-before-God, *The Pilgrim's Progress* leaves intact—indeed strongly reinforces—women's socialization.

V

This brings us to another feature of the pilgrimage metaphor that needs examination, namely, the individualism of the pilgrimage. Devotional manuals insist that to think of one's life as pilgrimage it is necessary to focus one's entire attention on oneself and one's own salvation. An individuation that we are inclined to read as individualism was advocated in historical devotional manuals because authors assumed—rightly or wrongly—that most of their readers felt little initiative to change themselves and needed to be prodded.

In spite of explicit and forceful injunctions to forget others and focus on achieving one's own salvation "without tarrying for any," however, metaphorical pilgrimages like *The Pilgrim's Progress* as well as actual pilgrimages occurred in the company of others. In fact, the pilgrim's attitudes toward others became the topic of detailed and lengthy discussions in devotional manuals precisely because other people were understood as *connected* to oneself. The problem addressed by manuals is the problem of the differentiation of an individual from family, friends, and society. In contrast to modern discourse about relationship, in which the problem addressed is the existential alienation and estrangement of individuals from one another, Bunyan's analysis

---

29. Bunyan, *Pilgrim's Progress*, 48–49.
30. Ibid., 210.

of what was needed in the seventeenth-century led him to urge individual responsibility rather than interdependence. Similarly, after emphasizing the imperatives of individual decision and initiative and of keeping a psychic distance between oneself and loved ones throughout his sermon on pilgrimage, Edwards acknowledges in the last paragraph that "Christians help one another in going this journey." Even then, however, the danger of "company" seems in the forefront of his mind as he concludes the sermon with a warning against hindering one another.[31]

We must question the usefulness, in the twentieth century, of the pilgrimage metaphor's focus on the individual. Devotional manuals have contributed to the formation of that fictional character, "autonomous Western man." In a nuclear world, people who could die together must learn to live together in interdependence, recognizing our need for mutuality rather than for individualistic competitiveness. We must seek the metaphors that emphasize, and the social arrangements and forms of institutional organization that actualize, our interdependence.

At the same time, we must not ignore another consideration. The diagnosis of a contemporary need for strengthening our awareness of human connectedness with one another must not obscure the fact that, even in the twentieth century, not everyone needs to be reminded of interconnection rather than of individuation. Although the phrase "autonomous Western man" has frequently been used to characterize contemporary North American Society as a whole, it is not equally applicable to all people. White, educated, professional men are more tempted to think of themselves as independent of others than are women, racial minorities, and those who live beneath the poverty level. So, people who have not enjoyed the social and economic conditions that make individuation possible must not be included in indictments of the individualism of contemporary society.

In the same manuals that advocate regarding other people as "mere shadows," however, readers are often urged in the strongest possible terms to love them. Augustine's teaching has been influential on this issue also. In his treatise, *On Christian Doctrine*, he describes how other people are related to one's Christian life: "Among all these things only those are to be enjoyed which we have described as being eternal and immutable; others are to be used so that we may be able to enjoy those."[32] Other people, Augustine said, are to be "used," but not "enjoyed" as ends in themselves. Although "use"

31. Edwards, "Christian Pilgrim," 149.

32. Augustine *On Christian Doctrine* 122 (Robertson, 18).

in modern parlance has come to connote a cavalier disregard for the other, in Augustine's usage some things that are to be "used" must also be loved. His examples are other human beings and one's own body.[33] One can love while realizing that the child, woman, or man one loves is like oneself—not a "blessed immortal," but fragile, vulnerable, and mortal. The best way to love a mortal being, Augustine said, is to include this person in the central concentrated river of one's love that flows ultimately toward God: "Whatever else appeals to the mind as being lovable should be directed into that channel into which the whole torrent of love flows."[34] Besides loving the neighbor in God, however, Augustine is clear and insistent that Christians must love God in the neighbor: "Neither should we let this question disturb us, how much love we ought to spend upon our brother, how much upon God. . . . We love God and our neighbor from one and the same love."[35]

Nevertheless, the connotations of "use" in the modern world so strongly imply devaluation of the person or object used that Augustine's formula cannot characterize our regard for either the natural world or the social world. Rather, if we are to state the role of others in our practice of Christianity in Augustine's terms, we must choose "enjoyment" as the most accurate description. Enjoyment, however, includes both responsibility and critical perspective. At the same time that we "love our neighbor" and are vividly aware of the interconnection and interdependence of all human beings, the social world needs our continuous critical examination. We cannot simply "enjoy" a world of unjust social arrangements, unfair food distribution, exploitation and oppression. But we must enjoy the natural world, other human beings and the delightful objects of our physical senses to a degree and in a way that results in the spontaneous response of gratitude and responsibility. Such enjoyment is a moral responsibility in the nuclear world.

Christian authors, in attempting to correct what they saw as a debilitating hemorrhage of attention and energy onto objects in the world and onto other people as objects, often exaggerated their descriptions of the necessity to ignore, disdain, and neglect everyone and everything in order to orient oneself solely to God. In the nuclear world, in which human beings are, in fact, one human community in life and death, love of "neighbors" takes on a newly critical meaning. If we are to find the metaphor of pilgrimage usable in the late twentieth century, we will need to reject historical suggestions that

33. Ibid., (Robertson, 19).
34. Ibid.
35. Augustine *On The Trinity* 8.8.12.

other people are to be seen merely as help or hindrance in the individual's pursuit of salvation.

VI

In conclusion, we must reconsider the usefulness of the metaphor of Christian life as pilgrimage for contemporary Christians. Does the metaphor contribute anything of importance to twentieth-century Christians in our threatened and threatening world? Some historical instructions associated with Christian life as pilgrimage, we have seen, are particularly dangerous when we scrutinize them in our own context: disparagements of human life in this world in comparison to life after death; denial and glorification of death; and individualism that fantasizes independent agency and autonomous action. We have also considered some historical interpretations that could be valuable in our world: for example, an emphasis on loving other people in a way that is not compulsive or possessive, but regards others as themselves "before God," engaged in their own pilgrimage. Moreover, in the practice of actual pilgrimage, a sense of the natural world as rich with spiritual meaning was stimulated; the dissolution of daily habits and habitual responses also suggested the need for practices that relieve, refresh, and reinvigorate body and spirit.

Pilgrimage as a metaphor for Christian life can still retain in the twentieth century one of its most highly valued historical functions. Realization of the impermanence of the world of human experience—of one's own mortality and that of others—can produce a heightening and intensification of experience, a strong treasuring of the moment. Awareness of finitude can infinitely increase our delight in the kaleidoscope of sensible beauty provided daily by the natural world and the human community. Instead of making us long for a future life in contrast to which the one we know seems shabby, we will perhaps come to think of a future life as the necessary fulfillment of a present world too colorful, too vibrant with meaning, too precious to end—the continuation of a pilgrimage too engrossing and rewarding to have a final destination.

18

Imitation of Christ

Is It Possible in the Twentieth Century?

The care and cultivation of an interior life have fascinated human beings for many centuries. Certainly, human life contains an irreducibly high instance of gratuitous conditions and events, but the possibility of shaping one's subjectivity and one's life in society within the wider parameter of the unpredictable—variously named as fate, the will of God, luck, or simply "life" continues to intrigue thoughtful people. Socrates may have overstated his plea for self-awareness and conscious choice when he said, "The unexamined life is not worth living." But the alternative—reliance on the social conditioning provided by one's culture—has frequently been experienced as confining or even dangerous.

In order to live a Christian life, one must first imagine such a life, must visualize what it might look like, might feel like. In the history of Christianity, metaphors have been a primary device for providing a setting and lending vividness to the ideas and practices that embody Christian life. Metaphors govern understanding by suggesting that an unknown and ineffable entity—life—can best be understood as an activity one knows something about—pilgrimage, for example. This comparison of an unknown to a known entity, Sallie McFague writes, is "the way language and more basically, thought works."[1]

In the twentieth century, for example, the metaphor of revolutionary struggle informs the Christian practice of thousands of base communities in Central and South America. In Christianity understood as revolutionary struggle, people worship, pray, study scripture, and participate in sacraments in order to achieve the communal solidarity and empowerment necessary for acting in society to bring about political change. A generation ago, another metaphor,

---

1. McFague, *Metaphorical Theology*, 37.

the metaphor of exodus—God's leading of an oppressed people to freedom—informed the deeply religious civil rights movement in the United States. Both of these metaphors—revolutionary struggle and exodus—highlight engagement and action, vigorous participation in the public world of politics and society. Before the twentieth century, metaphors usually focused less on struggle against unjust social arrangements and oppressive governments than on individual struggle to renounce the social world. Society and the "transient" rewards of the social world have frequently been understood as enemies of a Christian life.

I

How were metaphors of Christian life circulated in the historical societies of the Christian West? A voluminous literature of manuals of instruction in the practice of Christianity—self-help manuals—existed: *Meditations on the Life of Christ*, Thomas à Kempis's *The Imitation of Christ*, John Bunyan's *Pilgrim's Progress*, Erasmus's *Enchiridion of the Christian Soldier*, the nineteenth-century Russian Orthodox manual *The Way of a Pilgrim*, and Francis de Sales's *Introduction to the Devout Life*, to name only a few. Before the printing press was invented at the end of the fifteenth century, advice on how to live a Christian life was given in sermons, catechetical instruction, religious drama, and hymns, as well as in hand-copied texts. It was in devotional manuals, however, that metaphors of Christian life were most thoroughly and extensively articulated.

Perhaps the most frequently developed traditional metaphor of Christian life is that it is essentially an imitation of Christ. Interpretations of precisely what it meant to imitate Christ varied widely, however, from St. Francis of Assisi's stigmata, a literal participation in the suffering of the crucified Christ, to less flamboyant imitations of the virtues of Christ's life and ministry.

Devotional manuals advocated the imitation of Christ on the basis of the scriptural statement that human beings were created in the image of God. If humanity was made in God's image, they reasoned, the actualization of human nature lies in developing this similarity to the divine. Likeness to God was lost in the sin of Adam and Eve, however, so that all that remains is the faint image. Nevertheless, the image is built-in, indestructible, a lifelong characteristic of human beings. Thus, although the image of God cannot be effaced, it cannot be developed without divine help because of its badly warped condition. Patristic authors like Athanasius and Gregory of Nyssa used the image of a damaged painting to describe the state of the image in sinful humanity; Christ, because of his love for humanity, became himself an "image of the invisible God."[2] Christ revealed, in living flesh, what God is so that human beings could see, in this translation of divinity into body, the possibility of rehabilitating—as one restores an old and damaged painting to freshness of line and vividness of color—the image of God in oneself.

But perplexingly diverse interpretations of what it means to imitate Christ appear in instructional manuals in the practice of Christianity. We will explore several representative descriptions: Thomas à Kempis's *The Imitation of Christ*, Gregory of Nyssa's *On Perfection*, *The Little Flowers of St. Francis*, and the illustrated fourteenth-century manuscript *Meditations on the Life of Christ*. Each urges the imitation of Christ but describes the practices informing such an imitation very differently.

II

The Imitation of Christ was the most popular devotional text of the fifteenth century and one of the most popular manuals in the history of Christianity. It was written by a monk, Thomas à Kempis (1380–1471), who participated in the late medieval popular religious movement the *Devotio Moderna*, or New Devotion. Although it was founded by monks of the Brethren of the Common Life under the direction of Gerhard Groote (1340–1384), the New Devotion quickly became a lay movement, inspiring gatherings of hundreds of groups of people in the Netherlands and eventually reaching into southern Europe—the "base communities" of the fifteenth century. Motivated by the then-novel idea that life in the world did not necessarily exclude one from being a real Christian but could become spiritual discipline, the New Devotion had no vows. The movement was simultaneously a rejection of the "full-time" model of Christian practice, a denial that one could only engage in a complete religious life in the setting of a monastery or convent, and an attempt to describe what a different kind of full-time engagement in Christian life might look like for people who worked, loved, and lived "in the world." Members were expected to continue their accustomed lives, informed by communal study and discussion of scripture and prayer. Education was important to the movement, and free education accompanied the spread of the New Devotion. The revolutionary potential of the idea of an ordinary life as spiritual discipline is attested by the rapid growth of the movement. By shaping the inner life of the individual around meditation on the life and passion of Christ, the imitation of Christ could be achieved in the midst of the most demanding of secular lives.

2. Athanasius *On the Incarnation* 68.

From *The Imitation of Christ* we can gain some understanding of how an unaccustomed pressure was brought to bear on individuals in order to create a new relation "of the self to the self," a new relation of the individual to the group, and a new sense of relationship to God. The New Devotion represented, in its own time, a skillful reconstruction of the "self," an intensification of Christian life that *produced* the "self" it addressed. In *The Imitation*, the individual is no longer seen as primarily a social entity, gripped by conditioning, limited by economic and political restraints, but as a unique self constituted by listening and speaking to God. The forceful pressure on the individual to exchange her or his "natural" predilections toward a comfortable life for a life focused on relationship to God was balanced by the support and counsel of a group of similarly engaged people.

Thomas à Kempis defines the imitation of Christ as a meditation on the inner life of Jesus. By meditation, one's life begins to conform to "the pattern of Christ's life." Since the inner life of the historical Jesus is not readily accessible, and since Thomas does not, in *The Imitation*, exegete the Gospels for suggestions about Jesus's inner life, Thomas's translation of Jesus's inner life into attitudes, practices, and lifestyles was dependent on two sources: Christian tradition—especially the monastic devotional tradition of which he was a part—and his own experience in cultivating a Christian life.

Much of the advice of *The Imitation* is not congenial to twentieth-century people. Thomas à Kempis spoke in violent imagery of "crushing one's natural feelings," of "killing the old impulses"; he names as enemies the passions, emotions, desires, and even one's own body. "The highest and most profitable form of study is to understand one's inmost nature and despise it," he wrote. This rhetoric attempts to demonstrate the value of a chosen, consciously shaped, cultivated Christian life in contrast to a life thoroughly programmed by cultural conditioning. Thomas's use of the word "natural" also needs careful interpretation: in context he seems to mean that feelings that seem to appear "naturally" are not to be regarded as either inevitable or normative, but can be changed.

Twentieth-century people, many of whom have learned that one's socialization or cultural conditioning is frequently inadequate and confining, and have set out to change habitual responses, can perhaps understand Thomas à Kempis's project even if the violence of his language makes us recoil and the enemies he names are not our perceived enemies. Anyone who has tried to change her conditioning in order to cultivate a richer life, a wider repertoire of responses to people and events, and a greater energy for love and work knows both how difficult it is to change settled habits, attitudes, and feelings *and* that it can be done. Reading Thomas à Kempis with a hermeneutic of generosity requires that we bring to his advice the experience we have that matches the sense of intensity and urgency we get from his rhetoric.[3]

III

Much more could be said about *The Imitation of Christ*, and we will return to this enormously popular manual. Our purpose is first to recover a range of historical interpretations of what it meant to understand Christian life as an imitation of Christ. St. Gregory of Nyssa (d. 395) was a bishop in Cappadocia, the brother of St. Basil and friend of St. Gregory Nazianzus. The influence of his thought on the Eastern Orthodox Christian Churches has been profound. Gregory considered spiritual perfection—or deification—to be the goal of Christian life and to be attainable in this world by the earnest seeker. Deification is the doctrine that human beings can, through liturgy, participation in the sacraments, and devotional piety share in the divine energy brought into the world of human experience by the incarnation of Christ. Although intellectual knowledge of God beyond what has been revealed in scripture is not possible for human beings, through human cooperation with God—synergy—full participation in the divine energy of love is a present possibility for Christians.

Gregory of Nyssa's definition of the imitation of Christ appears in his treatise *On Perfection*. Human beings, created in God's image, can learn by imitation of Christ—who participated fully in both the divine and the human realms—how to actualize the image of God. Gregory lists the attributes of Christ, analyzing them into two categories: those that human beings can imitate, and those that cannot be imitated and must simply be worshiped.

> The marks of the true Christian are all those we know in connection with Christ. Those that we have capacity for we imitate, and those which our nature does not approximate by imitation, we reverence and worship. Thus, it is necessary for the Christian life to illustrate all the interpretive terms signifying Christ, some through imitation, others through worship.[4]

---

3. I do not use the word "rhetoric" in a pejorative sense; I indicate by it simply the style and emotional quality of an author's effort to persuade.

4. Gregory of Nyssa *On Perfection*, 110.

Gregory further divides Christ's attributes into two kinds: attributes associated with wisdom, and those associated with power. Both kinds of attributes are accessible to Christians. Christ as peace, as light, as redemption, as life, and as spiritual nourishment makes the reality of these characteristics available to the one who bears Christ's name. Gregory's proposal for the imitation of Christ, then, focuses on scriptural—especially Pauline—accounts of Christ's wisdom and power, and the Christian's realization that his participation in Christ's life and body permits him to share Christ's attributes. Gregory carefully limits his account of the imitation of Christ to what is revealed in scripture, abstaining from "theories concerning the divine nature."[5]

Gregory's method is scholarly and biblical—but it is also passionate. Yet Gregory names the passions as the factor of human life that is most likely to alienate the Christian from God. Why write a passionate treatise about the evil of the passions? Why understand Christ as "passionless," and the source of passionlessness in contradiction to gospel accounts of Christ's anger, sadness, and compassion? A partial answer to these questions lies in an enriched understanding of the Greek word *apatheia*.

Apatheia is an extraordinarily difficult word to translate, and the English word "passionlessness" is a misleading translation in terms of twentieth-century connotations. *Apatheia* took different nuances of meaning from the different contexts in which it was used, and can mean lack of feeling, or insensibility, freedom from emotion, detachment and tranquility, or—as frequently in Gregory's usage—freedom from sin.[6]

Gregory of Nyssa's *On Perfection* presents a design for a particular kind of Christian life, that of an educated intellectual, skilled in study and contemplation, a life characterized by "intellectual beauty" in which there is no "civil war" between body and soul. By identifying distractions from one's chosen life as caused by "passions," Gregory did not intend to preclude integrated passion. Indeed, as a Christian Platonist he understood that all intellectual endeavor must be motivated by an original passionate interest in the world of the senses.[7] However, passion that remains stuck on the surface of the sensible world, passionate interest that cannot move more deeply into sensual objects in order to contemplate their origin in the intelligible world (for the Platonist), or (for the Christian) their creator, becomes the enemy of the cultivated life. It is important to notice that it is not the sensible world

5. Ibid., 105.

6. Lampe *A Patristic Greek Lexicon*, 170ff.

7. Plato *Symposium* 210a; also *Phaedrus* 251a.

itself that is dangerous or threatening, but the inability of the passionate lover of sensual objects to move beyond their surfaces into contemplation of the implications of their existence.

IV

A third conception of what it meant to imitate Christ is that of St. Francis of Assisi (1181 or 1182–1226), who introduced into Christian tradition what is perhaps the most dramatic interpretation of the imitation of Christ. St. Francis was the first saint reputed to have received the stigmata, a "marvelous imprint of the passion of Christ in his flesh," an event witnessed and reported by his disciple and friend, Brother Leo.[8]

Francis's distinctive practice of Christianity was organized around the poverty, humility, powerlessness, and vulnerability of the historical Jesus: "He was always thinking about Jesus," his first biographer wrote; "Jesus was in his mouth, in his ears, in his eyes, in his hands; Jesus was in his whole being."[9] Although Francis's physical participation in the crucifixion of Christ was only one result of his long imitation of Christ's life and ministry, the stigmata have, understandably, received a greater share of attention than his less dramatic daily imitation of Christ.

The late fourteenth-century *Little Flowers of St. Francis*, a compilation of earlier documents, reports Brother Leo's account of Francis's stigmatization. As Francis was praying in a solitary place on Mt. Alverna, he experienced a vision of Christ in which he conversed with Christ at length. When the vision disappeared,

> it left a most intense ardor and flame of divine love in the heart of St. Francis, and it left a marvelous image and imprint of the Passion of Christ in his flesh. For soon there began to appear in the hands and feet of St. Francis the marks of nails such as he had just seen in the body of Jesus Crucified, who had appeared to him in the form of a Seraph. For his hands and feet seemed to be pierced through the center with nails, the heads of which were in the palms of his hands and in the upper part of his feet outside the flesh, and their points extended through the back of the hands and the soles of the feet. . . . Likewise, in his right side appeared the wound of a blow from a spear,

8. Habig, *Acts of St. Francis and His Companions*, in *St. Francis of Assisi*.
9. Thomas of Celano, *First Life*, in Habig, *St. Francis of Assisi*, 329.

which was open, red, and bloody, and from which blood often issued from the holy breast of St. Francis.[10]

The enormous popularity of St. Francis in his own time guaranteed that his version of the imitation of Christ became one of the marks of sainthood in the Christian West for the next several centuries. Francis's celebrated love for—and power over—the natural world, his embrace of poverty in a time of steadily increasing commercialism, and his frequent visions and ecstatic states made him the most popular saint of all time in the Christian West. Over the centuries between Francis's time and our own, many have claimed that they received the stigmata from Christ, including Catherine of Genoa, Gertrud of Delft, Veronica Giuliani, and Therese Neumann (d. 1962); Catherine of Siena and Teresa of Avila claimed to have invisible—but painful—stigmata. Even today, outside North America, there are reported cases of stigmatization that have a wide popular following.

V

The illustrated devotional manual *Meditations on the Life of Christ*, dating from the end of the thirteenth century, gives yet another interpretation of the imitation of Christ, the final one we will examine before discussing the present usefulness of each of these models. As in St. Francis's interpretation, it is the humanity of Christ that the anonymous author urges the reader to imitate. The imitation of Christ advocated in the text and pictured in the illustrations, however, is not the colorful and extreme practices of St. Francis, but a devotion more adapted to the daily lives of ordinary people. Here the imitation of Christ is described as a deeply felt empathy with Christ and with the scriptural characters who surrounded Christ during his life on earth.

The necessary condition for feeling with the scriptural figures, the *Meditations* says, is to imagine oneself participating as an actor or an observer in the events of Christ's life; the necessary condition, in short, is "being there": "If you wish to profit you must be present at the same things that it is related that Christ did and said, joyfully and rightly, leaving behind all other cares and anxieties."[11]

It is not enough simply to recall a verbal story, however; one must also place oneself in a visual setting. As another author, contemporary with the author of the *Meditations*, wrote, images

10. Brown, *Little Flowers of St. Francis*, 192–93.

11. Ragusa, *Meditations on the Life of Christ: An Illustrated Manuscript*, 5

move the mind more than descriptions; for deeds are placed before the eyes in paintings and thus appear to be actually carrying on. But in description, the deed is done as it were by hearsay, which affects the mind less when recalled to memory. Hence, also, it is that in churches we pay less reverence to books than to images and to pictures.[12]

Since the goal of the *Meditations on the Life of Christ* was to render scenes from the life of Christ vivid, the best way to accomplish this immediacy was to aid the visual imagination of the reader.[13] Illustrations for every narrative were planned for the manuscript of the *Meditations*.[14] With simple but eloquent gestures, the figures in these drawings express their deep devotion to Jesus. Their relationship to Christ is presented as the model for all Christians.

VI

Interpretation of what it means to imitate Christ has covered a wide range of conceptual schemes, attitudes, and practices—from imitation as primarily a physical and literal imitation of Christ's suffering to intellectual cultivation of the attributes and characteristics of Christ. After identifying some emphases that these instructions have in common—emphases I take to be representative of the literature of Christian devotion—we will consider whether the metaphor of the imitation of Christ seems usable and fruitful in the nuclear world.

A common theme in treatises that use imitation of Christ as their dominant metaphor is the creation and development of a self organized and united by the practice of Christianity. "Keep watch on yourself, rouse yourself, remind yourself, and whatever happens to others, do not take your attention from yourself," *The Imitation of Christ* urges.[15] The fourteenth-century Dominican preacher and mystic Meister Eckhart wrote, "Begin, therefore, with yourself, and forget yourself."[16] The ambiguous use of the term translated "self" in contemporary English usage is puzzling until we recognize that the self cultivated by religious practices is not the socialized self, crusty with habits, embedded in a society that shapes and conditions desire around available and

12. Durandus of Mende *Rationale divinorum officiorum* 3.4.

13. Baxandall, *Painting and Experience in Fifteenth-Century Italy*, 45.

14. In the manuscript edited by Ragusa and Green, however, the sequence of pictures ends during the accounts of Christ's ministry.

15. Thomas à Kempis, *Imitation of Christ*, 82.

16. Eckhart, "Talks," 5.

approved objects and lifestyles. Rather, the self identified and strengthened in religious practice is the self in relationship to God. The goal of the practice of Christianity is to make *this* self strong enough to form the center around which the whole personality can be organized so that, as Gregory of Nyssa put it, the two aspects of the person, body and soul, can become one, and a "harmony of dissonant parts" can he achieved.[17]

It is important to remember that the imitation of Christ is not, even when contemplation is its major tool, simply a conceptual orientation or a mental attitude. The concreteness with which the metaphor is to be actualized, the precise practical instructions that enable imitation of Christ, is demonstrated by the care with which authors of devotional manuals describe them. The self does not become a unity by imagining itself so, but by acting in a unified way in hundreds of large and small ways every day. Michel Foucault's description of the philosophical "care of the self" in the first Christian centuries could equally well describe the agenda of most devotional manuals throughout the Christian centuries:

> It is important to understand that this application to oneself does not require simply a general attitude, an unfocused attention. The term *epimeleia* [cultivation] designates not just a preoccupation but a whole set of occupations. . . . The time is not empty; it is filled with exercises, practical tasks, various activities. Taking care of oneself is not a rest cure.[18]

Manuals in the practice of Christianity advise a number of practices: disciplines of the body like diet and sexual abstinence, and prayer, meditation, reading, spiritual direction, conversation with "holy" friends, and so on. All of these practices have the goal of embedding a preoccupation with the life of Christ in daily occupations, and, ultimately, in a lifestyle coordinated by imitation of Christ.

In addition to the construction of a new self, devotional manuals often agree on strategies for identifying, exercising, and strengthening this self. In general, their agenda is to achieve an incremental intensification of religious experience, an intensification that is simultaneously an interiorization and privatization of religious experience. Although communities of similarly engaged people may surround and support the seeking self, it was not communities that were addressed, but individuals. Only to the extent that an

17. Gregory of Nyssa *On Perfection*, op. cit., 121.

18. Foucault, *Care of the Self*, 50–51.

individual accepts a practice does she begin to experience the particular con-figuration of attraction and stern discipline that shapes the self in hitherto unimagined ways. Others may know about, may even practice, a program of development of a religious self, but the program itself is not teamwork, but an individual commitment and experience.

VII

What were the specific strategies for focusing an unfamiliar aspect of the person for cultivation and development? Scrutiny of one's body and what one does *as* body was the first exercise of the religious life. Every historical person who was adept in the spiritual life understood the energy to be gotten from naming the body as a field of conflict. For orthodox Christian authors the body could never simply be enemy, yet it is an undeniable fact of human experience—recognized by other religions as well as by Christianity—that abstinence from food and drink, sex, and sleep, as well as other disciplines can produce states in which the psyche is accessible and vulnerable, condi-tions necessary for work on the self. Philosophically inclined theologians of the past were often careful to state that such practices cast no doubts on the integrity and goodness of the body and created things.[19] However, authors of devotional manuals were not primarily theologians, and religious leaders of a more pastoral and practical bent tended to describe the distinction of body and soul in less nuanced terms, as a dichotomy in which one component was strengthened only at the direct expense of the other. "When the body is strong, the soul withers; when the soul is strong the body withers," one fourth-century desert ascetic wrote.[20] Although not many Christian authors were that direct in stating their sense of the hostility of body and soul, many of them described the experiential relation of body and soul in terms that were only slightly more appreciative of the body.

The energy to be gotten from rendering the body a field of struggle external to the self but able to affect the self seemed, to the authors of de-votional manuals, abundantly demonstrated in practice. St. Francis, his bi-ographer reports, achieved the ecstatic states for which he was famous by "great abstinence and severity, mortifying his body and comforting his spirit

---

19. See my *Fullness of Life: Historical Foundations for a New Asceticism* for a discussion of the care with which many historical authors discussed the role of human bodies in Christian life.

20. *Sayings of the Fathers*, in Chadwick, *Western Asceticism*, 139.

by means of fervent prayers, watchings, and scourgings."[21] *The Imitation of Christ* also describes a direct relationship between physical suffering and spiritual comfort and growth:

> The more his body is reduced by suffering, the more his spirit is strengthened by inward grace. His desire to be moulded to the cross of Christ makes him long for trials and difficulties; and he finds such strength in this that he would not want to be delivered from his sorrow and distress if he could, since he believes that as he bears more and heavier burdens for God's sake, so he becomes more acceptable to him.[22]

We must not, however, confuse and conflate a range of different experience all of which is referred to in devotional texts as "suffering." If we have in mind St. Francis's fastings and scourgings when we read a statement like that of *The Imitation of Christ* above, we will omit an important distinction between self-imposed suffering and involuntary suffering. *The Imitation of Christ*, for example, made it clear that involuntary rather than self-imposed suffering was being discussed, suffering that is inevitable and unavoidable in every life.

> Even if you arrange everything to suit your own views and wishes you will always find that you still have to suffer something, whether you want to or not. If you do not suffer physical pain, you will have inward trials of the spirit; sometimes God will abandon you, sometimes your neighbor will give you something to bear, and worse still, you will often be a burden to yourself. No remedy or comfort will be able to deliver or relieve you, but you will have to bear it as long as God wills it so.[23]

VIII

None of the historical interpretations of the imitation of Christ that we have explored can be adopted without reinterpretation in the nuclear world. Neither the voluntary physical suffering of St. Francis nor the cultivation of intellectual virtues and emotional tranquility of Gregory of Nyssa offers a viable spiritual discipline for most twentieth-century Christians. Similarly, reliving the heightened emotions felt by the family and friends of the histori-

---

21. Brown, *Little Flowers*, 183–84.

22. Thomas à Kempis, *Imitation of Christ*, 105.

23. Ibid., 104.

cal Jesus or contemplating and attempting to incorporate the inner life of Christ fails to recommend itself as an activity that offers concrete suggestions for the nuclear world. Moreover, there is an emphasis on an individualistic struggle and achievement embedded in the metaphor. Focus on individual development as an end in itself is neither realistic nor desirable in a world in which the human race must somehow learn to live together in order to avoid dying together in a nuclear holocaust.

There are other problems with imagining Christian life as an imitation of Christ as interpreted by devotional manuals. To what extent was Christ's vocation unique? Christian tradition's insistence that Christ was not only fully human but also fully divine casts doubt on the possibility of imitating his characteristics. The dissimilarities between Christ's life and the lives of Christians seem greater than the similarities. *His* death redeemed the world; the suffering and death of human beings do not. *His* self-sacrificial life, a life that led to martyrdom, was voluntary, tradition says, but countless people suffer both involuntarily and without "spiritual benefit." Even *The Imitation of Christ* recognized that "few people are improved by sickness."[24] Physical pain and illness should certainly not be sought in a world in which there is so much involuntary suffering.

Consider also the problems that arise when the model of Christian life as imitation of Christ is urged on women. Were women understood to be created in the image of God and therefore capable of imitation of Christ? This question was frequently raised and avidly disputed by theologians in the history of Christianity. It is not only a question that occurs to twentieth-century people sensitized to issues surrounding the social construction of gender; the volume of discussion on gender issues in Christian tradition indicates that the roles of women were a perennial source of conflict. The difficulty that Christian tradition has had in trying to decide whether women were created in the image of God may itself be deplorable, but perhaps not puzzling in western societies that subordinated women to male authority and limited their access to education and the public sphere. The argument reflects these social arrangements, but it also reinforces and supplements them, providing a rationale for continuing subjugation of women.

Theological discussions over whether women were created in the image of God, however, were not as important to most Christians as were the devotional models they received. Even in times when this question was being argued by theologians, not only were women implicitly included in injunctions

24. Ibid., 73.

to imitate Christ, but some of the most popular devotional manuals of the Christian centuries were specifically addressed to women—*The Meditations on the Life of Christ*, Juan de Valdez's *Christian Alphabet*, and Francis de Sales's *Introduction to the Devout Life*, to name only a few. Writers of devotional manuals who were more pastorally than theologically inclined clearly had no difficulty in recommending the model of Christ's life for women's emulation.[25] However, women were consistently directed to emulate, not Christ's qualities of intransigent self-possession, but his obedience, gentleness, and compassion for others.

Imitation of Christ, understood as self-sacrificing concern for others, is a highly problematic model for women. Rosemary Ruether's question, in *Sexism and God-Talk*, as to whether a male savior can benefit women needs to be examined, not in terms of biological differences, but in relation to the gender-specific conditioning in western societies.[26] Perhaps the imitation of a self-sacrificing Jesus has been a useful corrective for men, socialized to vigorous competition in societies that encourage male aggression. Self-sacrificing attention to the needs of others has, however, been part of the socialization of women, and therefore does not provide a correction to gender conditioning that encourages and rewards women's self-abnegation and single-minded attention to the needs of men and children. As Valerie Saiving, Judith Plaskow, and others have shown, women's characteristic temptations in western societies are not the same as men's. Women's temptations are to neglect their own talents and gifts, depending on others for self-esteem, and to scatter time and energy in a variety of tasks rather than to sustain a focus on a central task[27]

The imitation of Christ's gentleness, compassion, and self-sacrificial love is damaging to women in societies that socialize women to such attitudes and behavior. If twentieth-century women are to find the metaphor of imitation of Christ useful, it will need to be on the basis of the characteristics of Christ's life that confront and challenge women's social conditioning rather than those that sustain and reinforce it. Christ's anger at injustice, Christ's practices of self-remembering and centering, Christ's rejection of the social-

---

25. See my previous discussions of the role of images of the Virgin in medieval communities: *Image as Insight: Visual Understanding in Western Christianity and Secular Culture*, esp. chap. 4; "Images of Women in Fourteenth-Century Tuscan Painting," and "The Virgin's One Bare Breast: Female Nudity and Religious meaning in Tuscan Early Renaissance Culture."

26. Ruether, "Christology: Can a Male Savior Save Women?"

27. Plaskow, *Sex, Sin, and Grace*.

role expectations of his day, and the creativity with which Christ met difficult situations and answered awkward questions about himself and his ministry; any or all of these could be useful to women in the twentieth century.

IX

Is the imitation of Christ a fruitful metaphor for Christian life in the context of the nuclear world? In responding to this question, let us first notice that the metaphor is simultaneously inspirational and flexible. Both of these qualities are advantages for twentieth-century interpreters. No stronger metaphor can be found for Christian life than to understand it as an imitation of Christ. Yet how one identifies the characteristics of the Christ that one seeks to emulate is left open. To be heuristic in a particular concrete situation, a metaphor must enable both constructive conceptual grasp and responsible action.

Suppose, for example, that I were to think of myself as imitating a historical human being who was incarnated for the purpose of demonstrating the central claim of Christianity, namely that God *is* love. The metaphor is still vague; the loving response in every human situation is not immediately obvious. And Christian tradition contains many examples of questionable and even deplorable interpretations of what constitutes loving behavior. St. Augustine's famous injunction, "Love, and do as you will," has been used too often as a rationalization for religious, political, economic, and social oppression.[28] If, then, the metaphor not only *can* be abused, but has often *been* abused, does it hold any constructive possibility for the present?

We can begin to answer this question by acknowledging that every metaphor can be abused either by willful misuse, or by application in situations in which it is destructive. The simultaneous value and danger of metaphors lie in their capacity for interpretation and application in diverse situations. Metaphors cannot themselves guarantee their responsible use. To apply "imitation of Christ" fruitfully, the community or individual using it must define it in relation to an accurately analyzed present situation. Every attitude and act have a context, and the metaphor of Christian life as the imitation of Christ emphasizes the need for an accurate "reading" of the context as Christ himself had to discern both the requirements of his own integrity and the essential features of the context in which he acted. Christ's earthly life, according to gospel accounts, included moments of anger, distress, sadness, and feelings of abandonment and self-doubt as well as the loving generosity that we—and

---

28. Augustine *In epistulam Johannis* 7.8.

historical authors—seem to emphasize. Which of Christ's emotions, actions, or characteristics represent both an accurate interpretation of the needs of my present situation and my own capacity to respond?

Second, imitation of Christ as a model for Christian life inspires and demands strenuous engagement—hard work—rather than passivity. It raises questions; it does not provide answers. Yet its inspirational value is potentially great. In an entertainment culture in which there is little encouragement to develop and articulate an interior life, the metaphor of imitation of Christ can provide a reminder and an impetus for an active rather than passive attitude toward self and society. Because twentieth-century Christians live in a predominantly secular world, we frequently do not think of ourselves as purposely and continuously engaged in the creation of Christian life. The metaphor of imitation of Christ can provide, not a blueprint that can be automatically applied, but a challenge and an inspiration to twentieth-century Christians to engage our clearest self-knowledge and our most perceptive analysis of the situation in which we must act in beginning to ask ourselves, How might I imitate Christ in *this* moment?

19

Hermeneutics of Generosity and Suspicion

Pluralism and Theological Education

The paper will be an exploration of the changes in style and method of discussion that become necessary in a genuinely pluralistic setting. Drawing upon my experience in teaching hermeneutics to doctoral students in theology at Harvard Divinity School, I will first examine the present pluralism of theological education as a situation in which new and exciting questions are being asked of traditional texts. These questions do not arise from Enlightenment assumptions, nor do they yield to traditional hermeneutics characterized largely by examination of the relationships of ideas within a text. The recent participation of women, blacks, and third world people in theological discussion, in large enough numbers to form a "critical mass," is producing a new discourse, a discourse that is not chaotic, but is beginning to shape a method of understanding and interpretation that demands examination of the assumptions, language, and style of theological work.[1] Far from understanding this collapse of Enlightenment hermeneutics as disastrous—the "end of civilization"—I will argue that hermeneutics of generosity and suspicion must be integrated to reconstruct the historical antecedents of people who, until recently, have been excluded from theological discourse. Finally, some concrete issues concerning historical evidence and interpretation will be explored—for example, the use of visual images as historical evidence, gender as a category of historical analysis, and the sociology of hermeneutics.

1. I would like to thank my student and faculty colleagues with whom, and from whom, I learned to own in myself, to value in others, the complex perspectives we bring to theological discussion. This is not merely a polite nod, but a real indebtedness, which makes vivid for me the communal adventure of understanding and interpretation. It was in company and conversations with my colleagues in theology, Gordon D. Kaufman, Richard Niebuhr, and Sharon Welch, and with members of the theology doctoral colloquium, and the Common Doctoral Seminar that I learned to trust and delight in pluralism—not the idea of pluralism, but the people who embody the reality of pluralism.

What is pluralism, and how have we come to an educational situation defined by it? In the late fifties, when I first encountered theological education as the wife of a seminary student, the few women enrolled in the San Francisco Theological Seminary were studying to be Directors of Education in Presbyterian churches. The BD class of 1960 consisted—if memory serves me accurately—entirely of white males from similar "melting pot" ethnic origins and middle-class backgrounds. In the classrooms, "objective," rational theological arguments commanded consent, and most differing "opinions" could be negotiated in the steady approach to Truth. Intractable differences of ideas or values were dismissed as perverse, and the few who held them quit the seminary to find other occupations than the ministry or other seminaries where they could find support and reinforcement for their beliefs.

This situation was soon to change. In the next two decades increasing numbers of women were admitted to BD and MDiv degree programs; more and more frequently, blacks came to liberal seminaries, and third world people began to enter. These new participants in theological education were taught by the same professors who had taught the young ministers of the fifties, and at first the new participants tried to fit in, to show they were as bright and could do as well as the young men who felt at home in theological institutions. Gradually the new people came into theological discussion in sufficient numbers to begin to find support for their questions, concerns, and interests. They began, tentatively and hesitantly, to raise these questions, not only in the halls and refectories of theological schools but even in classrooms. Persistently, their professors insisted that rational argument was the key to overcoming differences of "opinion" and, since they were masters of language, the professors could rather easily dispose of proposals for alternative interpretations raised by their students. Appeals to a rationality grounded in a transcendental subjectivity could still compel consent.

But the questions became more persistent. Often students asked how the ideas of a particular author related to his historical situation, the political, class, and institutional affiliations of his thought. Sometimes the questioner insisted on the reduction of the author's ideas to his allegiance to a class, an institution, or to a socially-constructed gender ideology. This historicism was deeply offensive to the professors whose lives had been shaped, enriched, and altered by the beauty and profundity of the ideas of theological authors. In vain they urged objectivity and generosity in interpretation. Some of them even experienced the new questions as threatening the "end of civilization," the demise of rationality itself. They insisted that the modern interpreter of historical texts should try to understand and evaluate only the coherence and comprehensibility of ideas within a text. They felt keenly that objectivity and even "Truth" itself were endangered, that the only alternative to the Enlightenment faith in rationality was "anything goes," chaos.

Pluralism in theological education came into existence in something like the process I have sketched. Pluralism is *not* different emphases within an agreed-upon system of ideas and values. Nor is it the *representation* of different life experiences and perspectives. It is different *people*, new people, in the sense that our historical antecedents were not here, participating in reality-defining theological discourse, people who are new to institutions of graduate theological education.

So here we all are with strong longings, with intractable fears, with a desire powerful enough to prompt the commitment of our lives to understanding each other and the texts we study. Our naive illusions of the intuitive rightness and universality of our ideas and practices have been irreversibly challenged by our confrontation with each other. Where do we go from here? Where do we go from the realization that our differences are irreducible, our beliefs and even our feelings the products of our different perspectives? What is beyond the impasses of our efforts to change one another? Where do we go from the unsettling recognition that there is no value-free interpretation of each other or of our texts? Is it possible to understand as fruitful and exciting a situation that at first gave the impression of an abyss?

In his November 1985 address at Austin Presbyterian Seminary, James Gustafson criticized the *Wissenschaft* model of scholarship as incompatible with a vision of the theological school as "intellectual center of the church's life." The "ideal of scholarly competence and disinterestedness," he said, does not stimulate the kind of scholarship that benefits and energizes Christian churches. His listing of the characteristics of intellectual work that *would* accomplish this service is the following: "wisdom and insight, probing and suggestiveness, creative reformulation of the conventional ways in which issues have been dealt with, novel comparisons with anticipated materials which enlarge if not explode perceptions and reflections, setting religious issues in wider intellectual contexts."[2]

If this kind of critical, innovative, exploratory, contextual scholarship that works the areas of the confrontation of theological issues and human lives is what is called for in theological education, we have it in the concerns,

2. Gustafson, "Vocation of the Theological Educator," 6.

the commitment, and the intellectual work of the present pluralistic theological community. The issues are different than those traditionally pursued. I seldom hear arguments about Christian doctrine in the halls and classrooms of Harvard Divinity School. I hear instead a great deal of *theological* reflection on issues of world hunger, peace, aging, violence against women, public policy, and gender. Many of our MDiv students will pursue traditional ministries with a continuing commitment to activity with these concerns. A growing number will enter nontraditional ministries; they will direct soup kitchens, shelters for battered women; they will work in the Peace Corps and in peace activism. They will bring their theological education to this work and will test the strength and resilience of their theological preparation on the potentially overwhelming problems they will face in the public and private spheres.

How do we educate for ministry when ministry takes such varied forms? Neither "scholarly competence and disinterestedness" nor the "traditioning" of a classical theological education will meet the needs of women and men confronting the massive social and political issues of the contemporary world, not only—or even primarily—in sermons, but in the secular organizations that address these issues.

This pluralism in ministries, as well as the pluralism of people of other religions and nations, of a diversity of Christian affiliations, and of race, gender, and class, *mandates* a starting point of respect for the personal knowledge—the lived experience—of the people who constitute the new pluralism. If I understand them to be entering theological institutions in order to "overcome their ignorance and [to find themselves] a place from which to view the world,"[3] I will not conceive my task as theological educator in a realistic and productive way, that is, as a continuing reappraisal of the resources and methodology of theology in order to better serve the pressing theological needs of students. They *have* a "place from which to view the world;" what they seek is the conceptual and practical tools with which to *change* the world they see. They are shaping "the tradition"—which is itself consistently and insistently pluralistic—as surely as their locations in the Christian traditions are shaping them.

Let us be honest about the losses. Objectivism, faith in the possibility of a value-neutral understanding of each other and interpretation of the texts we study, is decisively undermined. Relinquishing objectivism, we fear, will throw open the doors of the academy to skepticism, historicism, dogmatism, fanaticism, and ultimately, nihilism. In the demise of objectivism,

3. Ibid., 8

relativism looms—the fear that ultimately no statement, no description, no belief is universally normative, doubt that there is any value in even talking together if all positions and perspectives are to enjoy equal validity, fear that our judgments cannot be grounded on universal values. Lurking in the darkness beneath these intellectual fears, is the real terror that if relativism is *what there is*, in the great world outside theological education, nothing but force can ultimately adjudicate our differences, and so our differences will come to nuclear blows.

At Harvard Divinity School, unlike many denominational schools and seminaries, pluralism is featured: not only are people with different Christian affiliations in constant conversation in every classroom and hall, but also, there are people from other religious persuasions and no religious persuasion, from other parts of the world, from different racial and class and gender experiences. We even insist that people studying Christian ministry must take courses in the study of other religions, and people from other religions certainly get mammoth doses of Christian ideas and values in most of their classes. If Harvard Divinity School has gone further than most theological institutions in fostering pluralism, the problems of pluralism have also become more acute. But we are also learning some things about pluralism that might be useful for other groups—churches and schools—in which pluralism exists, but, perhaps, not quite so prominently. Sometimes we experience the difference of each from each as richness, sometimes as shattering. Should pluralism be understood as wealth, or as problem? It is on the basis of working with the concrete and rich pluralism of Harvard Divinity School that I make the following observations and suggestions.

I do not think that pluralism can be reduced either to being understood as wealth or as problem. We must neither underestimate the stimulation, the delight, the diversity and complexity of the present community of theological scholars, nor must we romanticize away the difficulties, the potential and actual misunderstandings, the dismay we feel when we lack each other's support for our ideas, beliefs, and feelings. I do not intend either to dismiss or to dispose of the many problems of pluralism, but to suggest how these problems can be worked with in education for Christian ministry. We must work in new ways; we must create and invent and experiment and risk and respond in our work together; we must build a new kind of discussion that is neither chaotic— "anything goes"—nor one that constantly strains back to the old situation of rational "transcendence" of differences.

Where might a discussion that does not attempt to overlook the "accidents" of particularity in favor of a "universal" human subject begin?

Let me give an example that is very immediate and vivid in the minds of those of us who participated in an experiment in the theology doctoral colloquium of Harvard Divinity School this past semester. For the past several years, the theology colloquium has been reading and discussing, in alternate terms, an author or a problem with theological implications. We have read Barth, Foucault, Descartes, and Spinoza, and explored such issues as the imagination, the problem of evil, and understandings of nature in American literature. The theology faculty, sometimes with other interested faculty members, participates, together with doctoral students in theology—an international group of women and men, Asians, Black and White, North, Central, and South Americans, and assorted Europeans.

For some time now, many of these women and men have been raising awkward questions about the texts we were reading, questions that seemed to some of us to have "nothing to do with" understanding the text and what it was trying to say. Again and again, we urged a hermeneutics of generosity in order to try to establish the discussion on the level of the ideas presented in the text, in order to dismiss questions about the author's political commitments, institutional loyalties, and gender assumptions and imagery. One member of the colloquium coined the striking phrase, "textual harassment" to describe the demand that we shelve questions about the function and allegiances of the text in order to examine only the relationships of ideas within our texts. Finally, at the beginning of the spring term, 1986, when we were scheduled to read Descartes and Spinoza, it occurred to several of us that *this*, this variety of questions on the level of the assumptions, revealing metaphors, and political loyalties of our texts, this *is* what genuinely pluralistic discussion looks like. A blanket consent to address only the rational argument of texts cannot be the starting place for people whose experience has alerted them to the way that books always and inevitably carry a host of assumptions undercover of their conscious agenda.

A pluralistic discussion starts by examining these assumptions, affiliations, and loyalties. Once these have been acknowledged and examined, we found, the ideas within the text may take on unexpected meanings. Gordon Kaufman stated in the first meeting of the term that questions about the historical situation of the author would not only be tolerated in the colloquium, but would be solicited, by asking students to write short papers each week, raising the features of the text they wanted to discuss, whether historical or systematic. As moderator of the colloquium, Gordon would study these questions in advance of our meetings, grouping them in an agenda for discussion. What we found, I think—though I am now speaking for people who might better speak for themselves—was that a hermeneutics of generosity is possible for those of us who are new to theological discussion *only* when we can see, as fully as possible, the historical situation of the author and can analyze the social context of his concerns, interests, polemics, and metaphysics. Only then can we understand the pressures, fears, and longings that motivated his authorship. Only when we are able to acknowledge openly that the author's universalizing prescriptive statements are in fact directed toward particular people in a particular situation do we relax a bit from bristling at the unexamined elitism, racism, sexism, etc. we find woven through the text. We found we could then practice a realistic objectivity based on our ability to distinguish our own agenda from those of the text. Objectivity, in contrast to objectivism—objectivity as doing our best to respect the integrity of the other with whom we converse, whether human being or text—is still an important commitment if we are not shamelessly to project our sensitivities and sometimes our blindnesses on the text or the person we claim to be trying to understand.

Respect for our own historicity and for that of the other with whom we dialogue comes into being simultaneously. Objectivity requires the willingness to be honestly explicit about the particular situation and perspective from which any human speech comes. We came to recognize historicity as the ground of all discourse. If anything is "universal," it is the historicity of theological statements. Awareness of historicity, in contrast to historicism, does not reduce human speech to its historical location, but immeasurably enriches our understanding of that speech by attention to its place in a particular discourse. It is attention to historicity that makes us conscious of the fragility, beauty, and poignancy of human speech that, if it is lifted out of its imbeddedness in particular human lives can be so disastrously misapprehended, misrepresented and misappropriated. In fact, most of our discussion in the theology colloquium under this new experiment centered around the ideas of Descartes and Spinoza; we found that we could entertain these without resentment once the historical situation of the author was clear to us.

In another seminar of the year just past, the Common Doctoral Seminar, across the theological disciplines, for entering ThD students, another group of racially and religiously diverse people explored some new methods for implementing pluralistic theological reflection. We asked ourselves how we should imagine our relationship to the people and ideas we study. Would we think of ourselves as entering a privileged elite that gave us and our perspectives a universal validity? Would we think of ourselves as disengaged, *The Seeing Eye* as described in a book of that name by Walter Brenneman, Stanley Yarian, and Alan Olson? The authors, in the last paragraphs of the book, describe the role of the phenomenologist of religion as one of the attentiveness to "other tales of power" than those of the dominant culture. They write:

> Like the third son in the fairy tale, we have left the sacred home of our father, the king, and have gone on the search for some other tales of power. . . . Now it is time to return to the king laden with the knowledge of new tales of power . . . that we have gained from the folks in the forest.
>
> The implication of this metaphor [they continue] lies in its symbolic relationship to the historian and the phenomenologist of religion. We too are sovereigns who oversee the sacred realm that lies spread out before us from our lofty thrones within the castle of the university. . . .[4]

Are we to think of ourselves as surveying from thrones in a castle the ordinary people whose "tales of power" can be used to reinforce and augment the university? Surely this model cannot be our view of our work in theological institutions. On the other hand, are we "new people" to donate our energies and those of our historical antecedents and contemporary communities to the support of academic and ecclesiastical institutions that, far from being our advocates, have actually marginalized or excluded us? Or must our participation in theological education change the content and methods of that education? Can we find ways to speak, not for, but in solidarity with those who have not been a part of the shaping of theological ideas and institutions.

In the Common Doctoral Seminar we explored some methods that enabled us to speak for ourselves, from our own experience and with the sensitivities created by our experience, but in solidarity with the people who are our communities of support, concern, and challenge. We employed a "hermeneutics of suspicion,"[5] not in the spirit of reducing the text's significance, beauty, or profundity, but precisely to understand these in relation to the author's assumptions and allegiances. We read the "advocacy scholarship"

---

4. Olson, *Seeing Eye*.

5. Gadamer, "Hermeneutics of Suspicion."

of Vincent Harding[6] and Elisabeth Schüssler Fiorenza.[7] We examined the strength with which they presented the history of people who have not *had* histories. The history of women in the nascent Christian churches and the history of American Black struggles for equality does not, both Schüssler Fiorenza and Harding insist, merely supplement the history of the prevailing powers and ideologies, but demands a re-vision and a rewriting of those histories, a reconstruction on the level of "what happened," not just an addition to the history of the Christian churches and the American people as we learned it in high school and college.

We experimented with writing our own advocacy scholarship, which we then discussed and critiqued, critiqued in the interest of strengthening, not in order to dismiss. One of us wrote a paper on the treatment of Jews by Christians; one paper by an Asian woman examined the history of American policy in relation to Korea; an American Roman Catholic woman analyzed the grounds for exclusion of women from priesthood and advocated a reversal of this position. Exploring the possibilities and limitations of advocacy scholarship, we asked ourselves: is there a point at which a historian loses credibility because of her explicit involvement in the practices and ideas she describes? What are the self-regulating devices by which one can correct one's temptations to exaggeration, to ignoring evidence that may suggest another interpretation than one's own, while arguing forcefully that an underrepresented perspective be entertained?

We discussed the possibility of using different kinds of historical evidence for the interpretation of theological texts than have traditionally been a part of the methodological repertoire of historical theologians. Current studies of historical communities by social and cultural historians are correcting the one-sidedness of intellectual histories. These studies frequently give profoundly different pictures of historical communities from the often profoundly unhistorical tradition we have received concerning them. Even this valuable evidence of the living roots of ideas in the lives of the people of the past, however, can be seriously partial if the visual images that informed and accompanied the worship life of Christian communities of the past is not taken into account.[8] The search for different kinds of evidence of the attitudes, motivations, and loyalties of historical Christians can nuance or enrich or even alter our interpretation of the ideas of the Christian tradition.

6. Harding, "Historian as Witness."

7. Schüssler Fiorenza, *In Memory of Her.*

8. Miles, *Image as Insight.*

In the seminar we also investigated theoretical approaches to historical, scriptural, and comparative study, seeking—and finding—the methods
and questions that do not *reduce* one's interpretation to sociological analysis,
marxist analysis, feminist analysis, but which use the tools of these approaches
to enrich, to render more complex and accurate one's interpretation, which
take into account more, not fewer, aspects of the context of a text, which
help, in short, to define the *historicity* of a text.

We explored the ways in which gender assumptions imbedded in ourselves and in our texts are not "women's issues," but serious issues for everyone.
We found that absence—the frequent absence of women and marginalized
religious and racial groups—from the "great" texts of western Christianity is
a problem; absence constitutes a judgment, assuming a lack of value of the
thoughts and practices of such people. We became more adept at the use of
gender—the social construction of feminine and masculine roles and characteristics—as a category of analysis. We learned, for example, to recognize
gender asymmetry, that is, the construction of masculine and feminine characteristics in a relation of uneven value to one another. If "manly" is valued
as courageous, strong, and active behaviour, while "womanly" is thought of
as weak, vacillating, and passive, we have gender asymmetry. People who are
not, even by projected sympathy, among the intended readers of a text, are especially sensitive to the specific strategies employed by the author to engage,
convince, and seduce readers. These sensitivities, in pluralistic theological
discussion, must not be dismissed, but must be cultivated in the direction of
becoming sophisticated methodological tools.

A hermeneutics of suspicion must also investigate the strategies of historical and contemporary authors. It must question the traditional device
of scholars in which one's own position is constructed over against, and by
attacking, the interpretation of someone else. Theological education in a
pluralistic setting must proceed by cooperation rather than by competition.
This is not to say that we will never hope to convince someone else of the
adequacy and accuracy of our interpretation, but it does mean that we will
realize that competition is not a fruitful method for imaginatively entering,
and learning from, the other person's perspective in order to see—if only
momentarily—the world through her glasses.

The imperative need of the newcomers to theological education is to be
able to identify, in theological books and in theological discussion, aspects
that are not designed to energize or empower them, but rather to seduce
them into "understanding" the ideas of the text at the expense of ignoring its

implicit or explicit rejection of their particularity. As one black man in the seminar described his necessity for constant alertness: "I have to get the white bias out of every book I read and out of every newscast I watch."

Once the newcomers to theological discussion have been permitted, encouraged, and trained to sharpen their skills in identification of the white, or the male, or the class, or the political or institutional loyalties with which the author writes, a hermeneutic of generosity, an understanding of the struggle, the integrity, and the limitations of the author, follows spontaneously. A generous interpretation cannot be advocated in order to stifle inquiry, but emerges among people who are not prevented from asking their own questions but encouraged to develop those questions into self-conscious and effective interpretive tools.

People new to theological education are very pressingly aware of the need to learn the skills of disciplined inquiry. We often need to learn objectivity, to develop the ability to distinguish our commitments and sensitivities from those of each other and the texts we study so that we can see both our own and the other with more clarity and precision. But what of the so-called "problem" of relativism. If all descriptions of reality and beliefs are valid—even valuable—will no beliefs or values be considered universally normative?

The way that the newcomers to theological discussion have often dealt with the problem of relativism is to privilege a certain social experience; for example, feminist theologians have "started from" women's experience; Latin American theologians have privileged the experience of the poor. This, I think, is a dangerous move. For one thing, all women and all poor do not have the same experience, as black women were quick to point out to white feminists.

Secondly, the claim to ontological status for certain perspectives does nothing but duplicate the ontological claim of philosophical hermeneutics. Identifying a different recipient of imputed privilege, it simply makes explicit what had been masked and unacknowledged in traditional hermeneutics, namely that skill in the use of language privileged the perspective of the educated. This claim, developed explicitly from Heidegger to Gadamer, and implicitly long before, is that if language is the house of being, the more skillful interpreter of the world actually holds a place of greater ontological plenitude than the less skilled linguist. Thus it is this linguistic skill—definitely an educated skill—that becomes normative in reality-defining discourse. Everyone who has not had the leisure and money for a long and intensive training in the use of language is automatically excluded. To privilege one's own perspective ontologically, even in the interest of including the excluded seems to me to be an ultimately indefensible theological move, though it may be historically an important beginning toward a rebalancing of the old privilege available only to the educated and the articulate. What we are left with, however, is conflicting claims for ontological status and normativity, in other words, with relativism.

In order to sketch, not a "way out," but a way to work with the relativism that seems to accompany the pluralistic situation of theological discussion in our time, I need first to suggest an understanding of the "other" with whom I converse and with whom I need to act in solidarity even if I cannot think in uniformity. In a world recently made more dangerous than ever before in history by the ominous presence of nuclear weapons, the importance of being able to agree on action even though we may disagree on ideas becomes incrementally more pressing. Who is the other with whom I must negotiate this action? Who is this "other" to whom I also am "other"?

First, the other is not the *object* of my understanding and interpretation. If we relate to each other as object, my attention will remain on the effect on *me* of the other's beliefs. That grammar permits us to list "my house, my job, my car, and my wife," should not blind us to the fact that the last item listed is incommensurable in the series.

Secondly, the other must not be construed, as I have already said, as the Kantian transcendental subject, constituted by rationality and accessible in language, without any necessary and largely determining historicity.

The other, in a pluralistic discourse, must rather be understood as *historical* subject. To understand the other as historical subject is to catch a glimpse of the richness and complexity of his perspective; it is to honor her particularity, to respect the very aspects of his life that had seemed, from the perspective of the "transcendental subject" formulation, to be nothing but the "accidents" of her birth and culture, the idiosyncrasies of personality and conditioning. To see the other as historical subject is to honor his subjectivity equally with my own, to understand that we are, as Herder put it, "equidistant from God."

The other in a pluralistic discourse, like myself, is both privileged and limited by historically particular experience. While claiming the privilege of particularity of experience, we all need to acknowledge and specify also the limitedness of our experience, the partialness of our sensitivities. In this situation of our equality of privilege and limitation grounded on the condition of historicity, we can still do two things together, even though we cannot "overcome" or transcend our differences: we can talk together, and we can act together.

Remembering that our dialogue will have a different goal than the Platonic goal of exposing the misapprehensions of the other's thought and the misrepresentations of his speech, a pluralistic discourse will seek to articulate the complexity of the dynamic of our perspectives and understandings. I do not think that the commitment to a dialogue in which another person can be understood is different in *kind* from the kind of conversation between a text and a reader that must occur if a text is to be understood. "Each person who has read the same text," I tell my classes in historical theology, "has read a different text, because we are all differently educated, experienced, and thus sensitized, to notice different aspects of the text in its context." In discussing the text together, it will then be our delight to listen to and understand the many readings of the text that will emerge, finding most illuminating those readings in which the interpreter has managed simultaneously to engage her own perspective, in the form of alertness to features of the text, *and* has managed to recognize the otherness of the text and therefore the partialness of her interpretation. It is not merely enjoyable or educational to discuss texts, but *necessary*, since no one of us enjoys the privilege of an absolute perspective from which to give a final interpretation. This does not mean that we cannot argue about more and less adequate interpretations, nor does it mean that we cannot protest interpretations that reflect the concerns of the interpreter more than those of the text, but it does mean that no one set of questions, no single method can claim finality. This kind of relativity, not a relativism that posits in advance that the other—whether text or person—can never really be understood, is not the end of rationality, but a different kind of rationality, simultaneously a more generous and a more critical rationality than the rationality that claimed to transcend difference by means of a competition for the normative interpretation. Moreover, I notice that when we are not driven toward uniformity of interpretation, we seem to find more commonality than we had expected.

Finally, we as participants in theological education in a pluralistic setting can act together against the destructive forces that threaten to end human life on our mother, planet earth, forces that threaten not only human bodies, but the body of the planet that is our home. *Can* we act together, though, without first negotiating agreement on what are the issues, on who are the villains, and on the principles we represent? *Can* we have commitment without the foundation of a universalizing rationale? I think we can. I think we can do without Kant's categorical imperative, which asks us to choose and to evaluate our actions by imagining whether they would still be good or beneficial if everyone in the world imitated them. The alternative to consensus on a rationalizing rhetoric for our actions is the understanding that each of us is a historical subject, sensitized by the particularity of our experiences to notice some things and to ignore others—beyond belief.

The recently deceased French philosopher, Michel Foucault, practiced commitment to action without the claim to universal rightness. He was frequently asked to explain. "The ethico-political choice each of us has to make every day," he said in an interview, "is to determine what is the main danger and to focus our efforts there." We do not have to agree on what is the "main danger" if we can agree that the "main danger" is probably not a single danger. We can each focus our efforts against the "main danger" we identify, content in the awareness that others are focusing their efforts on what they detect to be the "main danger." To act as a historical subject is to take the risk and responsibility of deciding on the focus of my efforts without a rhetoric that exaggerates the importance of my efforts by diminishing or dismissing the efforts of others. It is to be grateful that my efforts are not conclusive, the direction of their focus not normative for everyone, but that my colleagues in theological discourse are addressing dangers that my experience has not prepared me to detect. To act in this way, in absolute responsibility for my own actions, and with respect and gratitude for the actions of others, is to act *together* without needing to agree on principles, strategies, or immediate targets. It certainly requires that I remain open to hearing and possibly becoming convinced of, and involved in, another's analysis of "main danger," but it does not mean that I should neglect to direct my efforts to the "main danger" I detect because of the universal claims of a privileged rhetoric.

The transcending of real differences of who we are, what we believe, and what we value can never be the goal of theological education in a pluralistic setting. Rather, dialogue in which particularity is respected as opportunity for the correction of the limited vision of each, and action in the face of death, the ancient enemy in its thousand guises, can become the basis for a pluralistic theological community. The necessary humility for this enterprise comes readily when we recall that ultimately theological education is a luxury. If the wider community had a choice between getting rid either of its theologians or of its garbage collectors, which do you think it would choose to eliminate? But the appropriate response to a gift and a luxury is not guilt, but gratitude and responsibility.

20

Theory, Theology, and Episcopal Churchwomen

Questions surrounding a theory of women's participation in past and present American Episcopal churches may take two foci. First, the particular question about the present: Why do—or, more pointedly, how can—women participate in the Episcopal Church? The second focus is more general; it assumes that work on a particular content—women in Episcopal congregations—may also yield the possibility of a critique or nuancing of more wide-ranging theoretical questions, such as why women support patriarchal institutions. No doubt there are many problematic reasons for doing so, but are there any "good" reasons, and how can legitimate reasons be recognized and theorized? This essay will consider the second set of questions first, exploring some theoretical approaches to women's activities in established institutions. I will turn then to the particular question, asking whether the theories we have examined can contribute to understanding women's contemporary situation in the Episcopal Church.

I

Historically, the dominant Christian rhetoric defined the place of women in Christian communities as one of privileged subordination. The character traits to which women have been socialized in Christian societies—obedience, humility, submissiveness, and attentiveness to others' needs are privileged, in devotional manuals, sermons, religious art, and theological treatises, as central to the "imitation of Christ" and thus to Christian behavior. Cultivation of these virtues may indeed have represented, for men, a correction of their socialization to aggressive and competitive self-interest. For women, however, they reinforced—rather than corrected—their socialized subordination to male authority. It would seem to follow that women, already socialized to humble acceptance of the roles and behavior to which they were assigned in male-designed and -administered societies, should have been recognized as ideal Christians. And so they were, when their self-abnegation assumed heroic proportions, as in asceticism and martyrdom.

Yet the attitudes and roles that were thought natural for women seem not to have been as appropriate for men to imitate as they should have been if they were really seen to represent ideal Christianity. Although many men were martyrs and ascetics, self-sacrifice was only *one* of the behavioral choices for Christian men; they could also achieve esteem as ecclesiastical leaders, as teachers, fighters, or thinkers. The *theologically* privileged position of subordination failed *practically* to empower women because they were, without alternatives, consigned to it. It must also be acknowledged, however, that by the exercise of individual creativity some women were able to use the condition of privileged subordination to play roles in the patriarchal church and in society that they might otherwise not have achieved. In Christian churches women have sometimes gained alternatives to the social and sexual arrangements in patriarchal societies. Nevertheless, Christian churches have usually displayed a wide disjunction between women's engagement, allegiance, and concrete support and their access to leadership roles in which the design and direction of the church as a social institution were debated and decided.

For example, women's associations have always existed in Episcopal churches. Often these organizations were task-oriented, but there were also study groups whose purpose was mutual support and learning. In these groups women frequently found both a form for their energies and considerable personal gratification. Women's groups have also provided crucial financial as well as emotional support for their churches. They have usually, however, achieved personal satisfaction and community esteem at the expense of suppressing a critical evaluation of their roles in churches that were grateful for their hard work but that offered them little formal institutional power. Traditional women's groups did not "rock the boat"; they "fit in." Neither did these groups— individually or communally—examine their own feelings of gratification in order to ascertain whether these feelings rested on socialized compliance with patriarchal domination.

It is important to say at the outset what I mean by *patriarchal,* whether I use that particular term or a synonymous phrase. Minimally, *patriarchy* is descriptive, indicating that Western Christian and post-Christian societies are and have been designed and administered by men. By *patriarchal,* I also mean, however, that the formal and informal institutions of these societies are designed to embody and support the agenda of male psyches.

In the early twentieth century Freud described the psychological roots of patriarchal domination in the relationship of the male infant to the mother. Freud's theory, though it should not be presumed to illuminate all historical and contemporary human interaction, suggests one interpretation of the intersubjective origin of male authority and control. He located the decisive dynamic in the dual and contradictory need of the infant on the one hand for recognition by the (m)other, and on the other hand for independence from the (m)other. He described male individuation as a difficult and dangerous process of creating a self-other distinction, a development in which "merging was a dangerous form of undifferentiation, a sinking back into the sea of oneness."[1] The male infant's task, then, was to resist the chimera of dependency by striving for omnipotence and control.[2] On the level of society, patriarchal institutions reflect the psychic agenda of the male infant: domination and control.[3]

Where do women "fit" in this scenario? The interplay between love and domination is a "two-way process, a system involving the participation of those who submit to power as well as those who exercise it."[4] For the dominated, "the pain that accompanies compliance is [often] preferable to the pain that attends freedom." Using Dostoevsky's "The Grand Inquisitor" as a paradigm of male dominance and female submission, Jessica Benjamin notes, "The awesome nearness of the ultimate power embodied in the Church makes pain tolerable, even a source of inspiration or transcendence. This ability to enlist the hope for

---

1. Benjamin, *Bonds of Love*, 47. Benjamin criticizes Freud's analysis of infant development, proposing instead a theory of intersubjectivity in which the infant's task is to achieve a "paradoxical balance between recognition of the other and assertion of self." Struggle for domination and control, according to Benjamin, is not a "psychological inevitability" but the result of a specifically male-gendered process of psychic development.

2. The little girl, because she can grow up to be like the mother, need not, like the boy, struggle to control the mother. Freud did not theorize the dynamic of female psychic development beyond positing an opposite but parallel development in relation to the father. Benjamin, *Bonds of Love*, revises Freud's theory and argues for a specifically female development.

3. For example, in a revealing passage in *City of God*, Augustine explicitly says that the Christian ruler—whether in household or state—should be motivated not by a "lust for domination" (*libido dominandi*) but, rather, by a "dutiful concern for the interests of others." He states in the same passage that "domestic peace" depends on an "ordered harmony about giving and obeying orders among those who live in the same house. . . . husband gives orders to the wife, parents to children, and masters to servants." *City of God* 19.14 (Bettenson, 874).

4. Benjamin, *Bonds of Love*, 5.

redemption is the signature of the power that inspires voluntary submission . . . [a] power that inspires fear and adoration simultaneously."[5]

It is also possible, however, to understand women's allegiance to, and support for, institutions they neither designed nor administered without invoking female masochism. There can be no doubt that the "hope of redemption" offered by Christianity has been as attractive to women as to men. Moreover, women have supported patriarchal institutions because these institutions often provided the only *real* opportunities accessible to them.[6] To say that most women have accepted without question their exclusion from leadership roles in public institutions, their subordination, and the appropriation of their energies for male projects is not, I think, to honor sufficiently the integrity and creativity of historical women. The psychological explanation of a theory of intersubjectivity offers reasons for male domination, but it does not adequately explain women's complicity with the male project. It reiterates mothers' failure to require from their sons a parallel recognition of the mother's subjectivity as a result of societies' neglect in failing to affirm the mother as subject of her own experience—in the family as well as in social institutions. We must turn, then, to social theories of subjectivity.

II

A social theory of the subject must be preliminary to any effort to understand women in relation to institutions. Michel Foucault, Frigga Haug, Rom Harré, Bryan Turner, and others have argued convincingly that there is no preexisting entity called "the self" that is subsequently appropriated, trained, or manipulated to activities that maintain and reproduce society. Humans are fundamentally social beings whose "selves" are socially constructed. These authors describe the so-called repressive hypothesis, according to which "docile bodies" and behavior are engineered, as distorting without a parallel hypothesis that highlights the social *production* of motivation, desire, pleasure, and reward. According to these social theorists, although oppression of women existed, exists, and should not be underestimated, women are not *only* coerced by the male-designed institutions of "compulsory heterosexuality," family, and society; rather, the simultaneous processes of socialization, sexualization,

5. Ibid.

6. Daly's thesis that women's energy has always been usurped and used by patriarchal institutions (repressive hypothesis) does not recognize that energy is not a "thing" possessed by individuals and appropriated by power but is actually socially produced (productive hypothesis); see *Gyn/Ecology*.

and subjectification are also pleasurable learning processes in which effective social competencies are developed.[7] The gratification to be earned from progressively learning how to engage, control, and reap the rewards of the social order are inextricably linked to women's self-insertion into society.

These benefits, of course, are not undiluted. While women's attention has been on the increments of opportunity offered, for example by Christian churches, they have tended not to notice the continuity of the patriarchal project of domination and control across secular and ecclesiastical institutions. If the continuity of male-designed and -dominated institutions across historical and contemporary societies and religions were noticed and taken seriously, the conclusion might be, as Mary Daly has pointed out, that the establishment of patriarchy is itself the slenderly disguised agenda of both social and religious organizations.

Thus, a productivity hypothesis of women's socialization cannot simply replace the repressive hypothesis but, instead, must balance it by positing a continuum along which female socialization and subjectification occurs. At one end is the pleasurable sensation of empowerment by self-discipline and achievement; at the other end are the forceful forms of women's socialization—domestic and other forms of violence against women, and legal restriction of women's prerogatives and activities. Education, socialization, and force, Foucault argues, lie along a single continuum in which socialization is anticipatory force; it attempts, by training people to docile behavior, to forestall the necessity of coercion. Western institutions have affected women in oppressive as well as in productive ways that are seldom easy to distinguish and categorize. Social theories of the construction of subjectivity can help to account for women's complicity in supporting male domination and control without invoking female masochism. They describe some of the conditions women need in order to rectify present social arrangements, but they analyze neither the public sphere in which social arrangements are determined and maintained, nor do they identify any points of access for women to the public sphere. For this we must turn to feminist political theorists.

III

How do private and semipublic conversations and events relate to a broader sphere of public discourse? However misguided in theory and ineffective in practice the modern public sphere has been, it was nevertheless imagined as

---

7. Haug, *Female Sexualization*, 166.

an ideal arena in which all men—at least—were granted voice. In the late twentieth century, however, mass communications have produced a "pseudo-public sphere" characterized by the "homogenizing and universalizing logic of the global megaculture of modern mass communication."[8] Another essay would be required to demonstrate that media communications inevitably reflect and reproduce the male interests that dominate the public sphere. Perhaps it is enough, for the present essay, to note that in a recent survey of images of women and men in a single issue of the *New York Times*, approximately 90 percent of the images of men appeared in news stories, and the same percentage of images of women appeared in advertising. These percentages reiterate ancient gender expectations in which men were assigned roles associated with rationality—thinking and acting—while women remain objects for the gaze of the male rational subject, achieving social esteem to the extent that they succeed in attracting that gaze.

Over and against pseudopublic spheres, groups with political, social, and religious concerns form what Rita Felski has recently called "counter-public spheres," or "critical oppositional forces."[9] In contemporary North American communication culture, a plurality of counter-public spheres, Felski says, "voice needs and articulate oppositional values which the 'culture industry' fails to address":

> These new sites of oppositionality are heterogeneous and do not converge to form a single revolutionary movement; the current plurality of public spheres is united only by a common concern to establish "qualitatively new forms of social and political relations in which mutuality, discussion, and concern with concrete needs predominate."[10]

To be effective, counter-public spheres must identify with clarity and precision what it is they oppose in the discourse of the public sphere. For example, several analyses have recently identified aspects of the public sphere that marginalize women. Iris Marion Young has reconstructed a modern concept of "public life" that emerged in the mid- eighteenth century. It was, she writes, characterized by the positing of a public sphere based on a universal impartial moral reason in contrast and opposition to the affectivity and desire predicated of the private realm. This dichotomy of reason and desire underlay the essential difference between public and private, directing masculinity to

8. Felski, *Beyond Feminist Aesthetics*, 166.

9. Ibid.

10. Ibid.

the criteria of impartial reason and identifying femininity with privatized desire and the private sphere to which women were confined.[11]

Neglecting to notice that, masked by a rhetoric of impartiality, desire also permeated and motivated discourse in the public sphere, this theory of public discourse simultaneously marginalized women and affectivity. In opposition, then, counter-public spheres expose and criticize the illusion of "transcendent impartiality" that has operated to exclude not only the expression of feeling but also the people associated with affectivity and desire from the public sphere. Seyla Benhabib has also discussed what she calls the "generalized other"[12] posited by the collective male subject who defines the public sphere. Because of the confinement of women's self-expression to the private sphere, because women did not represent themselves in the public sphere, the impartial universality of that sphere remained unchallenged by a "concrete other."

To these suggestions about the strategies by which women's experience and perspectives have been isolated from public discourse, a further consideration needs to he added. Because body and the natural world were identified with women and the private sphere, and contrasted with the "reason" that governed the public sphere, recognition of, and respect for, bodies—their pleasures and their sufferings—were not understood as central to public discourse. The result of this marginalization of bodies from the public sphere has been that the suffering entailed by wars, ecological crisis, economic injustice, and epidemic disease, as well as issues surrounding childbirth, abortion, and child care have been seen as peripheral to politics and government. Each of these issues has generated counter-public spheres in which attention to them has been, with varying effectiveness, carried to the public sphere.

The adversarial role of counter-public spheres should, however, not be emphasized at the expense of their constructive and reconstructive capacities. Ultimately, it is not a permanent condition of playing gadfly that defines the role of a feminist counter-public sphere but, rather, of weaving feminist critique and revision of the public sphere as it was inherited from earlier centuries into public discourse. The creation of a public discourse defined equally by women's and men's concerns, experiences, and perspectives should be the goal of a feminist counter-public sphere.

Integrated with Benjamin's intersubjective theory and with the social theories I have sketched, feminist political theory suggests new ways to envi-

11. Young, "Impartiality and the Civic Public."
12. Benhabib, "Generalized and the Concrete Other."

sion women's participation in male-designed and -administered institutions. The contemporary question, then, is not whether women "should" support patriarchal institutions but, rather, whether there are ways in which already-existing institutions can work for women until they can be changed *by women* and men in the direction of an equality, mutuality, recognition of interdependence, and a distribution and circulation of power that can, at present, be envisioned only dimly and must eventually be worked out in myriad details and "on location." Instead of seeing women's leadership in patriarchal institutions as inevitably entailing the appropriation of women's time and energy for the reproduction of those institutions, a two-stage strategy of institutional change is needed.

In the first stage, women must achieve institutional positions in which they *can*, in the second stage, revise these institutions. This is a dangerous first step. Individuals, once they have achieved institutional power, have often succumbed to the pleasure of achievement and enjoyment of the rewards of such power and have forgotten their commitment to a project of reform. The only antidote to intoxication with such rewards is the ongoing support and critique of a self-critical community. Continuous and vigorous communal self-criticism can continuously monitor whether women's participation is effecting real change in the direction of *institutionalizing* equality.

Significant institutional change, it must be acknowledged, cannot be brought about by individuals but requires the construction of women's collective voice in the public sphere, a voice that women have gained only occasionally and briefly in the patriarchal Christian West. However, both of these critical terms—*collective voice* and *public sphere*—need further exploration.

Through talking and working together women are currently gathering—by induction rather than by deduction from an assumed and/or coerced "unity"—a feminist collective voice. Rooted in the diverse experiences of many women, collective voice need not mask the real differences among women in order to acknowledge the similarity of the subordinated experience of women as a "caste"[13] in patriarchal societies. This similarity of women's experience, however, must be a precisely defined, rather than a generalized, similarity. It refers specifically to the myriad social and sexual arrangements, customs, and laws by which women's access to self-representation in the public sphere has

13. Daly's term; the danger in speaking of women as a caste, or in invoking a women's "collective voice" is described in Young, "Ideal of Community and the Politics of Gender." Nevertheless, it is important not to glaze over women's similarities in recognizing and respecting their differences.

been, and continues to be, limited. Collective voice is constructed, then, by women's conversations, first with one another and eventually also with men in public or semipublic locations. In discussions in classrooms, churches, and interest and support groups, women learn simultaneously about the similarity and the diversity of one another's experience and begin through honest speaking and generous listening to identify with one another, not by pretending a universalizing impartiality but precisely by communicating the particular affectivity of their experiences. Suzanne R. Hiatt's account of the "irregular" ordinations of eleven women to the priesthood on July 29, 1974, emphasizes the process of gathering a self-critical collective voice in bringing about these ordinations that effectively forced the Episcopal Church to recognize women's ordination, and, by January 1977, to regularly ordain women to the priesthood.[14] The Episcopal Women's Caucus was organized in 1971 to organize and educate toward women's ordination; the caucus was itself the result of an earlier gathering of women in April 1970. Through building a network and an organization, this national group "built a ground-swell of enthusiasm for women's ordination."[15]

In addition to the conversations of small groups of women and organizations of larger groups around issues of common concern, at least two other strategies for constructing collective voice are crucial. First, women in groups that tend to be composed of women of similar class and race must intentionally correct the ghetto assumptions that can be communicated and reinforced by conscious self-identification with women of other races, with battered women, poor women, sexually abused women. Groups on the model of the consciousness-raising groups of the 1970s can facilitate identification with women as a caste so that a response of identification with women with whom one may not be in face-to-face contact becomes spontaneous. Second, public events that acknowledge and celebrate women's public achievements are occasions on which collective voice is strengththened. The "irregular" ordination in 1974 was, for many women who attended or who heard descriptions of the event, such an occasion of joyous bonding. So was the consecration of Barbara Harris as Suffragan Bishop of Massachusetts in 1989. Let us now turn to examining the role of women in the Episcopal Church in relation to these theories of the social construction of the self and the public role of counter-public spheres.

14. Hiatt, "How We Brought the Good News from Graymoor to Minneapolis: An Episcopal Paradigm." See also "Episcopalian Story."

15. Hiatt, "How We Brought the Good News," 579.

IV

Is the Episcopal Church a valid form for women's energy? For many women, participation in Christian churches in general, and the Episcopal Church in particular, remains an ongoing question. Those who answer this question in the affirmative often feel that it would constitute a denial of their experience to withdraw from a community, a common story, and a practice that has—in addition to causing them much frustration and anger—provided and continues to provide challenge, support, encouragement, and comfort. If they no longer experienced spiritual and emotional nourishment in the Episcopal Church, they would be able to acknowledge with gratitude the role played in their lives by Christianity thus far and move beyond it. Nevertheless, in remaining in the Episcopal Church, they frequently examine their own intentions and motivations; they also ask whether the *effect* of their participation counts on the side of institutional change or on the side of maintaining the church as it is and has been. How long would they have waited, they ask themselves, for women's ordination to the priesthood before becoming convinced that the church is not in the process of coming to accept women's leadership? How long, they wonder, would they have waited for a woman bishop before deciding that institutional change is not occurring, or, if occurring, is happening as slowly as rocks grow when left in soil? It happens, Plotinus said, but don't expect to see it in a single human lifetime! Although the inertia of an establishment church continues to distress them, when they regard the developments of the past twenty years in the Episcopal Church in relation to women, they are forced to acknowledge that at least one form of institutional change—women's participation in leadership roles in the Episcopal Church—is advancing remarkably rapidly. The question concerning how women's leadership will *change* the church remains to be examined.

A global perspective makes it no easier to evaluate whether gains outweigh impediments and problems: on the one hand, the WASP and class affiliations of the American Episcopal Church are dramatically reversed in African Anglicanism; on the other hand, however, the Church of England, in spite of voting to "proceed toward" ordination of women to the priesthood, has not yet done so. The picture remains frustratingly mixed, and this ambivalence, many Episcopal women feel, is sustained on the global level.

In short, there are both concrete reasons for entertaining hope about the openness of the Episcopal Church to women's concerns and leadership, and reasons to despair. If we ask, then, what gender analysis reveals about the church rather than what the church says about gender, it is difficult to identify advantages for women without also noticing some dangers attached to and interwoven with these advantages. I will proceed, therefore, by discussing linked pairs of advantages and dangers.

First, the Episcopal Church in the United States, like Anglican churches throughout the world, has an institutional structure similar to the political structure of the American state. It is easy to locate power in this hierarchical structure. The clearly articulated distribution of power provides a ready-made strategy for establishing women in positions of leadership, authority, and power. This is not to say that a hierarchical distribution of power is desirable or unproblematic but only to recognize that it gives outsiders—such as women—a clear map as to which offices come first in the order of access. Although this refers mainly to clergywomen, not to laywomen who may seek to gain empowerment from the Episcopal Church for leadership in social and political spheres, laywomen benefit from the religious leadership of clergywomen who are in solidarity with their experience and concerns. The danger connected to the advantage of an explicit "ladder" of ecclesiastical power is obvious and need not be discussed at length: namely, the risk that having gained institutional validation, a woman may take on the institution's perspectives, forgetting that she has pursued power in order to redistribute it, to circulate it more widely and specifically to those who have formerly held lesser shares. A Spanish proverb warns, "You must change the world quickly, before it changes you." Women in leadership roles in patriarchal institutions must find that warning important to heed.

Second, the mainline Christian churches, in the context of Western culture, have consistently offered support and reinforcement for women's subordination. This agenda has been more subtle at some times than at others, but it is one of the most remarkable continuities of Christian theology and practice across the diverse societies of the Christian West.[16] From representational practices in which female nakedness symbolized and signaled sin to the massive witch persecutions of the sixteenth century, Christianity has accepted and reiterated women's secondary, derivative, and inferior nature in relation to men. In participating in the detection, exposure, and elimination of sexism within a mainstream Christian tradition, then, women can address male domination in one of its primary bastions, in a major social institution

---

16. See my *Carnal Knowing: Female Nakedness and Religious Meaning in the Christian West* for discussion of the figuration of women's bodies as symbol of sin, sex, and death in the textual and pictorial representational practices of the Christian West.

that maintains patriarchal society.[17] If sexism could be eradicated in Christian churches, patriarchy would lose one strong source of institutionalized support. On the other hand, the marginalization of Christian churches in secular society clearly means that the depatriarchalization of Christianity, if this can be achieved, will not affect society as much as the loss of ecclesiastical support would have done before a post-Christian age. Nevertheless, the dismantling of Christian sexism would certainly affect the culture as a whole and women in particular. The attendant danger is evident: it is the difficulty of distinguishing women's participation for purposes of changing an institution from support by the marginalized for a marginalizing structure.

A third reason for women to continue working within the Episcopal Church relates more directly to the possibility of constructing churches as counter-public spheres. A church can be understood and function as a semi-public arena in which women can construct the collective voice by which they can address and revise both the church as an institution and the secular public sphere. The intense, cumulative process by which women come to know—and say—what they think, listen to the perspectives of other women, and develop analyses, critiques, and plans for social action can occur in the context of a space that is simultaneously public and, in a post-Christian society, sheltered by its very marginalization from the assumptions, demands, and values of public life.

Male collective voice, informed by the male infant's project of domination and control of the (m)other, has governed the public sphere and its institutions. The conscious construction of alternative institutions will require another collective voice, a voice not automatically available from women who have been isolated from, and placed in competition with, one another in patriarchal institutions. Women's collective voice must be gathered in the process of speaking intimately, honestly, and at length with one another. This is a project that can begin in churches, moving out into home and society when sufficient strength and configuration have been gained. Churches that in the past have assimilated women's support and work without permitting them voice and leadership roles can now function as places to develop the

17. I do not agree with Turner (*The Body and Society*) that "patriarchy," defined as legal and political oppression of women, no longer exists. Turner believes that the dismantling of women's subordination and oppression is gathering a momentum that will soon sweep away remaining vestiges of institutionalized sexism. He has not taken into account, however, the very class and gender variables that have always oppressed some women more than others; for example, most women—for financial, emotional, or other reasons—do not have access to the courts of law in which sexist situations may be examined and overturned.

individual and collective self-confidence necessary to come to voice, to ana-lyze, criticize, and revise the patriarchal organization of church and society. Moreover, Christian churches, at present marginalized in a commercial and entertainment-oriented culture, could rediscover an ancient religious role of providing a countercultural or prophetic voice in relation to the values and interests of secular culture. Churches could become effective both in empow-ering members and in functioning as counter-public spheres.

Thus far I have been speaking primarily of Episcopal churches as in-stances of Christian churches in general. Now I would like to suggest that Episcopal churches in particular are "pregnable," even liable to women's revisionist participation. In "Feminist Theology and Anglican Theology," Owen Thomas argued that because Anglican theology has always toler-ated—even encouraged—people with diverse theological perspectives held together by a common liturgical and sacramental practice, it is theoretically more open to feminist critique and revision.[18] Christian churches with a greater emphasis on confessional formulae, he says, find it more difficult to admit feminist revisions of the creeds that are seen as defining the character of these denominations. Although the religious "weight" may be somewhat more distributed in Anglican practice from language to ritual, however, it is still true that liturgy entails language. And it has not, thus far, proven easy to alter the androcentric language of the *Book of Common Prayer* and the mass. Nevertheless, the Episcopal emphasis on practice—on movement, pos-ture and gesture, reading and listening, eating and drinking—does facilitate women's participation, rendering the verbal content of worship less crucial. Moreover, precisely because liturgy and sacraments have traditionally been the prerogative of an exclusively male priesthood, the exhilaration of hearing those words and seeing those gestures performed by a woman priest is—or can be—powerful and empowering for women.

Our exploration of several kinds of theories of social interaction—psychological, social, and political—has led to a theory of women's participa-tion in Episcopal churches as one counter-public sphere in which collective voice can be developed as a base for challenging the "pseudopublic" sphere of mass communications.

If the persistent continuity of gendered socialization is to shift to mu-tuality in designing and administering a society in which opportunity and social roles are accessible to women and to currently marginalized men, however, the present plurality of counter-public spheres with their criticism

18. O. C. Thomas, "Feminist Theology and Anglican Theology."

and revision of publicly circulated values must continue to gather strength, voice, and courage to address—each group from its own collective voice—the communication media's limitations of the public sphere to the economic interests and class affiliation represented in mass communications. Theories, even those that are temporarily useful in imagining a more just society, must ultimately "collapse into immediacy,"[19] that is, they must be translated into the *practices* that make them concrete and move the concerns and values they represent beyond private conviction and into public attention. The communal practices—worship, discussion, social action—of Episcopal churches often bring together diverse people who would not otherwise speak with one another, women and men, people with different sexual orientations, the homeless and the affluent, educated and uneducated, to name only some of the most obvious diversities. Churches, as semipublic spheres, can become an arena in which counterpublic collectivities can be constructed.

19. Robin George Collingwood's phrase.

21

From the Garden to the Academy:
Blame, Battle, or a Better Way?

Exploring Sex and Power in the Academy

My personal history with theological education goes back to the 1950s, when my first husband was a seminary student in the San Francisco Bay area. In those days, as in all seminaries at the time, the few women enrolled were not studying for ordination, but to be Directors of Christian Education. The only other women in sight were wives. I was a wife, and for the wives of seminary students, an organization called Parsonettes endeavored to help us to anticipate and prepare for our roles as ministers' wives.

My life, since those long ago days, has reflected the amazing and rich and painful changes in theological education and in our society and world. When I was twenty-two, I had an ulcer that threatened to perforate. The ulcer was painful enough to get my attention, to say to me, in the words of Rainer Maria Rilke, "You must change your life."[1] Thereafter I was fortunate enough to have about seven years of effective psychotherapy that taught me, in Augustine's words, to "relax a little from myself."[2] At the same time, the energy that had devoured my stomach lining began to appear in my head. I learned that, as Abraham Maslow put it, "a capacity is a need."[3] I began to read hungrily, for dear life. As Doris Lessing said in her autobiography, *Under My Skin*, "I read, I read, I read. I was reading to save my life."[4] When my children reached school age, I went to the nearest junior college. One thing led to another, and I have been happily addicted to learning ever since.

1. Rilke, "Archaic Torso of Apollo," 181.
2. Augustine *Confessions* 7.14
3. Maslow, *Toward a Psychology of Being*, 399.
4. Lessing, *Under My Skin*, 399.

An incident midway between my Parsonette days and the present will illustrate another moment in women's uneven advance into theological education. Around a decade ago *Newsweek* decided to do an Easter cover story on women studying for ministry They came to Harvard Divinity School, where I taught at the time, to interview and photograph, using my office as headquarters. When Easter approached and the edition appeared, imagine our surprise when the cover pictured not women studying for ministry, but Jim and Tammy Faye Bakker! That scandal had broken in time to bump earlier plans for the cover story and was seen as more interesting than women in ministry in the context of a media culture.

I have been the Dean of the Graduate Theological Union in Berkeley for five years. This has given me a new perspective on theological education, a rather strikingly different perspective than the one that accumulated in my eighteen years as a faculty member at Harvard Divinity School. I want to emphasize at the outset that my remarks about women in religious studies emerge from my experience. My perspective will need to be corrected by others' experience.

Theological education changed radically in the two decades after my introduction to it. Increasing numbers of women were admitted to BD and then MDiv degree programs. African Americans, Asians, and people whose origins were in the two-thirds world came to seminaries more and more frequently. The new participants in theological education were taught by the same professors who had taught the young ministers of the 1950s, and at first the new participants tried to fit in, to prove that they were as intelligent and could think as well as the young white men who felt at home in liberal theological institutions. Gradually, however, the newcomers gained sufficient numbers to find support for their questions, concerns, and interests. They began, hesitantly and tentatively, to raise their own questions, not only in the halls and refectories, but also in the classrooms. The questions became more persistent. Often students asked how the ideas of a particular author related to his historical situation and the political, class, and institutional affiliations of his thought. They inquired not so much about the author's intentions, but about the effects of his ideas. Sometimes the questioners went so far as to reduce the author's ideas to his allegiance to a class, gender, or institutional ideology. This historicism was deeply offensive to their professors, whose lives and careers had been altered, enriched, and shaped by the beauty and profundity of theological authors. In vain the professors urged objectivity and generosity in interpretation. Some of them even experienced the new questions as threatening the demise of rationality itself, the end of civilization as "we" knew it.

Diversity in theological education came into existence in something like the process I have sketched. So here we are, all of us with strong longings, with intractable fears, with a desire for understanding powerful enough to motivate the commitment of our lives to understanding each other and the texts and religious traditions we study. Our naive impressions of the intuitive rightness and universality of our ideas and practices have been irreversibly challenged by our confrontation with one another. Where do we go from here? What lies beyond the impasse of our efforts to change one another? Where do we go from the unsettling recognition that there is no value-free interpretation of each other, or of our texts and traditions?

Let us focus specifically on women in religious studies. Women presently play at least two different roles in religious studies institutions: faculty and administrative roles. I will eventually argue that the success of faculty women relies at every point—from hire to tenure—on women in administration and urge that more women consider accepting administrative roles. But first, what is the situation for faculty women? Eloise Rosenblatt's carefully researched article on "The Present and Future Status of Women in Religion," forthcoming in the journal of *Feminist Studies in Religion*,[5] presents a good news/bad news picture of women's participation in religious studies institutions.

On the one hand, the number of degree programs in gender and feminist studies has increased nationwide in the last decade. On the other hand, although the number of women with PhDs in religion/theology has increased during the last decade, since 1994 the number of women hired for tenure-track positions has declined. And women doctorates are expected to continue to increase from 37.9 percent of all doctorates in 1996 to 49.5 percent by 2006. Yet Rosenblatt concludes that despite increased opportunities for training, women seeking full-time employment in religion face a number of obstacles. Once hired, the category of "institutional fit," used in evaluation for promotion and tenure, can mask judgments against women. Rosenblatt found that women who devote their scholarly articles to male historical figures and academic authorities may fare better in the academy. Women who join men's academic projects may be viewed as a better institutional fit than those who devote themselves to feminist themes and female historical figures, and who cite other women academics as their scholarly authorities. For racial/ethnic minority women, the picture is even bleaker.

5. Rosenblatt, "Present and Future Status of Women in Religion."

After an increase of appointments in the early 1990s, racial/ethnic minority women in the field of religious studies suffered more acutely the general decline in hiring women of all races and ethnicities. The American Theological Association's statistics for 1999–2000 report that "although the percentages of Asian, Black, and Hispanic faculty members have increased slightly since 1995, the increase has been only a fraction of the percentage point for each group over the five-year period."[6]

Hiring practices in the 1990s have also disadvantaged women. Part-time and adjunct appointments are more likely to go to women than to men, a statistic that also has the effect of widening the gap between women's and men's salaries in religious studies. For full-time senior positions at large research universities, a national survey shows an average salary gap of $6,980.

A 1998–1999 survey of hiring conducted by Richard Rosengarten for the Council of Graduate Studies in Religion offers finely-tuned data that permit us to see with some clarity where the gender gaps occur in hiring practices. The survey included data on new hires from 176 institutions, most of them liberal arts colleges, private and state universities, and theological seminaries. Most of these positions were tenure-track, and search committees received an average of fifty to one hundred applications for each position. A gender gap occurs first at the application stage: for every one hundred applications, male applicants averaged seventy, compared to thirty female applications, a slight leveling of the gender pool from 80/20 in 1996–1997. A 50/50 applicant pool was achieved by only 2 percent of hiring institutions. Seventy-eight percent of the polled institutions hired one of their applicants. Seventy-two males were hired, compared to forty-seven females. There was virtually no change here from the 1996–1997 figures of seventy-six male hires, forty-seven female. The study also reveals that religious studies institutions are increasingly hiring faculty who were trained in other fields, such as American history; anthropology; medieval studies, philosophy, and sociology: in 1998–1999, twenty-nine candidates with training in fields other than religious studies were hired, as contrasted with five such candidates in 1995–1996. This trend may also work against women with PhDs in religious studies. Three years ago, a discussion at the American Academy of Religion Executive Board meeting examined this trend. We concluded that the statistics are still too slight to allow meaningful interpretation. Perhaps we should see the hiring of people trained in disciplines other than religious studies for

6. The Association of Theological Schools, 1999–2000 *Fact Book on Theological Education*, 73.

religious studies positions as a much-needed freshening of the field. But only if a commensurate number of people trained in religious studies are hired in other disciplines.

Many religious studies institutions have made real progress in hiring women faculty and a few women administrators. Often this progress is cited to rebut the urgency of further progress. But the "add women and stir" recipe for reform is not sufficient to make institutions genuinely user-friendly for women and other newcomers to higher education in religious studies. Nor do numbers guarantee that misogyny has disappeared. Once hired, women continue to experience institutional misogyny at all levels. Annette Kolodny's excellent book, *Failing the Future: A Dean Looks at Higher Education in the Twenty-first Century*, discusses the anti-feminist intellectual harassment endured by women faculty.[7] Within the academy, Kolodny writes, women tend to hit the glass ceiling at two points: at the point of initial promotion and at promotion to full professor. Although "there is no comprehensive national survey of the obstacles to advancement encountered by women faculty," there is an embarrassment of riches of anecdotal evidence that women faculty continue to suffer on the basis of research areas unfamiliar to colleagues who have not continued to educate themselves on new topics and methods of scholarship and differential standards.[8] Kolodny found that women faculty also experience hidden workloads: course assignments far from their research interests, disproportionate committee assignments, and advising loads that go far beyond academic advising to time-consuming mentoring and simply listening to students who perceive women as good listeners. As Kolodny puts it, "The emotional cost is enormous."[9] Moreover, workloads at home for married parents are greater for women than for men. A study quoted by Kolodny found that married female parents spend forty hours at work and an additional forty-five hours per week in home chores and child care, while married male parents spend an average of forty-four hours per week at work, but only fourteen hours in home chores and child care.

Given this less than reassuring forecast for women, Eloise Rosenblatt urges that women form political alliances across color lines and seek the support of sympathetic male colleagues, and that they develop strategies to counteract the hiring setbacks that are presently consigning women to part-

---

7. Koloduy, *Failing the Future*.

8. Ibid., 83

9. Ibid., 86.

time, adjunct, and community college teaching positions and reducing their presence at graduate institutions.

I also have a suggestion. It is that women accept administrative positions. When I came to the GTU, I had been a faculty member for my whole career. Against the advice of colleagues, family, and friends who predicted that I would hate administration after the comparative luxury of working with students, books, and ideas, I felt a conviction that, if the institutions of church and academy are going to change in the direction of becoming more friendly and welcoming to women, women need to learn how to govern them.

Women administrators need to design and implement the changes that would equalize women's and men's opportunities in the field of religious studies. Desperately needed changes include: developing hiring strategies for diversifying faculty, curricular changes that acknowledge demographic shifts, clarifying promotion/tenure procedures, establishing team approaches to problem-solving, involving faculty in policy making, and creating family-friendly policies and flexible schedules for faculty and staff. None of these changes will be easy to make. For some time to come, it may be that a number of women faculty should think in terms of relatively short administrative appointments; for example, Annette Kolodny served for five years as Dean of the College of Humanities at the University of Arizona, Tucson, before burning out to the point of endangering her health. Nobody is arguing that it's easy and fun, but if a number of women faculty were prepared to do five-year appointments, changes could be sustained without the dramatic human sacrifice one woman would suffer over a longer period.

But I have discovered that becoming an administrator for change is not as easy as simply accepting an administrative job. I have needed to do a great deal of emotional and intellectual work in order to adjust to an administrative role. For example, there was (and is) difficult psychological work to be done to revise the cynical expectations I have developed in relation to institutions and to learn to work effectively and productively in them. For women have a difficult past with institutions. These are, after all, the same institutions that have marginalized us, denied us leadership roles, and often simply excluded us. We are very aware that they have not been designed and administered with our support in mind. Moreover, difficult intellectual work was necessary in order to discern what aspects of my training and experience in academic institutions are useable, and which of the attitudes and styles I have learned—which knowledges need to be substantially revised.

More than a decade ago, Audre Lorde questioned whether the Master's tools can be used to dismantle the master's house. Perhaps we should ask instead whether the master's house can be redesigned with the tools provided. The answer must ultimately be no. Here a generation gap comes into the picture. The first generation of women engaged in an enterprise new to women must demonstrate their ability to fit in, to do the job as well as—meaning essentially, better than—a man. While women are engaged in this stage, there is little leisure for revision of institutions. But we are presently in approximately the second generation of women in educational administration. And I believe that it is now time for women in administration to think together about how institutions can and should change to reflect women's perspectives, experience, and expertise.

The importance of women thinking together, rather than following the Lone Ranger model of professional work, should by now have been well learned. As long ago as the 1960s we learned in consciousness-raising groups to identify with women as a caste in American society. Later we learned by painful experience how next-to-impossible it is for a lone woman to change even a classroom conversation much less an institution without the audible support of others. As graduate students we developed simple and effective strategies for seconding one another's voices, for repeating points another woman had made. As teachers we discussed and experimented with feminist pedagogies. Yet at the stage of leadership roles, women often allow ourselves to be institutionally isolated from others who could share, criticize, and refine our perspectives. Why? Speaking from my experience, several reasons appear.

First, workloads preclude even sitting together over a cup of coffee or lunch. Second, the relative rarity of women leaders means that if we do make friends, we will make them among women students and faculty. Fine, but these are the very people we are prohibited from confiding in by protocols of professional confidentiality. Wrenchingly painful experiences teach us that we will be punished for operating, even occasionally, outside the traditional protocols of institutional politics. We become isolated from those we have learned to trust and work with. We become lonely, and ultimately ineffective, unconvinced of the soundness of our decisions in situations in which the simple expedient of talking them over with others is closed to us. There are, as yet, no "clubs" where women administrators can consult, criticize, and support one another. Suspicious as we should properly be of constructing old girl networks that parallel the old boy networks by which institutions used to work, it nevertheless goes against everything we have learned from feminist politics to deny ourselves one another's company and advice.

But perhaps at this point we should ask an even more fundamental question: do women need institutions at all? Should we perhaps be prepared to invent our own from the ground up? I think we do need institutions and that we need not start from scratch. Consider: what institutions do best is to provide space and support for people to discuss ideas with others, to circulate those ideas and, over time, to refine them. If women do not claim institutional space in which to do our work, with one another and with male colleagues, we will be restricted to our informal networks—mother to daughter, friend to friend. In other words, we will need to reinvent the wheel in every generation. If, however, we can make a place for ourselves within institutions, we will have space in which to work on our ideas, to criticize, revise, and celebrate them.

One of the requirements for effective institutional leadership is that we must be very good historians. We must constantly ask whether this is the right cultural and institutional moment for whatever we are proposing. We will, of course, often want to advocate change that from a sober historian's perspective is definitely premature. What I refer to here, however, is how to discern the best form, at any particular moment, for women's fragile and conflicted relationship with institutions. For example, there was a historical moment in which women needed to have segregated space and time in which to think together about their identity as women and their agendas in those institutions. Women's colleges, women's classes, women's centers within universities, divinity schools, and seminaries were crucial for providing women with institutional space. But there is also the need to mainstream women's perspectives, questions, interests, and concerns. Perhaps the discipline that has best achieved mainstreaming is history, in which male and female historians now routinely research women's roles in societies as well as women's intellectual influence and the lives of individual women.

It is not easy to identify what is needed in a particular situation at a particular time. Without opportunity for segregated discussion among women, no agreement about purpose and goals can emerge. Yet without mainstreaming, male faculty and students never understand that their education is strikingly incomplete without training in gender analysis throughout the curriculum. Both segregation and mainstreaming are potentially dangerous. But that awareness should not lead to passivity, but rather to the development of self-critical awareness in academic work, the refinement of any field (in this case, women's studies, gender studies, feminist theory) requires the concentrated attention across time of well-trained scholars. Because of the classes, the colleagues, and the conferences in which gender theory and studies are debated and refined, the field has achieved great sophistication in a remarkably short time—roughly twenty-five years. (The same can be said for several other new fields of study, like, for example, gay and lesbian studies, and queer theory.)

One of the strongest indications that religious studies institutions bear a continuing gender bias despite strongly worded commitments to recruitment at the faculty, staff, and student levels is the present unreformed style of institutional politics. Institutional politics that have worked well for men have usually not worked to women's advantage. So women often find ourselves unwilling to support the institutional protocols that men have designed and administered. For example, in my observation, a traditional male administrator's first instinct when a question or problem arises is to keep it secret. He will then typically talk it over and resolve it with one or two other men in positions of power, requiring confidentiality all around. This is a very slightly updated version of smoke-filled-room politics in which a small number of men make decisions for the community or nation. Typically, when confronted about this management style, male administrators will be upset that they are not trusted to make the best possible decision. But for many women, "trust me," said by a man, is a major danger signal! Ever since I got pregnant at eighteen by accepting that advice I have not been reassured by this plea! Consider: women have no confidence that men in power will make the decisions that forward women's interests (or, for that matter, the institution's interests). Indeed, there is abundant evidence to the contrary! What women have learned from our rocky institutional experience is that women need to stick together, to inform one another of issues as they arise, and to use concerted (political) efforts to address and resolve the issue. We typically rally one another to write letters, sign petitions, and make telephone calls to whomever has the authority to make the decision. The assumption is that pressure needs to be brought to bear on authorities who do not have one's interests at heart. This model of institutional politics features grassroots politics for people without direct access to power/authority. We learned this kind of politics in a variety of political arenas, not only in academic institutions. Women are routinely accused of politicizing the issue; it is seldom recognized that the confidentiality model is at least equally a political move.

Neither the confidentiality model nor the grassroots model is adequate for the religious studies institutions of the twenty-first century. There are other ways to work together more effectively. For example, a method alternative to both the confidentiality model and the grassroots model is one I call the modified town meeting model. It works by exposing issues to the primary stakeholders as they occur, for discussion, argument, and negotiation, for thinking together. This model assumes and requires generosity and a commitment to listening (as well as speaking) honestly. The administrator's responsibility is to provide the forum in which all perspectives can be heard, relinquishing the illusory safe spaces of either secrecy or of being sequestered with one's political friends.

The modified town meeting model is modified in that the community knows from the beginning who has the authority to make the decision, informed and guided by the town meeting discussion. But good decisions are not made at town meetings. There is too much peer pressure, too much reliance on skillful rhetoric, and too much possibility of bandwagoning. The person or group of people responsible for making the decision must do it on the basis of hearing with attention and sympathy all the stakeholders perspectives and advocacy. She must consider the damages, to certain groups, of decisions they perceive as harmful. She must weigh the advantages, in the short term and in the long term, of the available range of decisions. And she must be accountable for her decision. She must be willing to state the values and commitments that inform it. What is different about this decision-making process is that the decision-maker will have direct access to the heated interests of all interested people. She will not insulate herself from dissenting voices but will carefully consider each of them.

A complicating factor: Institutions, like societies, have primarily at stake their survival. And survival is a profoundly conservative interest, one that stimulates retreat into what has worked in the past. Unarticulated survival anxieties can also be profoundly at odds, even, on occasion, contradictory to the same institution's mission statement, which may state with unambiguous resolution its concern for justice, diversity, and equal opportunity for all. How can change and survival be simultaneously administered? An administrator is certainly responsible for the health and longevity of the institution she serves. Finding the decisions that best serve both the institution's flourishing and the mission statement's commitments usually takes more than one brain. We who have always thought of wisdom as the personal acumen of a single person must develop a new idea of distributed, negotiated, and critical wisdom, by which I mean the ability to take account of all the engaged perspectives and to state the values and assumptions that inform them.

Let me suggest a further possible result of employing the modified town meeting model: There is at present a shortage of leaders in theological and religious studies institutions. Several recent presidential searches in divinity schools, graduate schools, and seminaries have developed the same short list of "the usual suspects." Meanwhile, several excellent administrators have left theological education to accept important posts in universities. Those of us interested in the well being of the field of religious studies should worry about this. Why are religious studies institutions apparently not attractive or challenging, or even—is it too much to expect?—rewarding to people with talent, vision, and proven administrative skills? On a bad day I could wax eloquent in answering this question. The real answer must be more complex than the one I'd give on a bad day, though. My sense is that because we have not found effective forms of institutional politics, adequate to the diverse perspectives now within religious studies institutions, our institutions are fragmented. Leaders are distracted from leading by dealing with financial crises, conflicting values, and disagreement. Sidetracked in this way, they are frustrated by finding themselves unable to articulate a persuasive vision and build toward that vision.

We need, and need desperately, to find an institutional politics that furthers the common good. We live in a historical moment in which identity politics must be balanced with attention to the common good. We have not identified adequate ways of conducting civil conversation among people who assume the best (not the worst) of one another. Though we cling to them tenaciously, neither the confidentiality model nor the grassroots model serves us well in the midst of real diversity, i.e., not token diversity, but critical mass diversity. I suggest that the modified town meeting model might be tried and refined on location. It offers the possibility of negotiating differences—not transcending or overcoming differences—but giving voice and weight to difference in a complex process of decision-making capable of gathering enough agreement to move forward.

Unless women are willing to accept the difficult and often thankless labor of administration, the institutions that lure and promote faculty women and that train women students will not change sufficiently to make religious studies institutions a place where women and our scholarship can flourish. I do not presume to say what values women administrators will bring to institutional decisions. I resist the easy claim that all women are more relational, more humane, better listeners, and more caring than all men. Original sin is not confined to one gender. But most women have a different experience of body and society than most men do, and the perspectives gained from women's experiences should help to inform the commitments and politics of institutions as they have not in the past, and often still do not in the present.

On a good day, this all looks like a challenge. On a bad day, it seems that despite our dedication and hard work, institutions change at a snail's pace. And so—what else is new?—we live by faith, not in our individual efforts, but in our common, cumulative, committed work. We work supported by the conviction that the inclusive, just, freeing, and authorizing community for which we work is right. Nobody actually likes to live by faith. We would rather have a vision, plot our course, set measurable goals, and implement them. However, if we think that's what we're doing, we position ourselves for disappointment and burnout. No, we do live by faith, and the only options are to recognize and embrace this fact of life, or to ignore it and pretend that we don't. It is always easier to complain of our institutions than to take responsibility for them. But, as Toni Morrison wrote in *Jazz*, "Oh shoot! Where the grown people? Is it us?!"[10]

10. Morrison, *Jazz*, 110.

Bibliography

Agger, Ben. *Cultural Studies as Critical Theory*. Washington DC: Palmer, 1992.

Alter, Jonathan. "The Fight for High Ground." *Newsweek*, March 15, 2004, 42.

Aristotle, *Nichomachean Ethics*. Translated by J. A. K. Thomson. Baltimore: Penguin, 1953.

Armstrong, Nancy. "The Death and Sinister Afterlife of the American Family." In *Body Politics: Disease, Desire, and the Family*, edited by Michael Ryan and Avery Gordon, 18–31. San Francisco: Westview, 1994.

The Association of Theological Schools. *1999-2000 Fact Book on Theological Education*. Pittsburgh: ATS, 2000.

Athanasius, *On the Incarnation*. In *Christology of the Later Fathers*, edited by Edward Hardy, 55–110. Philadelphia: Westminster, 1974.

Augustine. *City of God*. Edited by David Knowles. Translated by Henry Bettenson. Middlesex, England: Penguin, 1972.

———. *The Confessions of St. Augustine*. Translated by Rex Warner. New York: Mentor-Omega, 1963.

———. *De bono conjungali*. In Treatises on Marriage and Other Subjects, translated by Charles T. Wilcox et al., edited by Roy J. Defarrari. Fathers of the Church 27. New York: Fathers of the Church, 1955.

———. *De musica*. In *Patrologiae, Cursus Completus, Series Latina*, vol. 22. Edited by J. P. Migne. Paris: Migne, 1845.

———. *Enarrationes in Psalmos 121*. In *An Augustine Synthesis*, arranged by Erich Przywara. New York: Harper, 1958.

———. *Homily 7*. In *Augustine: Later Works*, edited by John Burnaby, 312–20. Library of Christian Classics. Philadelphia: Westminster, 1955.

———. *In epistolam Johannis ad Parthos tractatus*. In *Augustine: Later Works*, edited by John Burnaby, 251–348. Library of Christian Classics. Philadelphia: Westminster, 1955.

———. *On Christian Doctrine*. Translated by D. W. Robertson Jr. Indianapolis: Bobbs-Merrill, 1958.

———. *Sermon 80*. In *An Augustine Synthesis*, arranged by Erick Przywara. New York: Harper, 1958.

Barry, David. "Screen Violence: It's Killing Us." *Harvard Magazine* 96 (1993) 38–43.

Barthes, Roland, *The Pleasure of the Text*. Translated by Richard Miller. New York: Hill & Wang, 1975.

Baudrillard, Jean. "Hyperreal America." *Economy and Society* 22 (1993) 243–52.

Baxandall, Michael. *Painting and Experience Fifteenth-Century Italy*. Oxford: Oxford University Press, 1972.

Bedell, Kenneth B. *Yearbook of American and Canadian Churches*. Nashville: Abingdon, 1994.

Bell, Robinette, et al. *Violence against Women in the United States: A Comprehensive Background Paper.* New York: Commonwealth Fund Commission on Women's Health, 1995.

Benderly, Beryl Lieff. "Rape Free or Rape Prone." *Science* (1982) 40–43.

Benhabib, Seyla. "The Generalized and the Concrete Other." In *Feminism as Critique: Essays on the Politics of Gender,* edited by Seyla Benhabib and Drucilla Cornell, 77–95. Minneapolis: University of Minnesota Press, 1986.

Benjamin, Jessica. *The Bonds of Love: Psychoanalysis, Feminism, and the Problem of Domination.* New York: Pantheon, 1988.

Bernstein, Richard J. *Beyond Objectivism and Relativism.* Philadelphia: University of Pennsylvania Press, 1983.

Bethge, Eberhard. "The Challenge of Dietrich Bonhoeffer's Life and Theology." *The Chicago Theological Seminary Register* 51 (February, 1961) 1–38.

Bleicher, Josef. *Contemporary Hermeneutics: Hermeneutics as Method, Philosophy, and Critique.* London: Routledge, 1980.

Boguet, Henri. *An Examen of Witches Drawn From Various Trials.* Edited by Montague Summers. Translated by E. Allen Ashwin. London: Rodker, 1929.

Bonhoeffer, Dietrich. *Ethics.* Translated by Neville Horton Smith. New York: Macmillan, 1955.

———. *Letters and Papers from Prison.* Edited by Eberhard Bethge. Translated by Reginald H. Fuller. London: SCM, 1953.

Bonner, G. I. "*Libido* and *Concupiscentia* in St. Augustine." *Studia Patristica* 6 (1962) 303–14.

Bordo, Susan. *Unbearable Weight: Feminism, Western Culture, and the Body.* Berkeley: University of California Press, 1993.

Brenneman, Walter L. Jr., and Stanley O. Yarian with Alan M. Olson. *The Seeing Eye: Hermeneutical Phenomenology in the Study of Religion.* University Park: Pennsylvania State University Press, 1982.

Brooten, Bernadette. "Paul's Views on the Nature of Women and Female Homoeroticism." In *Immaculate and Powerful: The Female in Sacred Image and Social Reality,* edited by Atkinson et al., 61–87. Boston: Beacon, 1986.

Brown, Raphael, editor. *The Little Flowers of St. Francis.* New York: Doubleday, 1958.

Bruns, Gerald L. "The Problem of Figuration in Antiquity." In *Hermeneutics: Questions and Prospects,* edited by Gary Shapiro and Alan Sica, 147–64. Amherst: University of Massachusetts Press, 1982.

Bunyan, John. *Grace Abounding to the Chief of Sinners.* Grand Rapids: Baker, 1978.

———. *The Pilgrim's Progress.* Glasgow: Collins, 1979.

Butler, Judith. "The Lesbian Phallus and the Morphological Imaginary." *Differences* (1992) 133–71.

Bynum, Caroline Walker. *Holy Feast and Holy Fast: The Religious Significance of Food to Medieval Women.* Berkeley: University of California Press, 1987.

Bywater, Tim, and Thomas Sobchack. *Introduction to Film Criticism.* New York: Longman, 1989.

Camporesi, Piero. *The Incorruptible Flesh: Bodily Mutation and Mortification in Religion and Folklore.* Translated by Tania Croft-Murray and Jelen Elsom. Cambridge: Cambridge University Press, 1988.

Carson, Tom. "To Disneyland." *Los Angeles Weekly,* March 27–April 2, 1992.

Chadwick, Owen, editor. *Western Asceticism*. Library of Christian Classics. Philadelphia: Westminster John Knox, 1958.

Cohen, Kathleen. *Metamorphosis of a Death Symbol: The Transi Tomb in the Late Middle Ages and the Renaissance*. Berkeley: University of California, 1973.

Cronin, William. *Changes in the Land*. New York: Hill & Wang, 1983.

Daly, Mary. *Gyn/Ecology: The Metaethics of Radical Feminism*. Boston: Beacon, 1990.

de Lauretis, Teresa. "The Essence of the Triangle or, Taking the Risk of Essentialism Seriously: Feminist Theory in Italy, the U.S., and Britain." *Differences* 1:2 (1989) 3–37.

Dinnerstein, Dorothy. *The Mermaid and the Minotaur: Sexual Arrangements and Human Malaise*. New York: Harper & Row, 1976.

Dray, W. H. "Conflicting Interpretations in History." In *Hermeneutics: Questions and Prospects*, edited by Gary Shapiro and Alan Sica, 239–57. Amherst: University of Massachusetts Press, 1982.

Dworkin, Andrea. *Pornography: Men Possessing Women*. New York: Perigree, 1981.

———. *Woman Hating*. New York: Dutton, 1974.

Eck, Diana L. *On Common Ground: World Religions in America*. New York: Columbia University Press, 1997.

Eckhart, Meister. "Talks." In *Meister Eckhart: A Modern Translation*. Translated by Raymond Blakney. New York: Harper & Row, 1941.

Edwards, Jonathan. "The Christian Pilgrim." In *The Works of President Edwards*. Vol. 2, edited by S. B. Dwight, 135–46. New York: Carvill, 1830.

Eisenstein, Elizabeth. "The Advent of Printing and the Protestant Revolution: A New Approach to the Disruption of Western Christendom." In *Transition and Revolution: Problems and Issues of European Renaissance and Reformation History*, edited by Robert M. Kingdon. Minneapolis: Burgess, 1974.

Eliot, George. *Middlemarch*. Edited by David Carroll. New York: Oxford University Press, 1986.

Felski, Rita. *Beyond Feminist Aesthetics: Feminist Literature and Social Change*. Cambridge: Harvard University Press, 1989.

Fortune, Marie M. *Sexual Violence: The Unmentionable Sin*. New York: Pilgrim, 1983.

Foucault, Michel. *The Archaeology of Knowledge*. Translated by A. M. Sheridan. New York, Pantheon, 1972.

———. "The Body of the Condemned." In *The Foucault Reader*. Edited by Paul Rainbow. New York: Pantheon, 1984

———. *The Care of the Self*. Translated by Robert Hurley. New York: Pantheon, 1986.

———. *Discipline and Punish: The Birth of the Prison*. Translated by Alan Sheridan. New York: Vintage, 1979.

———. "Docile Bodies." In *The Foucault Reader*. Edited by Paul Rainbow. New York: Pantheon, 1984

———. *Language, Counter-Memory, and Practice*. Ithaca: Cornell University Press, 1977.

———. *The Order of Things*. New York: Vintage, 1973.

———. "Polemics, Politics, and Problematizations." In *The Foucault Reader*. Edited by Paul Rainbow. New York: Pantheon, 1984

———. "Politics and Ethics, An Interview." In *The Foucault Reader*. Edited by Paul Rainbow. New York: Pantheon, 1984

———. *Power/Knowledge: Selected Interviews and Other Writings*. New York: Pantheon, 1972.

————. "Preface to The History of Sexuality, Vol. II." In *The Foucault Reader*, edited by Paul Rainbow. New York: Pantheon, 1984

————. *The Use of Pleasure*. Translated by Robert Hurley. New York: Pantheon, 1985.

————. "What is an Author?" In *The Foucault Reader*. Edited by Paul Rainbow. New York: Pantheon, 1984

Fussel, Kuno. "The Materialist Reading of the Bible." In *The Bible and Liberation*, edited by Norman K. Gottwald, 134–46. New York: Orbis, 1984.

Gadamer, Hans-Georg. "The Hermeneutics of Suspicion." In *Hermeneutics: Questions and Prospects*, edited by Gary Shapiro and Alan Sica, 54–65. Amherst: University of Massachusetts Press, 1982.

————. "On the Scope and Function of Hermeneutical Reflection." In *Philosophical Hermeneutics*, translated and edited by David E. Linge, 18–43. Berkeley: University of California Press, 1977.

————. *Philosophical Hermeneutics*. Translated and edited by David E. Linge. Berkeley: University of California Press, 1977.

————. *Truth and Method*. Translation edited by Garrett Barden and John Cumming. New York: Seabury, 1975.

————. "The Universality of the Hermeneutical Problem." In *Philosophical Hermeneutics*, translated and edited by David E. Linge, 3–17. Berkeley: University of California Press, 1977.

Glassner, Barry. *The Culture of Fear: Why Americans Are Afraid of the Wrong Things*. New York: Basic, 1999.

Gottwald, Norman K. *The Bible and Liberation*. New York: Orbis, 1984.

Gregory of Nyssa. *On Perfection*. Translated by Virginia Woods Callahan. Fathers of the Church 58. Washington DC: Catholic University of America Press, 1967.

Grünewald, Mattias. *Grünewald: The Paintings*. With two essays by J. K. Huysmans and a catalogue by E. Ruhmer. London: Phaidon, 1958.

Groth, Nicholas, and Jean Birnbaum. *Men Who Rape: The Psychology of the Offender*. New York: Plenum, 1979.

Gustafson, James M. "The Vocation of the Theological Educator." Lecture, Austin Presbyterian Seminary, November 15, 1985.

Habig, Marion A., editor. *St. Francis of Assisi: Writings and Early Biographies*. English omnibus of the sources for the life of St. Francis. Chicago: Franciscan Herald, 1973.

Haraway, Donna. "The Persistance of Vision." In *Writing on the Body: Female Embodiment and Feminist Theory*, edited by Katie Conroy, Nadia Medina, and Sarah Stanbury, 283–95. New York: State University of New York Press, 1997.

Harding, Vincent. "The Historian as Witness." In *Visions of History: Interviews of Radical Historians*, edited by Henry Abelove et al. New York: Pantheon, 1983.

Hardy, Edward Rochie, and Cyril C. Richardson, editors. *Christology of the Later Fathers*. Philadelphia: Westminster, 1954.

Harpham, Geoffrey Galt. *The Ascetic Imperative in Culture and Criticism*. Chicago: University of Chicago Press, 1987.

Haskin, Dayton. "The Pilgrim's Progress in the Context of Bunyan's Dialogue with the Radicals." *Harvard Theological Review* 77 (1984) 73–94.

Haug, Frigga, et al. *Female Sexualization*. Tranlsated by Erika Caner. London: Verso, 1987.

Heinrich Kramer and James Sprenger. *The Malleus Maleficarum*. Translated by Montague Summers. New York: Dover, 1971.

Hiaasen, Carl. *Team Rodent: How Disney Devours the World*. New York: Ballantine, 1998.

Hiatt, Suzanne R. "The Episcopalian Story." In *Women of Spirit: Female Leadership in the Jewish and Christian Traditions*, edited by Rosemary Ruether and Eleanor McLaughlin, 356–72. New York: Simon & Schuster, 1979.

———. "How We Brought the Good News from Graymoor to Minneapolis: An Episcopal Paradigm." *Journal of Ecumenical Studies* 20 (1983) 576–84.

Hollander, Anne. *Seeing through Clothes*. New York: Viking, 1980.

Howard, Roy J. *Three Faces of Hermeneutics: An Introduction to Current Theories of Understanding*. Berkeley: University of California Press, 1982.

Hutch, Richard A. *The Meaning of Lives: Biography, Autobiography, and the Spiritual Quest*. London: Cassell, 1997.

Hyman, Stanley Edgar. *The Tangled Bank: Darwin, Marx, Frazer and Freud as Imaginative Writers*. New York: Grosset and Dunlap, 1966.

Inglis, Fred. *Media Theory: An Introduction*. Oxford: Basil Blackwell, 1990.

Isozaki, Arata. "Theme Park." *South Atlantic Quarterly* 92 (1993) 175–82.

Jacobus, de Voragine. *The Golden Legend of Jacobus de Voragine*. Translated by Granger Ryan and Helmut Ripperger. New York: Arno, 1969.

Jeffrey L. Sheler. "Spiritual America." *U.S. News and World Report*, April 4, 1994, 49.

Jerome. *Epistle 108*. *Select Library of Nicene and Post-Nicene Fathers, Second Series* Vol. 6, 195–212. New York: The Christian Literature Company, 1893.

Johnson, Richard. "What is Cultural Studies Anyway?" *Social Text* 16 (1987) 38–80.

Johnson, Thomas, et al. "Faith in a Box: Television and Religion." Media Research Center Report. Alexandria, VA: Media Research Center, n.d.

Johnson, Thomas and Sandra Crawford, "Faith in a Box: Entertainment Television on Religion, 1994." In *Religion and Prime Time Television*, edited by Michael Suman. Westport, CT: Praeger, 1997.

Kahane, Garner, and Sprengether, editors. *The (M)other Tongue*. Ithaca: Cornell University Press, 1985.

Kass, Leon R. *The Hungry Soul: Eating and the Perfecting of Our Nature*. New York: Free, 1994.

Kellner, Douglas. *Media Culture: Cultural Studies, Identity, and Politics Between the Modern and the Postmodern*. New York: Routledge, 1995.

Kingston, Maxine Hong. *China Men*. New York: Knopf, 1980.

Kolodny, Annette. *Failing the Future: A Dean Looks at Higher Education in the Twenty-first Century*. Durham: Duke University Press, 1998.

Kristeva, Julia. *The Powers of Horror: An Essay on Abjection*. European Perspectives. New York: Columbia University Press, 1982.

Kuenz, Jane. "It's a Small World After All." *South Atlantic Quarterly* 92 (1993) 63–88.

Laertius, Diogenes. *Lives of the Most Eminent Philosophers*. Translated by R. D. Hicks. New York: Putnam, 1925.

Lampe, G. W. H. *A Patristic Greek Lexicon*. Oxford: Clarendon, 1961.

Leder, Drew. *The Absent Body*. Chicago: University of Chicago Press, 1990.

Lehman, Betsey A. "Fat: Globally, We're Expanding." *The Boston Globe*. August 1, 1994.

Lessing, Doris. *Under My Skin*. New York: Harper Collins, 1994.

Lippy, Charles H., and Peter W. Williams, editors. *Encyclopedia of the American Religious Experience: Studies of Traditions and Movements*. New York: Scribners, 1988.

Lorde, Audre. *Sister Outsider: Essays and Speeches*. Freedom, CA: Crossing, 1989.

MacFarquhar, Larissa. "The Populist: Michael Moore's Art and Anger." *New Yorker* February 16, 2004, 138.

Marcuse, Herbert. *Eros and Civilization: A Philosophical Inquiry into Freud.* Boston: Beacon, 1955.

Marling, Karat Ann, editor. *Designing Disney's Theme Parks: The Architecture of Reassurance.* New York: Flammarion, 1997.

Martin, Rex. "On Dray's 'Conflicting Interpretations in History: The Case for the English Civil War.'" In *Hermeneutics: Questions and Prospects,* edited by Gary Shapiro and Alan Sica, 258–69. Amherst: University of Massachusetts Press, 1982.

Maslow, Abraham. *Toward a Psychology of Being.* Princeton: Van Nostrand, 1962.

May, Herbert G., and Bruce M. Metzger, editors. *The Oxford Annotated Bible.* New York: Oxford University Press, 1962.

McFague, Sallie. *Metaphorical Theology: Models of God in Religious Language.* Philadelphia: Fortress, 1983.

Melton, J. Gordon, editor. *Encyclopedia of American Religion.* 4th edition. Washington DC: Gale Research, 1993.

———. *Religious Bodies in the United States: A Directory.* New York: Garland, 1992.

———. *Encyclopedic Handbook of Cults in America.* New York: Garland, 1992.

Menand, Louis. "Nanook and Me." *New Yorker,* August 9 and 16, 2004.

Merchant, Carolyn. *The Death of Nature: Women, Ecology, and the Scientific Revolution.* New York: Harper & Row, 1980.

Michener, James. *Poland.* New York: Fawcett Crest, 1983.

Miles, Margaret. *Carnal Knowing: Female Nakedness and Religious Meaning in the Christian West.* 1989. Reprinted, Eugene, OR: Wipf & Stock, 2006.

———. *A Complex Delight: The Secularization of the Breast, 1350–1750.* Berkeley: University of California Press, 2008.

———. *Desire and Delight: A New Reading of Augustine's Confessions.* 1997. Reprint, Eugene, OR: 2006.

———. *Fullness of Life: Historical Foundations for a New Asceticism.* 1981. Reprinted, Eugene, OR: Wipf & Stock, 2006.

———. *Image as Insight: Visual Understanding in Western Christianity and Secular Culture.* 1985. Reprinted, Eugene, OR: Wipf & Stock, 2006.

———. "Patriarchy as Political Theology: The Establishment of North African Christianity." In *Civil Religion and Political Society,* edited by Leroy S. Rouner, 169–86. Boston University Studies in Philosophy and Religion. Notre Dame, IN: Notre Dame University Press 1986.

———. *Practicing Christianity: Critical Perspectives for an Embodied Christianity.* New York: Crossroad, 1988.

———. *Reading for Life: Beauty, Pluralism, and Responsibility.* New York: Continuum, 1997.

———. *Seeing and Believing: Religion and Values in the Movies.* Boston: Beacon, 1996.

———. *The Word Made Flesh: A History of Christian Thought.* Blackwell, 2005.

———, and S. Brent Plate. "Hospitable Vision: Some Notes on the Ethics of Seeing Film." *CrossCurrents* 54:1 (Spring 2004) 22–31.

Miller, Alice. *For Your Own Good: Hidden Cruelty in Child-rearing and the Roots of Violence.* Translated by Hildegard and Hunter Hannum. New York: Farrar, Straus & Giroux, 1983.

Miller, J. Hillis. *Illustration: Essays in Art and Culture.* Cambridge: Harvard University Press, 1992.

Miringoff, Marc, and Marque-Luisa Miringoff. *The Social Health of the Nation: How America Is Really Doing.* New York: Oxford University Press, 1992.

Miringoff, Marque-Luisa, Marc Miringoff, and Sandra Opdycke. *The Social Report: Assessing the Progress of America by Monitoring the Well-Being of Its People.* Tarrytown, NY: Fordham Institute for Innovation in Social Policy, 2001.

Morrison, Toni. *Jazz.* New York: Knopf, 1992.

Murdoch, Iris. *Metaphysics as a Guide to Morals.* New York: Routledge, 1992.

———. *The Sovereignty of Good.* New York: Penguin, 1970.

Musurillo, Herbert, SJ. "The Problem of Ascetical Fasting in the Greek Patristic Writers." *Traditio* 12 (1956) 6.

Norris, Christopher. *Deconstruction, Theory and Practice.* New Accents. New York: Methuen, 1982.

Nussbaum, Martha. *Love's Knowledge.* New York: Oxford University Press, 1990.

Olson, Alan M. *The Seeing Eye: Hermeneutical Phenomenology in the Study of Religion.* Edited by Walter L. Brenneman and Stanley O. Yarian. Pennsylvania State University Press, 1982.

Pellauer, Mary D. "Moral Callousness and Moral Sensitivity." In *Women's Consciousness, Women's Conscience: A Reader in Feminists Ethics,* edited by Barbara Hilkert Andolsen, Christine E. Gudorf, and Mary D. Pellauer. Minneapolis: Winston, 1985.

Percy, Walker. *The Second Coming.* New York: Washington Square, 1980.

Plaskow, Judith. *Sex, Sin, and Grace: Women's Experience and the Theologies of Reinhold Niebuhr and Paul Tillich.* Washington DC: University Press of America, 1980.

Plato. *Symposium.* In *The Collected Dialogues of Plato,* edited by Edith Hamilton and Huntington Cairns. Princeton: Princeton University Press, 1961.

Plotinus *Enneads.* Translated by A. H. Armstrong. Loeb Classical Library. Cambridge: Harvard University Press, 1967–1988.

Ponticus, Evagrius. *The Praktikos and Chapters on Prayer.* Translated by John E. Bamberger. Kalamazoo, MI: Cistercian, 1978.

Proudfoot, Wayne. *Religious Experience.* Berkeley: University of California Press, 1985.

Rabinow, Paul, editor. *Foucault Reader.* New York: Pantheon, 1984.

Ragusa, Isa, and Rosalie B. Green, editors. *Meditations on the Life of Christ: An Illustrated Manuscript.* Princeton: Princeton University Press, 1961.

Renov, Michael. *The Subject of Documentary.* Minneapolis: University of Minnesota, 2004.

Ricoeur, Paul. *Interpretation Theory: Discourse and the Surplus of Meaning.* Fort Worth, TX: Texas Christian University Press, 1976.

Rilke, Rainer Maria. "The Archaic Torso of Apollo." In *Translations From the Poetry of Rainer Maria Rilke.* Translated by M. D. Herter Norton. New York: Norton, 1962.

———. *Letters to a Young Poet.* Translated by M. D. Herter Norton. New York: Norton, 1934.

Rorty, Richard. *Philosophy and the Mirror of Nature.* Princeton University Press, 1979.

Rosen, Jeffrey. *The Naked Crowd: Reclaiming Security and Freedom in an Anxious Age.* New York: Random, 2004.

Rosenblatt, Eloise. "The Present and Future Status of Women in Religion." Unpublished paper. 2000.

Ruether, Rosemary Radford. "Christology: Can a Male Savior Save Women?" In *Sexism and God-Talk: Toward a Feminist Theology.* Boston: Beacon, 1983.

Sanday, Peggy Reeves. *Female Power and Male Dominance: On the Origins of Sexual Inequality.* New York: Cambridge University Press, 1981.

Sanders, N. K., translator. *Epic of Gilgamesh.* Baltimore, Maryland: Penguin, 1960.

Schüssler Fiorenza, Elisabeth. *Bread Not Stone: The Challenge of Feminist Biblical Interpretation.* Boston: Beacon, 1984.

————. *In Memory of Her: A Feminist Theological Reconstruction of Christian Origins*. New York: Crossroad, 1983.

Segal, Lynne. *Slow Motion: Changing Masculinities, Changing Men*. New Brunswick, NJ: Rutgers University Press, 1990.

Seid, Roberta. *Never Too Thin: Women at War with Their Bodies*. New York: Garland, 1987.

Shapiro, Gary, and Alan Sica, editors. *Hermeneutics: Questions and Prospects*. Amherst: University of Massachusetts, 1984.

Shawn, Wallace, and Andre Gregory. *My Dinner with Andre*. New York: Grove, 1981.

Sheridan, Alan. *Michel Foucault: The Will to Truth*. New York: Tavistock, 1980.

Silverman, Kaja. *The Threshold of the Visible World*. New York: Routledge, 1996.

Sipe, Richard A. W. *Sex, Priests, and Power: Anatomy of a Crisis*. New York: Brunner/Mazel, 1995.

Smith, Sidonie, and Julia Watson, editors. *Getting a Life: Everyday Uses of Autobiography*. Minneapolis: University of Minnesota, 1996.

Smith, Wilfred Cantwell. *Towards a World Theology: Faith and the Comparative History of Religion*. Philadelphia: Westminster, 1981.

Stacey, Judith. *Brave New Families: Domestic Upheaval in Twentieth-Century America*. New York: Basic, 1990.

Staples, Brent. "Growing up in the Visiting Room." Review of *Life on the Outside*, by Jennifer Gonnerman. *New York Times Book Review*, March 21, 2004, 7.

Suleiman, Susan. "(Re)Writing the Body: The Politics and Poetics of Female Eroticism." In *The Female Body in Western Culture: Contemporary Perspectives*. Edited by Susan Rubin Suleiman. Cambridge: Harvard University Press, 1986.

Suman, Michael. "Do We Really Need More Religion on Fiction Television?" In *Religion and Prime Time Television*, edited by Michael Suman, 69–84. Westport, CT: Praeger, 1997.

Tertullian. *De cultu feminimurn*. Translated by S. Thelwall. *The Ante-Nicene Fathers*. First Series, Vol. 4. Buffalo: Christian Literature, 1885.

————. *De velandus virginibus*. Translated by S. Thelwall. *The Ante-Nicene Fathers*. First Series, Vol. 4. Buffalo, NY: Christian Literature, 1885.

Thomas á Kempis, *The Imitation of Christ*. Translated by Betty I. Knott. London: Collins, 1963.

Thomas, Keith. *Man and the Natural World: A History of the Modern Sensibility*. New York: Pantheon, 1983.

Thomas, Owen C. "Feminist Theology and Anglican Theology." *Anglican Theological Review* 68 (1986) 125–37.

Thompson, John B. *Critical Hermeneutics: A Study in the Thought of Paul Ricoeur and Jürgen Habermas*. Cambridge: Cambridge University Press, 1981.

Traherne, Thomas. *Centuries of Meditation*. London: Dobell, 1948.

Traube, Elizabeth G. *Dreaming Identities: Class, Gender, and Generation in 1980s Hollywood Movies*. San Francisco: Westview, 1992.

Trible, Phyllis. *Texts of Terror: Literary-Feminist Readings of Biblical Narratives*. Overtures to Biblical Theology. Philadelphia: Fortress, 1984.

Turner, Brian. *The Body and Society: Explorations in Social Theory*. New York: Basic, 1984.

Van Herik, Judith. "Excursus on Method." Chap. 2 in *Freud on Femininity and Faith*. Berkeley: University of California Press, 1982.

Wakefield, Gordon S., editor. *The Westminster Dictionary of Christian Spirituality*. Philadelphia: Westminster, 1983.

Watts, Steven. *The Magic Kingdom: Walt Disney and the American Way of Life.* New York: Houghton Mifflin, 1997.

White, Hayden. "The Modernist Event." In *The Persistence of History: Cinema, Television, and the Modern Event,* edited by Vivian Sobchack, 17–38. New York: Routledge, 1996.

Willis, Susan. "Disney World: Public Use/Private State." *The South Atlantic Quarterly* 92 (1993) 122–26.

Winkler, Mary, and Letha B. Cole, editors. *The Good Body: Asceticism in Contemporary Culture.* New Haven: Yale University Press, 1994.

Young, Iris Marion. "Impartiality and the Civic Public: Some Implications of Feminist Critiques of Moral and Political Theory." In *Feminism as Critique: Essays on the Politics of Gender,* edited by Seyla Benhabib and Drucilla Cornell, 56–76. Minneapolis: University of Minnesota Press, 1986.

———. "The Ideal of Community and the Politics of Gender." In *Feminism/Postmodernism,* edited by Linda J. Nicholson, 300–323. New York: Routledge, 1990.

Zulaika, Joseba. "The Self-Fulfilling Prophecies of Counterterrorism." *Radical History* 85 (2003) 194.